The Second
OLD HOUSE
CATALOGUE

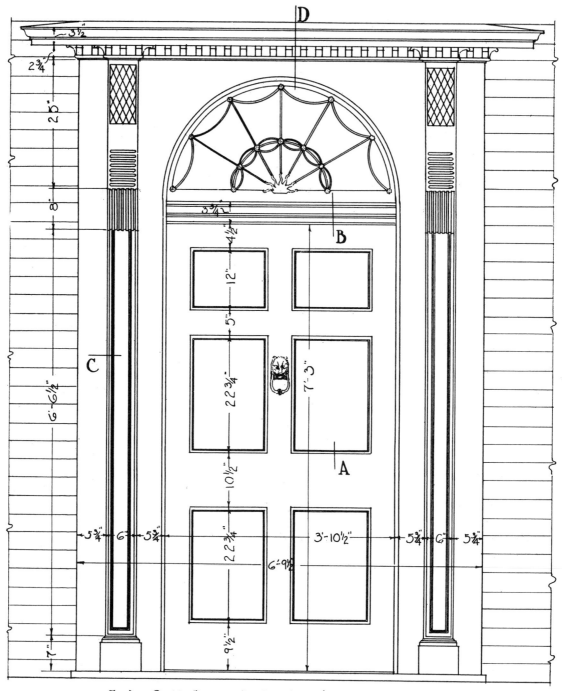

F R O N T   E L E V A T I O N

SCALE ½" = 1'-0"

The Second OLD HOUSE CATALOGUE

Compiled by Lawrence Grow

A Main Street Press Book
Universe Books　　　New York

First edition, 1978

Library of Congress Catalog Card Number 78-052201

ISBN 0-87663-986-4, paperback edition
ISBN 0-87663-315-7, hardcover edition

Published by Universe Books
381 Park Avenue South
New York City 10016

Produced by The Main Street Press
42 Main Street
Clinton, New Jersey 08809

Printed in the United States of America

Cover photograph by Eric Schweikardt

Contents

Foreword

Two years ago the first *Old House Catalogue* was issued, and, almost since that time, the question has been asked: When will there be another? Here, then, is *The Second Old House Catalogue*—not a replacement for the first or merely a revised edition of it, but a complete new book in itself. Some of the same suppliers of fine period materials will be found in the new volume, but products different from those listed in the first are featured. At least half of the companies and craftsmen included are brand new to us, and many are just reaching out for the first time to the ever-growing band of old-house enthusiasts. These suppliers are found in all parts of North America and in the British Isles.

The first book was described as "a modest step toward meeting the real needs of old-house owners and those who would like to take part in the growing movement to retrieve the livable past." *The Second Old House Catalogue* is no less modest an undertaking, but we believe that it is an even more ambitious and interesting sourcebook. It reflects the increasing diversity and energy present in the preservation/restoration movement of the late 1970s. Much more space has been devoted to basic structural needs as well as to period lighting fixtures and alternative heating sources.

Since *The Second Old House Catalogue* is not a directory, but combines sources and advice on how to use products and services, there is no way to update addresses, prices, and products effectively during the two-year interim between volumes, the third of which will be published in the Fall of 1980. Only a handful of companies listed in the first book, however, have disappeared from view since 1976. This is encouraging evidence of the increasing strength of the restoration-materials market. It is inevitable, nevertheless, that some sources will change their offerings during the next two years, or drop out of the picture entirely. In almost every listing telephone numbers have been given for the use of those who wish to shop by 'phone, and to aid in tracking down the suppliers who, like the rest of us, sometimes fall behind in answering correspondence. If, however, you find that a particular manufacturer or suppliers does not seem to be among the living, we hope that you will contact us at 42 Main Street, Clinton, New Jersey 08809. We'd like to correct our records, too, and will help you all that we can in finding an alternative supplier.

Once again we have refrained from listing electricians, plumbers, and most building contractors. Experts in these areas are best located on the local level where they are best known by reputation. Few will travel long distances and are therefore limited in their services to specific geographic areas. What has been increased in this volume, however, are the listings for regional restoration specialists who may be able to help with everything from pre-purchase inspection of an old structure to its rebuilding and furnishing. And we have even included some contractors who specialize in building fine period homes according to traditional construction methods.

To further aid the person who wishes to use some of the best in period-style fabrics and papers and finds the wholesale market difficult to enter, two appendices have been added to the book. The first is a list of department stores across the United States which feature materials from Scalamandré and Brunschwig & Fils in their decorating departments. (Fabrics and papers from other manufacturers listed in the book are generally available from the companies themselves or through various retail outlets.) The second appendix provides a listing of regional chapters of the American Society of Interior Designers. If you decide to seek such professional advice, you are urged to contact one of the chapters for assistance in selecting an experienced designer. He or she may also be able to help you in selecting and securing hard-to-get fabrics and papers.

During the past two years numerous people have freely contributed their suggestions for making *The Second Old House Catalogue* a useful resource book. Chief among them are the hundreds of craftsmen and manufacturers who make the "old-house" market as imaginative and quality-conscious as it is. They understand that there is no advertising space to be bought in this book, as there is in other directory-type publications, and that consequently, everything included in it has been chosen freely on its own merits. Without this willingness of producers to discuss their products openly, it would be impossible to proffer any objective recommendations or advice on their use. Those to whom we especially owe our thanks are Adriana Scalamandré Bitter and Serena Hortian of Scalamandré, Murray Douglas of Brunschwig & Fils, Mary Ellen Fuller of Schumacher, Bill Grage of The Decorators Supply Corp., Gary Kray of San Francisco Victoriana, and Kenneth Lynch of Kenneth Lynch & Sons.

Experts in the preservation field are busy every hour of the day engineering the salvation of the past. We are particularly grateful, then, for the advice given us by the following people in our travels across the country: Al Chambers, Historic American Buildings Survey, Washington, D.C.; Dana Crawford, Larimer Square, Denver; William Cross, Cultural Heritage Program, Pasadena, Calif.; John Frisbee, West Coast Office, National Trust for Historic Preservation, San Francisco; Wilbert Hasbrouck, Historic Resources, Inc., Chicago; Cheryl Krieger, Midwest Office, National Trust for Historic Preservation, Chicago; Clay Lancaster, architectural historian, Nantucket, Mass.; Barbara Sudler, Historic Denver; Jay Turnbull, The Foundation for San Francisco's Architectural Heritage; and Joseph, Olga, and Annette Valenta, artisans *par excellence*, Chicago.

An undertaking this complex could not have been undertaken without the assistance of members of the Main Street Press staff, in particular Richard Rawson who compiled information for several sections of the book. For special help with English materials, Alexandra Artley of the Architectural Press, Ltd., London, is owed our thanks. These, too, should go to Sally Held of Allanheld, Osmun & Co., for shepherding the manuscript through a complicated and tiring typesetting process.

"They Don't Touch Real Flowers"

In 1978 a resident of Flemington, New Jersey, reported to the local newspaper that artificial flowers left on his wife's grave were continually being stolen. Each day he would bring a new plastic bouquet to the cemetery, and each night it would disappear. Finally, he hit upon a solution to this unhappy dilemma: In place of plastic posies, he decorated the grave with honest-to-goodness growing things from the garden, for, in his own words, "They don't touch real flowers." So it has been with buildings in America for as long as anyone can remember. Most won't "touch real flowers": only the plastic. Old houses are therefore claimed only by Time, by those with taste and love, and—far too frequently—by the wrecker's ball.

All too often the ersatz is preferred to the real. It is the plastic which is still the most popular today. It is "new," easy to keep clean (so they say), and appears everlasting. Why then bother with materials that show age and cannot be considered up-to-date in any sense of the word? Why not just keep replacing the old and perishable with something of seeming permanence? As a Michigan realtor was heard to proclaim to a potential client: "For heaven's sake, you don't want a *used* house, do you?"

Well, maybe they and we and you *do*. Certainly lots of other people feel the same way—increasing numbers of them. The solution of "real flowers" is one that is enormously appealing at a time when new houses cost more than old, and present-day building materials fail to provide necessary protection from noise, heat, and dirt. To no one's surprise, an official of the Cleveland Wrecking Company reported in *The New York Times* that "new buildings are not as solidly constructed as they used to be." (He was rather downcast about this, naturally.) On a number of occasions, in fact, he had witnessed a wrecking ball bounce off a wall without even making a dent.

Unfortunately, many old houses—however well constructed—fall to the ground without a wrecker's help. They are merely left to die on their own without even a decent burial. America's cities and countryside are literally strewn with these gaping hulks. Everyone knows about the South Bronx, but perhaps closer to home are abandoned frame farmhouses or sagging and disfigured row houses. At a time when the average new home costs $50,000 to build, it seems particularly sad that the past should be allowed to decay. Improvement of the old, however, has not been encouraged on either aesthetic or economic grounds. Dependence on the property tax in most parts of the country has meant that fixing-up the old results in a higher assessment. And if a building has any historical value whatsoever, the taxable value will be raised even higher.

A Welsh friend of ours living in West Virginia always reported to the local tax assessor that the fine Italian Renaissance portraits in his home were ancestral paintings since those of "family" were not subject to personal property taxes. Ancestral or not, we need similar protection for legitimate architectural preservation of the past. Such legislative assistance is coming slowly. Hopefully, the property tax will continue to be challenged for its retrogressive and inequitable features. The Tax Reform Act of 1976 provides special relief for those whose properties are listed on the National Register of Historic Places or are located in one of the 150 historic districts throughout the country. Rehabilitation projects undertaken in these areas must be approved by the United States Department of Interior "as being consistent with the historic character of such property," a fair and necessary condition. Such legislation enables both investors in income-producing properties and private home owners to claim an accelerated depreciation deduction in their federal income tax for capital expenses incurred in rehabilitation. The effect is to make building restoration as financially attractive as new construction. In fact, it now can be more economical for an old building to be rebuilt than for it to be torn down.

Economic improvements such as these are the result of dedicated work by volunteers and professionals in the preservation field. Some are among the over 125,000 members of the National Trust for Historic Preservation; others are involved with the work of the Victorian Society, the Back-to-the-City Movement, and several thousand preservation and historical societies at the regional and local level. Increasingly the concern is with the general architectural environment in which we live and not with just *the* historic house or office building. *Recycling* is the key word these days: Waste not and want not in a time of dwindling resources, including money. This is all to the good. Preservation has for too long stood aloof from the movement to save the natural environment.

No one believes that everything can or should be saved. Not only are most buildings put up before World War II without architectural merit, but many are not even salvageable. And we cannot become so blinded by the old that we are insensitive to the new and adventuresome. Rather, what needs to be retained and reused are those buildings—homes, offices, stores, churches, schools—which are structurally sound and reflect something of the style

and texture of our past, whether they be showplaces or not. Shopping malls on superhighways do not take the place of downtowns made up of unique but complementary shops and offices of different styles and sizes. It is perhaps the diversity and the personal scale that we miss most, whether consciously or not. A contributor to *The New York Times* wrote recently about the sad changes to his home town, Lyndhurst, New Jersey. "This may be the most significant type of change in all small communities: The destruction of elegant, beautiful and friendly—but economically outdated—old homes and their replacement with unesthetic but more functional buildings."

One can only hope that the future will not be as bleak as this writer suggests. The sanctity of landmark zoning has just been upheld by the United States Supreme Court in the Grand Central Terminal case. Aesthetic considerations have thus been given standing with those of health and safety. If we can begin to untangle some of the socio-economic restraints inherent in our system of taxation which so hinder the preservation of some fabric of the real past, then a start can also be made on winning the battle against the fast-food mentality in architectural design. This is a matter of public education, and it will be a Sisyphean task. The desire to destroy and begin anew runs deep in the American grain. As our friend, the professional wrecker, put it (this time with glee): "I've torn down every structure known to man—high rises, tenements, churches, banks. Every building is fun."

Understanding the heritage of the past is the only way to gain appreciation of it. The effects of the Victorian period are enormously popular these days—stained-glass windows, Tiffany-style lamps, exuberant paisley and Morris prints, sturdy pieces of turned oak. In fact, a reading of current home-fashion magazines indicates that the traditional passion for all things "Colonial" is being challenged at last. Is there some way to channel this love for century-old styles into tangible action? Or is this revival to be only a cosmetic one of the sort played out in the latest boutique or café-restaurant?

The matter of knowledge of architectural styles is so basic that we begin *The Second Old House Catalogue* with it once again. The following illustrated survey of American architecture is simplified, but suggestive. It is conveniently divided into Colonial, early nineteenth-century, mid-Victorian, and late-Victorian categories. The examples shown are representative in enough ways to suggest the general outline of exterior and interior architectural treatment. In no way, however, should they be taken as the final word on any particular period. They are meant to lead one into a much deeper consideration of the special character and feeling which define a true period style and which make it something of real value.

All the illustrations are from the archives of the Historic American Buildings Survey, a National Park Service unit which has diligently and imaginatively documented our architectural past since 1933.

Colonial

Nathaniel Macy House
Nantucket, Massachusetts

built prior to 1745

Simplicity itself is personified in the Nathaniel Macy House. A braced-frame structure with a central chimney, it was moved to its present location in 1745 from another site. Perhaps this is when a lean-to kitchen was added to the original structure which had a kitchen and parlor on the first floor and two chambers above. A third and later addition, a modern kitchen, can be seen at the far left. It is with additions of this sort that rectangular Colonial houses assumed a saltbox profile. Clapboard and shingles form a solid sheathing for the frame, and standing out from the wall are neatly framed 9-on-9 sash windows. The classical entrance is the only bow to high-style elegance.

Many of the first New England homes were built of only two rooms, and most have a massive central chimney rather than chimneys at the gable ends. Little or no ornamentation was applied in the cornice or on other structural elements. The vast majority of buildings throughout the Colonies were built of wood, the most available and inexpensive of materials. There are, however, vast regional differences in the use of various kinds of lumber. Oak in New England was soon replaced by pine for both exterior and interior use, as it was in Nantucket.

Both the first and second floors of the Macy house are clearly outlined in these plans drawn in 1969. The original core of the building is seen at the left. Each principal first-floor room measures 14′ 6¾″ by approximately 17′. There is, of course, a large fireplace in each. The second story was originally reached by a narrow staircase to the left of the front door. With the addition of the lean-to, interior space was almost doubled. A third fireplace and a new oven were integrated into the center chimney, and a second set of stairs—these of the closet variety—lead to a basement and up to the second floor. The third (attic) floor is still only reached through the original section. The house was restored after 1934, but modernization has occurred primarily at the back of the building and includes new dormer windows to make the rear portion of the second floor more liveable.

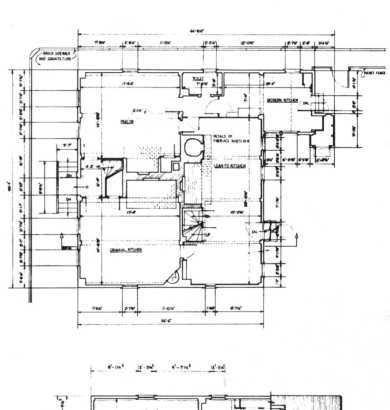

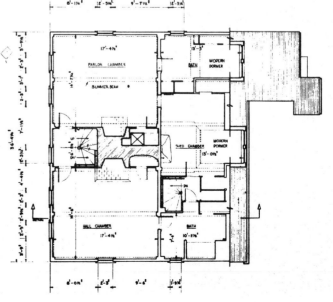

The front hall stairway is but a simple step and riser affair, a "tightwinder" in architectural parlance. The paneling is seen to be nothing more than stained pine boards with strips of lath covering the joints. The two-paneled door is to be found in other rooms in this section.

This is the original kitchen fireplace and is set in a paneled room end of a sort commonly found in many Colonial homes. The mantel is merely a carved series of mouldings. The hearth is very deep and extends into the room which is floored in pine. As can be noted, the floor has been covered with hooked and Oriental area rugs. The ceiling is low and the beams have been left exposed. The door to the left appears to lead to a storage area underneath the front stairs.

Early 19th Century/Federal

Robinson-Schofield House
Madison, Indiana

built c. 1820-21

The Federal style in America was introduced in the late 1700s. It derives in large part from the work of Robert Adam, an English architect and designer who influenced such American architects as Charles Bulfinch and Asher Benjamin. By the time of the settlement of Indiana, buildings in this style were to be found in all East Coast towns and cities of consequence. It is a much more restrained and dignified building form than that of the late Colonial or Georgian and perhaps more suitable to the new republic which was taking shape on the frontier of the Old Northwest Territory.

A chimney is situated at each end of the two-story building. The roof is typically low-pitched and ends in a simple cornice of brick. The windows and front entrance are slightly recessed below semicircular arches. Local legend has it that the home was the site of the founding of the Grand Lodge Free and Accepted Masons of Indiana in 1818. If so, the building, or some portion of it, must be somewhat older than can be documented.

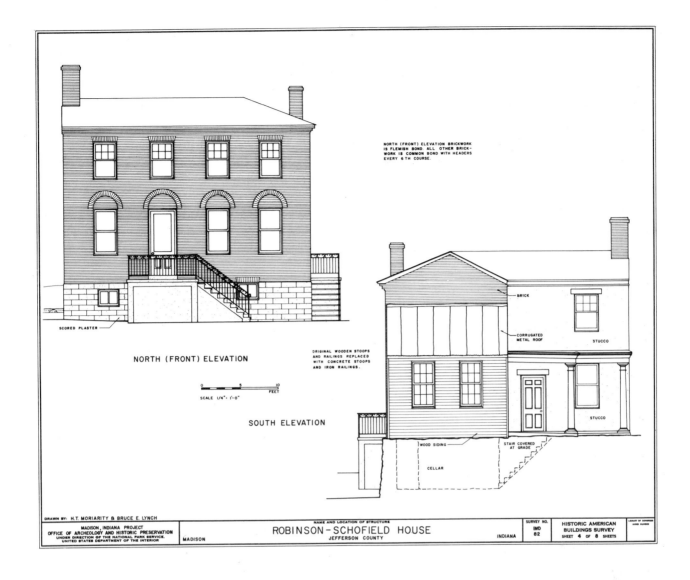

The measured drawing shows the front (north) and rear (south) elevations of the Robinson-Schofield House. The front brickwork is of Flemish bond, and all brickwork elsewhere is of common bond with headers occurring every sixth course. Both the front and side cement stoops with iron railings are replacements for wooden stoops and wooden railings. The odd shape of the front roof line can be explained by studying the rear elevation. The house is L-shaped. The original el probably consisted of only one room, and that now designated as the dining room may have been the kitchen. A study of the first-floor plan makes this even more clear. An L-shaped porch fills the rear right side of the building.

Although many Federal style buildings were built of wood, especially in New England, brick was the medium which was increasingly used. This is as true of homes and public buildings in Kentucky, Indiana, and Ohio as it was of such Eastern cities as Charleston, Baltimore, Philadelphia, and New York. These buildings were considered fireproof, at least in relation to wooden structures, and were required by statute in some cities which had suffered great property losses in devastating fires. A brick building was also considered a more substantial one for a citizen of some standing in the community.

The first-floor plan gives some idea of the interior make-up of the Robinson-Schofield House. Unfortunately, interior photos do not exist. The formal entrance to the house is found on the side rather than at the front. The stairway to the basement and the second floor is slightly more than a tightwinder. The rooms are generously spaced, and most certainly ceilings were lowered to cover structural beams. The placement of windows, doors, and fireplaces in the rooms now designated parlor, living room, and dining room is much more formal and regular than that found in the majority of Colonial houses. This structural regularity is quite typical of Federal-style buildings. The succeeding popular architectural style, the Greek Revival, was to stress this even more emphatically. Not until the mid-nineteenth century would there be a widespread popular retreat into the more eccentric and irregular forms of Gothic and Victorian.

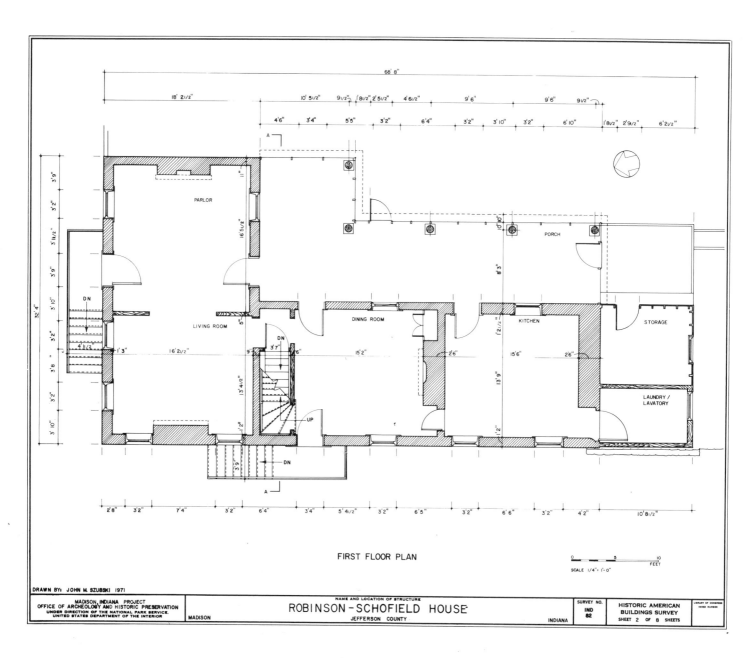

FIRST FLOOR PLAN

SCALE 1/4" = 1'-0"

DRAWN BY: JOHN M. SZUBSKI 1971

MADISON, INDIANA PROJECT
OFFICE OF ARCHEOLOGY AND HISTORIC PRESERVATION
UNDER DIRECTION OF THE NATIONAL PARK SERVICE.
UNITED STATES DEPARTMENT OF THE INTERIOR

NAME AND LOCATION OF STRUCTURE

ROBINSON-SCHOFIELD HOUSE

MADISON   JEFFERSON COUNTY   INDIANA

SURVEY NO.
IND
82

HISTORIC AMERICAN
BUILDINGS SURVEY
SHEET 2 OF 8 SHEETS

Mid-Victorian

Morris-Butler House
Indianapolis, Indiana

built in 1864

John D. Morris's fine Victorian manse is attributed to architect Dietrich Bohlen of Indianapolis. In 1881 it was sold to Noble C. Butler and remained in his family's possession until 1964 when the Historic Landmarks Foundation of Indiana acquired it for use as a house museum. The building combines many of the popular architectural forms of the mid-nineteenth century—an Italianate tower, Second Empire mansard roof, arched window heads and entryways of Romanesque Revival inspiration. It is a massive building of brick and stone of rich textures and fine proportions.

The main entrance to the house is through the towering center pavillion. Here there is nothing fussy or gloomy to depress those with a distaste for the Victorian. The arched entryway is gracefully shaped and appropriately decorated with a sculpted keystone. The recessed double entrance doors have etched glass decoration and in style repeat the rhythmic arch of the exterior.

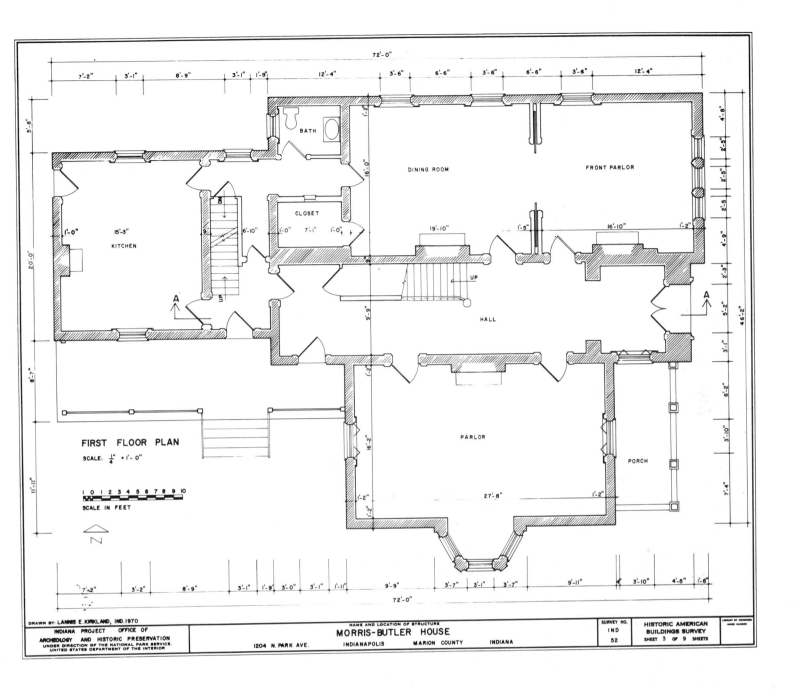

FIRST FLOOR PLAN

SCALE: $\frac{1}{4}$" = 1'-0"

SCALE IN FEET

DRAWN BY: LANNIS E. KIRKLAND, IND. 1970

INDIANA PROJECT OFFICE OF
ARCHEOLOGY AND HISTORIC PRESERVATION
UNDER DIRECTION OF THE NATIONAL PARK SERVICE.
UNITED STATES DEPARTMENT OF THE INTERIOR.

NAME AND LOCATION OF STRUCTURE

MORRIS-BUTLER HOUSE

1204 N. PARK AVE. INDIANAPOLIS MARION COUNTY INDIANA

SURVEY NO.
IND
52

HISTORIC AMERICAN
BUILDINGS SURVEY
SHEET 3 OF 9 SHEETS

The first floor plan says a great deal about the leisurely pace of life of the wealthy Victorian. The principal rooms are appropriate for entertainment; the main hall and vestibule stretch over 35 feet. Dining room and front parlor may be opened up to each other by means of sliding doors. The large main parlor is pleasantly fitted with a bay window, a feature popular in homes since the 1840s. The staircase, of course, is suitably grand for such a fine town mansion. Some sense of the height of the rooms can be gained from the two photos on the following two pages. Note that the fireplace provides the focal point of interest in each of the three principal rooms. Even though it was no longer used for burning wood, it remained an organizing design principle.

The view from the foyer is splendid in the extreme. Ornate chandeliers hung from ornamental plaster rosettes; a heavy marble-topped pier table, a writing table, and upholstered chairs and settee appear right in place. Note also the painted motifs on the inside of the archway between foyer and hall and in the far corners of the hall ceiling.

The main parlor is the most extensively appointed room in the house, yet the effect is not one of clutter or vulgarity. The gilded mirror is hardly an exercise in restraint, but neither this object nor the marble mantel seem out of keeping in a room of this style and size. Only the crystal chandelier can rival these elements in elegant beauty. The furniture is typical of the second half of the nineteenth century—highly carved and liberally upholstered. The richly ornamented ceiling and cornice in white, as well as the subdued carpeting, serve to soften what could be a stiff atmosphere. Brocade has been lavished at the window, which is topped with a tasseled lambrequin. A fine lace liner serves as a permanent filter of light. Note that this room was also used for musical entertainment.

Late Victorian

John H. Houghton House
Austin, Texas

built in 1886–87

One of the great glories of old Austin *was* this towering Queen Anne/Victorian Romanesque mansion; it was demolished in 1973. Mr. Houghton was a very prominent man, and the architect he chose, James Wahrenberger, was similarly well-known in central Texas. The roof line is the most interesting feature of the house with its numerous projections and imaginatively placed windows. In a state of disrepair when this photograph was taken, the building had obviously lost some of its details, particularly those of the conical and pyramidal-roofed towers. The hideous shapeless pile behind the Houghton mansion is typical of the "progress" that overtook it.

The detail of the center tower roof perfectly illustrates the lavish and eclectic use of building materials.

The floor plan shows how extremely complex the form of the Victorian structure had become by the late nineteenth century. The dining room has an octagonal shape; the music room makes use of the circular space of the corner tower, perhaps providing a stage for performers; the hallway not only reaches straight back from the vestibule but also turns to form a grand stair hall. The parlor and ballroom are more regular spaces, but both these rooms extend into an enclosed porch. Only the service areas, neatly separated from the rest of the house, appear to be at all conventional.

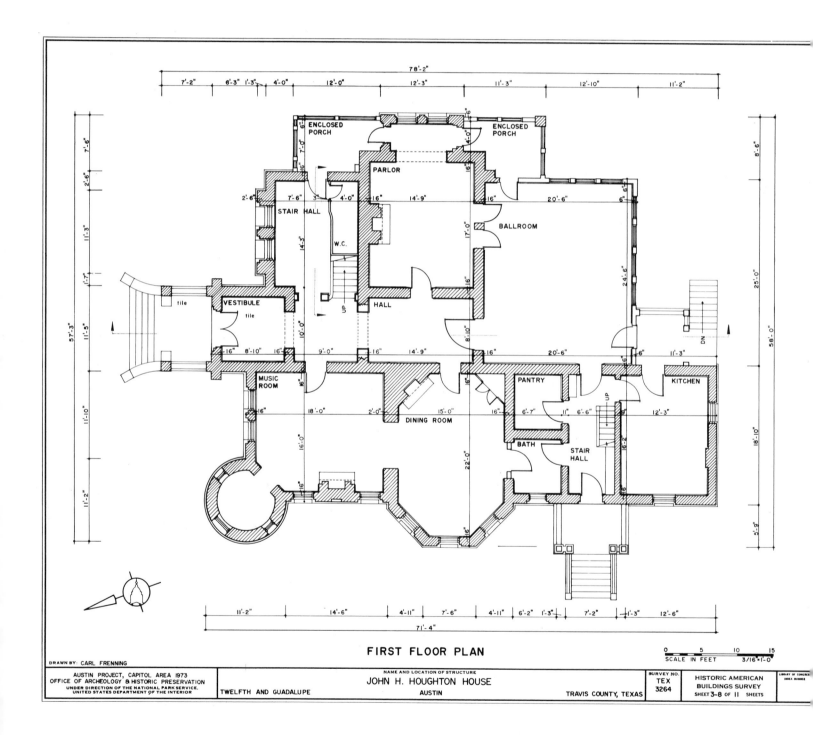

FIRST FLOOR PLAN

SCALE IN FEET

DRAWN BY: CARL FRENNING

AUSTIN PROJECT, CAPITOL AREA 1973
OFFICE OF ARCHEOLOGY & HISTORIC PRESERVATION
UNDER DIRECTION OF THE NATIONAL PARK SERVICE.
UNITED STATES DEPARTMENT OF THE INTERIOR

NAME AND LOCATION OF STRUCTURE
JOHN H. HOUGHTON HOUSE
AUSTIN

TWELFTH AND GUADALUPE

TRAVIS COUNTY, TEXAS

SURVEY NO.
TEX
3264

HISTORIC AMERICAN
BUILDINGS SURVEY
SHEET 3-8 OF 11 SHEETS

LIBRARY OF CONGRESS
INDEX NUMBER

Only this one built-in cupboard in the dining room remained to be photographed before the building was torn down. Particularly interesting is the combination of classical and Gothic motifs. Presumably the original furnishings would have been similarly eclectic.

Raised-panel front entrance door by Townsend H. Anderson; hand-forged thumb latch by Robert Bordon. *See* page 39.

I   Structural Products & Services

Structural materials are by definition the most important components in any house—new or old. In substance, they provide a structure's form; in design, they define its style. First and foremost, a building must be structurally sound. Load-bearing walls will settle with age, and joists and rafters may show some stress, but as long as these elements are not badly out of line, rotted, or diseased, problems of a structural sort can be kept to a minimum. Future deterioration may be prevented by the use of collar beams, extra supports, and careful attention to any moisture problems in the foundation or roof. The secondary structural elements—windows, doors, siding, paneling, decorative columns, steps, chimneys and fireplaces, railings and balusters—are more likely to require frequent attention. And these are also the elements which may have changed the most with age. It is somewhat difficult to change the basic structural framework of a house, but stylistic modifications were easier and less expensive to make. It is with these secondary structural appurtenances that most restoration work is concerned.

This first and most important section of *The Second Old House Catalogue* covers a great deal of the structural territory. It is primarily concerned with those elements which define a house style. Such items as structural beams are not ignored, but the basic work of re-building a house or restoring it to its original form is the business of a skilled contractor with knowledge of building technology past and present. There are few home owners who will attempt such work. Catalogued in this chapter are some of the best professionals to consult.

Supplies of antique building materials are becoming somewhat more difficult to obtain. Since old-house living has become a popular option, there has been a natural tendency for prices to rise with the decrease in available resources. It was once a relatively easy matter to find what you needed—shutters, doors, complete stairways—in junk or salvage yards. Anyone who became active in preservation work in the 1950s knows that there was a surfeit of old materials on hand thanks to the misguided efforts of so-called "planners" to renew our cities and towns and to transform the countryside with interstate expressways. Progress of this sort has slowed down to a rush hour crawl. Even the new highways are now becoming antique, and, if taxpayers continue to revolt, they may just stay that way.

What has been "lost" in antique materials in the 1970s has been gained in quality reproduction work. Educational and cultural institutions have assisted in the revival of traditional craft skills among the young and their preservation among the elderly. The restoration craftsmen of the first half of the twentieth century were a hardy but small band, and we all owe them a great debt of gratitude for keeping alive a small fire of practical antiquarianism. It is easy to laugh at the pretension of so much early restoration work of an upper-class sort, but without it we would be lost today. The new housewrights, blacksmiths, woodworkers, and masons have learned from their courtly peers the value of graceful old age.

Now that the preservation cause has swelled to movement importance, however, one must be on guard. Beware the prophet bearing false witness, or, in this case, the supplier pushing bogus goods. The "old" look is "in"—from early Colonial to late Victorian. There is no local, state, or national consumer protection agency to blow the whistle on "authentic" reproductions. And more and more people are choosing to visit a large-scale plastic recreation park than such a careful recreation of the past as Colonial Williamsburg or the period rooms of Winterthur. The temptation grows greater to substitute surface appearances for goods of long-lasting quality. Read on and you will discover that no one needs to accept the second-rate in houses any more than they do today in automobiles or clothing, and especially not when it comes to something as important as the very fabric of an old house.

Primary Materials

Good basic structural materials can be as hard to come by as well-made doors and windows. Real wood—as opposed to laminated composition—has escalated some 20% in price within the past year alone. Hopefully, the home restorer will not need vast quantities of lumber and will be able to make do with supplies readily available in his area—whether antique or newly sawed. Quality stone is just as "pricey." And there are bogus varieties which just won't pass muster. Stone-like blobs of some polymer are sold across the country under several different commerical names. They are called, of course, "authentic" and "faithful reproductions." It would be better to gather your own fieldstones one-by-one in the country on weekends than to create such an instant horror.

We can offer several sources for new and old wood in case you cannot locate supplies nearby. Structural stone is more regional in distribution and variety, and, of course, extremely expensive to ship any long distance. Whether it be for Colorado sandstone, Illinois limestone, Connecticut brownstone, Pennsylvania fieldstone, or any other regional variant, visit your nearest quarry or stone supplier. Masons can also help you to locate sources or supply.

Paneling

Both Simpson and Potlatch offer new solid-wood planks. Simpson features redwood paneling as well as pine, alder, Douglas fir, cedar, and juniper. Most of these are available in tongue and groove patterns which vary from 4″ to 10″ in width and do not appear to have been smeared with a laminate. The Townsend wall planks from Potlatch are less natural in appearance than those of Simpson because of treatment with a alkyd-urea finish which is baked on. But there is much greater variety in hardwoods—walnut, various oaks, ash, cypress. cottonwood, pecan, and cherry. Most of the woods are ½″ thick and measure from 4″ to 8″ in width.

You may wish to send for Potlatch's "Designer's Kit" of 14 samples, $5. Both Simpson and Potlatch products are distributed throughout North America.

Simpson Timber Co.
900 Fourth Ave.
Seattle, Wash. 98164
(206) 292-5000

Potlatch Corporation
Wood Products, Southern Division
P.O. Box 916
Stuttgart, Ark. 72160
(501) 673-1606

Those fortunate enough to live in old homes built of California redwood—an extremely durable material—and who are thinking of restoring or just preserving a building of such timber will find the literature offered by the California Redwood Association especially helpful. There are over 100 "idea booklets," technical data sheets, and bulletins distributed through architects, builders, and dealers. Ask one of them to show you what they have, or write:

California Redwood Association
617 Montgomery St.
San Francisco, Calif. 94111

If you can't abide the commercially-available lumbers, then there are specialists you can turn to for help. Wagon House Cabinetmaking is one of these and will make up walnut, cherry, oak, or ash paneling to order. This firm is also a specialist in random-width oak flooring.

The Wagon House Cabinetmaking, Inc.
Box 149
Mendenhall, Penn. 19357
(215) 388-6352

Diamond K. supplies old clapboards of 5″ widths. These are gray-brown, naturally-weathered boards which do not require stain or a sealer. Barnwood of weathered Eastern pine is also available and comes in golden brown, silver gray, or weathered red shades. Both clapboards and barnwood are priced at $1.50 a square foot.

Literature available.

Diamond K. Co., Inc.
130 Buckland Rd.
South Windsor, Conn. 06074
(203) 644-8486

Period Pine of Georgia was featured in the first *Old House Catalogue*, and so many readers responded favorably that we must report more good news. The pine—Virgin Longleaf Yellow Heart of Pine—which the company salvages and resaws, is now available not only for flooring and paneling, but can be made into wainscoting, chair rails, doors, mantels, mouldings, or can be supplied as beams. This is an extremely hard, clear antique wood that was largely timbered off by 1900. That which has replaced it, however, does not have exactly the same quality. The original trees were between 150-500 years old at the time they were cut.

Literature available.

Period Pine
P.O. Box 77052
Atlanta, Ga. 30309
(404) 876-4740

Don't be frightened off by the Weird Wood label. This is a product line begun by Green Mountain Cabins, and they may have what you need for replacing or patching small sections of paneling. You will want square edge stock, round edge, or a combination thereof. These shapes are available in white pine, butternut, cherry, sugar or rock maple, and yellow birch in various widths and grades. Everything will be done to see that you get as close a match to your old wood as is humanly possible.

Brochure available.

Weird Wood
Green Mountain Cabins, Inc.
Box 190
Chester, Vt. 05143
(802) 875-3535

Custom paneling will be executed by Accent Walls in whatever wood a customer specifies. This California firm will also provide custom-order wainscoting of the old-fashioned grooved variety and has some recycled lumber available as well.

Flyer available with stamped, self-addressed envelope.

Accent Walls
1565 The Alameda
San Jose, Calif. 95126
(408) 293-3082

For those seeking custom-order paneling of the most elegant sort, Architectural Paneling is the right answer. This firm is noted for its finely-executed wood interiors in the best of materials and traditional English and French styles. The contract division handles much more than panels; wainscoting, bookcases, mouldings, doors, and mantels are designed and executed—if so desired—in their entirety.

Brochure and color slides available, $3.50.

Architectural Paneling, Inc.
979 Third Ave.
New York, N.Y. 10022
(212) 371-9632

Beams

Such structural members connote rusticity. For many people, they practically define an "old house" style. Unfortunately, a goodly number of such wooden supports should never be exposed; the original builders knew this and provided a plaster ceiling. If most of the beams are indeed worthy of display, however, you may want to make them visible. By doing so you will at least automatically raise the height of the room, a not inconsequential achievement in a low-ceilinged Colonial interior that has to be lived in by today's considerably taller folk. And if you need to replace a few beams or are completely restoring a primitive country interior, there are sources of supply available. There is no need to depend on the fake, "wood-like" timbers of styrofoam teture which are purveyed in too many lumber yards.

The Broad-Axe Beam Co. derives its name from the chisel-bladed instrument seen being used in the picture above. This method of hewing timber is one of several traditional steps taken by the firm to insure that its products are correctly produced. Two types of beams —structural and decorative—are available in white pine. Structural beams are available sawed one side or hewed four sides, and are approximately 7½" x 7½" in lengths of 8', 12', 14', and 16'. These are available at $3.75 a linear foot. The decorative beam is a structural beam sawed in half lengthwise and measures approximately 3½" x 7½". The same lengths as for the structural are available at $2.75 a linear foot.

All the beams are air-dried for a period of at least six months, a process which assures that the lumber will gain in strength and properly shrink on the squared dimension. Broad-Axe will also undertake custom hewing jobs, including hardwood timbers, but they remind the customer that quality lengths greater than 24' are difficult to find and are expensive. In addition, they require much more drying time.

Illustrated literature available.

Broad-Axe Beam Co.
R. D. 2, Box 181-E
Brattleboro, Vt. 05301
(802) 257-0064

Most of Diamond K.'s beams are of the decorative sort. These are made from pine or spruce and are available in two grades: A at $2 a linear foot, 6" x 6" or 4" x 6" up to 30' in length; and B, $1 a linear foot, 4" x 4" or 3" x 5" up to 15' in length.

Hand-hewn structural beams of chestnut and pine can be ordered, and roughly 50% of these antique timbers will show peg and notch marks. The price of $5 a linear foot covers an 8" x 8" timber of up to 30' in length.

Literature available.

Diamond K. Co., Inc.
130 Buckland Rd.
South Windsor, Conn. 06074
(203) 644-8486

A wide variety of decorative ceiling beams are available from Guyon, Inc. They do not stipulate exactly what type of timber is used, but it is cut and sawed in Lancaster County, Pennsylvania. Sizes range from 4" x 6" to 8" x 10", and prices vary from $1.70 a linear foot to $9.35. Beams can be rough sawn or hewn on one side or three sides. All are given a linseed oil stain in one of 66 colors that you choose unless you request that the beams be left natural. The price is reduced 5% for no stain.

Literature available, $1.

Guyon, Inc.
65 Oak St.
Lititz, Penn. 17543
(717) 626-0225

Doors

Perhaps no feature in an old house attracts more attention than a well-crafted front door. Considerably more care has been traditionally lavished on these openings than on any other, and their very style and execution can determine the ultimate success of a restoration project. Fortunately, most old doors—if removed at one time—were saved. Nearly every supplier of antique house parts has a supply of different sizes and models available. These suppliers are listed later in this chapter. If, however, you must start anew, here are some leads to follow.

Walter E. Phelps is an individual craftsman who undertakes various types of architectural reproduction woodwork, including doors. He uses traditional methods of joinery and construction and works only from precise measured drawings or an exact sample.

Walter E. Phelps
Box 76
Williamsville, Vt. 05362
(802) 348-6347

Alan Amerian is an expert maker of custom raised panel and carved doors. His four-man shop makes use of select woods.

Literature available.

Amerian Woodcarving
282 San Jose Ave.
San Jose, Calif. 95125
(408) 294-2968

Bel-Air is a producer of commerical carved doors for entryways. Few of their models in solid mahogany or fir are appropriate for pre-Victorian houses, but they are certainly suitable for some later period homes. Illustrated is the "Heritage" model with a leaded glass design of tulips.

Literature available.

Bel-Air Door Co.
P.O. Box 829
Alhambra, Calif. 91802
(213) 576-2545
California toll free only outside Los Angeles (213) area:
1-800-242-4400

Homes in the Spanish Colonial or Mission style have special stylistic requirements, and these apply to doors as well. Spanish Pueblo Doors was founded over twenty years ago to meet the needs of a special group of home owners who, contrary to popular impression, are to be found almost everywhere in North America and not just in the Southwest. The company offers twenty basic reversible designs in quality-grade Ponderosa pine and Philippine mahogany. Each door is handmade and hand-finished, with each panel and samll part being cut, carved, and sanded separately. All doors are built from 1¾″ lumber. Custom-made doors are also available in such woods as red alder, red oak, and black walnut. Prices for the regular models range from $181.50 to $236; for custom-ordered, $219 to $468.75. Illustrated is regular style No. 160.

Literature available.

Spanish Pueblo Doors, Inc.
P.O. Box 2517, Wagon Rd.
Santa Fe, N.M. 87501
(505) 471-0811

Window Frames and Sashes

Windows are often a problem in an old house. Frames and sashes may have severely deteriorated over the years. If they cannot be adequately reconditioned, you have no alternative but to replace them. And it is quite unlikely that you will be able to use any sort of standard window that is commercially available. If you do not have a carpenter/woodworker in the area who can custom make what you need, all is not lost. There are competent firms that specialize in producing period window materials.

Maurer and Shepherd is one of the experts to consult. The firm makes Colonial-style small-pane windows, sashes, and frames. Mortise and tenon joinery is the method they follow in this carpentry work. Illustrated is a window that has been framed in this manner with 12 on 12 lights. Maurer and Shepherd will also undertake custom reproduction work in any other style you can name.

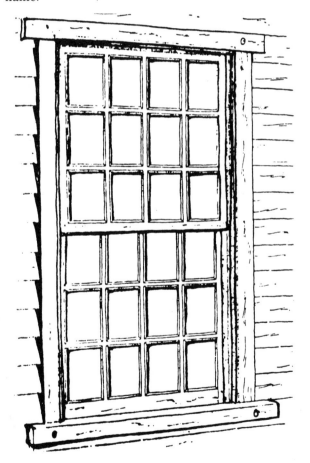

Literature available.

Maurer & Shepherd, Joyners
122 Naubuc Ave.
Glastonbury, Conn. 06033
(203) 633-2383

Michael Brofman is a very versatile woodworker. Although his company bears the name "Colonial," he enjoys working with more than plain rectangles. Quarter-circle, half-circle, full-circle, and Gothic triangle segment sash and frames are made to order.

Literature available.

Michael's Fine Colonial Products
22 Churchill Lane
Smithtown, N.Y. 11787
(516) 543-2479 after 6 p.m.

Expert advice is yours from the Preservation Resource Center. Their standard window sash is suitable for homes built from roughly the late eighteenth to the first decades of the nineteenth century. They can probably help you with other styles as well.

Data sheet, $1.

Preservation Resource Center
Lake Shore Rd.
Essex, N.Y. 12936
(518) 963-7305

If you can possibly save old windows, by all means do so. Replacements for antique glass panes are nearly impossible to find. Walter Phelps is one of a number of craftsmen who offers sash conservation, including glazing. It is delicate, precise work if properly executed, but very satisfying results may be achieved.

Walter E. Phelps
Box 76
Williamsville, Vt. 05362
(802) 348-6347

Shutters

Many architectural antiques supply houses carry a good stock of these traditional trappings. Search first in these haunts, catalogued separately in this chapter, before you turn to someone who can make them anew. Shutters were once used only for shutting out the outside and were, in essence, an early form of storm window. Now that a second layer of window or double-glazing has become customary, the utilitarian value of shutters has been replaced by decorative considerations. Shutters, however, may be hung so that in almost any situation they can be closed whenever desired, therefore providing an extra layer of insulation. If our winters are indeed growing colder each year, use of such devices may be one of the best investments we can make.

Michael Brofman is one woodworker who makes raised panel shutters. These are constructed of 1¹/₁₆″ white pine, and range in size from 2′0″ x 2′7″ to 3′ x 5′7″. Prices vary from approximately $36 to $67. Different sizes and styles are also made to order.

Literature available.

Michael's Fine Colonial Products
22 Churchill Lane
Smithtown, N.Y. 11787
(516) 543-2479

Glass

If we stop to think of glass at all in an old house, we probably only have an image of the clear variety used in windows. So standard have materials become in the twentieth century, that we are frequently surprised by the exception. Glass was once a luxury, and even that used for simple windows was used sparingly—if at all—in the seventeenth and early eighteenth centuries. But by the middle of the nineteenth century, various varieties of glass came into vogue, and their use multiplied at least through the 1920s. Stained, leaded, beveled, etched, chipped—the techniques were many and the effects quite stunning.

The atmospheric effects produced by using a decorative glass are widely admired today. In fact, many of the so-called restored commercial areas of our cities are awash in stained glass. Mediocre copies are widely available and are sometimes pawned off as the real thing to the unknowing. Yet there is much that is good in this renaissance of period-glass design. A recent exhibition at Los Angeles's Design Center graphically proved that there are a considerable number of contemporary artists who are skilled in this medium.

Judson Studios has been providing fine leaded-glass designs since the turn of the century and is heartily recommended by preservation experts in the Los Angeles area. Repair work, the creation of new designs, and traditional lead glass designs are undertaken by the firm.

The Judson Studios
200 S. Avenue 66
Los Angeles, Calif.
(213) 255-0131

Penco Studios is another expert designer and manufacturer of leaded-glass windows and has been in business since 1892. It divides its products into four categories: entry sidelights, general patterns, transoms, and miscellaneous windows. The Penco catalog features more than 100 standard patterns which can be used for various purposes. Illustrated are just a few of these.

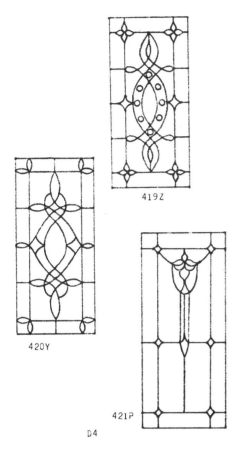

419Z

420Y

421P

D4

Virtu
P.O. Box 192
Southfield, Mich. 48037
(313) 357-1250

Cherry Creek provides hand- and machine-beveled glass for stained-glass artists, but can supply the home owner with standard blanks in many different sizes— which may be all that is necessary except for the framing. Two samples of the company's work are shown here along with an example of a hand-beveled

Penco will make any of these patterns (or others on a custom-order basis) with colored and/or beveled glass. The company has also developed a method of producing insulated leaded-glass windows by using an exterior protective sheet of glass and a vacuum seal.

Catalog available, $2.

Penco Studios
1110 Baxter Ave.
Louisville, Ky. 40404
(502) 459-4027

The artisans at Virtu work within the tradition of stained glass but seek to extend it with original new work. Much of this may be most appropriate for period interiors. One of the group's designs is illustrated here. Traditional patterns in leaded and copper-foiled stained glass can be produced as well.

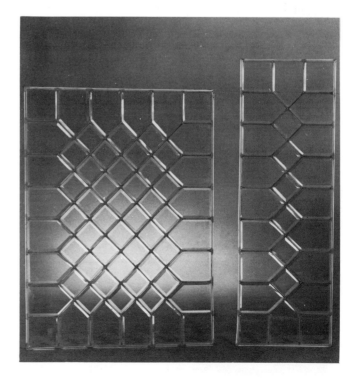

custom window panel. Standard pieces are made in a clear glass, but there are other colors and finishes of interest—bronze, mirror, frosted, miter, and something termed "glue chip." This last process—available on both plate and beveled glass—involves the use of animal glue and glass, a combination which produces a fern-like pattern. Such an appearance was popular in the early 1900s.

Catalog available.

Cherry Creek Ent., Inc.
937 Santa Fe Drive
Denver, Colo. 80204
(303) 892-1819

Era Victoriana specializes in antique American stained and beveled-glass windows. Many of these have required restoration, a process with which the firm is very familiar. This is an important source for windows, transoms, arches, skylights, and door panels that you should not overlook. Illustrated are two of their finest pieces, that below termed "Venus de Milo."

Illustrated brochure available, $1.25.

Era Victoriana
P.O. Box 9683
San Jose, Calif. 95157
(408) 296-5560

Bernard Gruenke of the Conrad Schmidt Studios is highly recommended by Chicago-area restorers. He will produce mosaics and beveled and frosted glass.

Bernard E. Gruenke, Jr.
Conrad Schmidt Studios
2405 S. 162nd St.
New Berlin, Wis. 53157
(414) 786-3030

Century is a good Texas outlet for clear or colored beveled plate glass. The glass used ranges from ¼″ to ¾″ in thickness. Various bevel widths are offered.

Price list available.

Century Glass Inc.
1417 N. Washington Ave.
Dallas, Tex. 75204
(214) 823-7773

Glass decorating and sculpturing have been specialties of Carved Glass and Signs in the New York area. They can duplicate sandblasted decorative glass and chipped glass panels and will undertake stained-glass work.

Carved Glass and Signs
767 E. 132nd St.
Bronx, N.Y. 10454
(212) 649-1266

Ceiling Materials

Metal ceilings have become almost as ubiquitous as stained glass. As is the way with architectural decoration, what was considered unbelievably dowdy, if not downright tacky at one time, is proclaimed ultra-chic a generation or two later. The story is somewhat the same with decorative plaster ceilings, but since these are extremely expensive undertakings, they have not achieved the same widespread popularity. Fortunately, suppliers who can provide new ceilings of both types, and craftsmen who can restore the old, are still very much with us.

AA-Abbingdon Ceiling Co is one of the two main suppliers of metal ceilings. These are available in 24″ x 96″ pieces. One of these plates contains 64 repeating designs or plates; most include only sixteen or four. A few are of one overall design. Illustrated are plates #507 (top) and #200 (bottom).

AA-Abbingdon also supplies the necessary sheet-metal moulding to finish off the ceiling.

Brochure available.

AA-Abbingdon Ceiling Co., Inc.
2149 Utica Ave.
Brooklyn, N.Y. 11234
(212) 236-3251

Shanker ceilings are identical to those of AA-Abbingdon, but this firm—a manufacturing source rather than just a supplier—also offers handsome metal cornices which nicely finish off a late nineteenth-century interior. These, of course, do not have to be used only with metal ceilings. Cornice designs #807 (top) and #906 (bottom) are illustrated.

Literature available.

Barney Brainum-Shanker Steel Co., Inc.
70–32 83rd St.
Glendale, N.Y. 11227
(212) 894-5581

The design and fabrication of plaster ceiling ornaments has been a specialty of Decorators Supply for many years. The demand for these is obviously very limited, but the individual ornaments are part of the company's regular offerings and can be supplied on demand for either new or restored work. The ceiling design illustrated is termed "Louis XIV."

Catalog available, $1.

The Decorators Supply Corp.
3610–12 S. Morgan St.
Chicago, Ill. 60609
(312) 847-6300

Felber Studios is one of the last firms that will undertake the design, execution, and installation of an ornamental plaster ceiling. In the first *Old House Catalogue* we presented their "Haddon Hall Modified" design, and here is a second, "Hopewood Inn." Like the

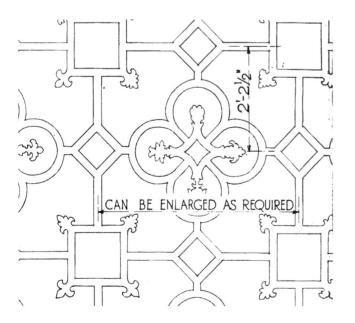

other, it is a Tudor design appropriate for a grand English Tudor mansion of the sort built between the turn of the century and the 1930s.

Felber also performs another most useful service—the reconstruction of antique plaster.

Catalog available.

Felber Studios
P.O. Box 551, 110 Ardmore Ave.
Ardmore, Penn. 19003
(215) MI2-4710

Roofing Materials

The importance of a particular roofing material and style is usually not appreciated until a new roof—of very different texture and appearance—replaces the old. This is especially true on those buildings of nineteenth-century style—French mansard, Queen Anne or Stick, and Spanish Colonial—which make use of either special materials or feature unusual multi-level roof treatments. The kind of shingling used on the exterior of many Victorian buildings, for instance, was continued on sloping façades which terminated in a flat or only slightly pitched roof. These shingles of various shapes are not always easy to find today. The terra-cotta tiles employed for homes in the Spanish Colonial or Mission style are similarly difficult to locate. Concrete imitations have taken their place.

Other kinds of materials—such as shakes and slate used for period buildings, including many pre-Victorian—have been more successfully imitated. There is still no real substitute for slate in either appearance or durability, but this has become prohibitively expensive. Fiberglass shingles are a considerable improvement on the first asphalt fire- and windproof materials and are worth the extra cost.

San Francisco Victoriana has provided San Francisco-area residents with traditional-cut cedar shingles for some time and is now offering these nationally. It is about time! These are needed just as badly in Boston and St. Louis as they are on the West Coast. Illustrated are the six different patterns available.

Included in their Book of Architectural Mouldings, *$1.*

San Francisco Victoriana
606 Natoma St.
San Francisco, Calif. 94103
(415) 864-5477

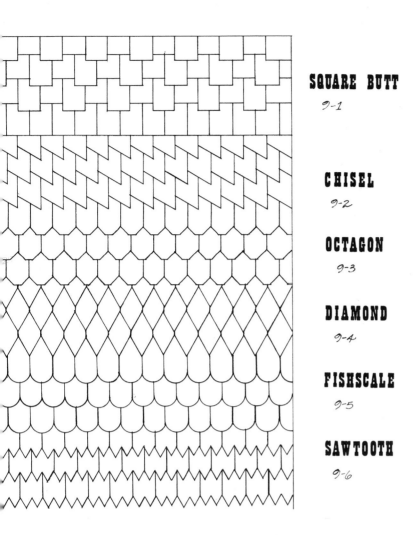

SQUARE BUTT

9-1

CHISEL

9-2

OCTAGON

9-3

DIAMOND

9-4

FISHSCALE

9-5

SAWTOOTH

9-6

more buildings are destroyed in future years. The only good that can come out of such urban warfare is a new supply of antique materials—a cold comfort, indeed.

Smith & Son Roofing
1360 Virginia Ave.,
Baldwin Park, Calif.
(213) 337-1524

Polyurethane Substitutes

Some purists may object to the inclusion of such an artificial material in a book devoted to honest, traditional materials and workmanship. We beg to disagree. A good number of molded forms available in modern polymers are useful for small-scale work of minor importance. Exactly how appropriate they might be for a particular purpose, however, is a matter which only the individual can determine. In any case, we feel that we have an obligation to announce their availability and to leave final aesthetic judgments to the prospective buyer. Bear in mind that products under discussion are not of the bogus "wood-like" sort being pushed commercially by too many major building suppliers.

Fypon, Inc. produces what they call "entrance systems" which feature pilasters, crossheads, and pediments for entryways. There are three product lines available—Eagle, Cardinal, and Sparrow—which reflect not differences in style but of quality and cost. All Fypon materials are made of high-density polyurethane which can be handled in much the same manner as structural millwork.

Literature available.

Fypon, Inc.
108 Hill St.
Stewartstown, Penn. 17363
(717) 993-2593

Dana-Deck offers machined and handsplit Western Red Cedar shakes. Both varieties have been treated with a fire retardant and are available in several sizes. The company· also supplies Western Red Cedar shingles for walls, mansards, and regular roofs. These come in ten fancy butt patterns—diagonal, half cove, diamond, round, hexagon, octagon, arrow, square, fish scale, and sawtooth.

Contact your local lumber dealer for supplies of these materials, or get in touch with Dana-Deck for help in this regard.

Dana-Deck, Inc.
P.O. Box 78
Orcas, Wash. 98280
(206) 376-4531 or 4787

Smith & Son Roofing warehouses handmade tiles of the sort suitable for Spanish-style dwellings. Just how long the supply will last probably depends on how many

The advantages of using polymers—they are molded in one piece, lightweight, and resistant to rot or insects—have been fully capitalized by Focal Point. The disadvantages—lack of precise details and texture—have been reduced as much as they probably can be. This firm does not attempt to create massive effects in the material, but rather concentrates on such features as domes, niches, ceiling medallions, and mouldings, the last category being one that is covered in the second section of this book. The domes and niches particularly interest us because these architectural elements are extremely expensive and difficult to achieve in natural materials. The Focal Point dome is illustrated here.

Brochure available.

Focal Point, Inc.
4870 South Atlanta Rd.
Smyrna, Ga. 30080
(401) 351-0820

Cleaning of Façades

Ever since the advent of the automobile, America (and the rest of the civilized world) has been getting dirtier and dirtier. Masonry buildings blacken; structures of wood just turn a grimy gray. Perhaps the recent imposition of stringent pollution controls will help matters considerably, but, frankly, we have little hope that the air will become that clean. The pollution of the past may not have been quite so bad for buildings—except in coal-mining towns—but it, too, was noxious. Today we are more conscious of the filth around us, and of the immense damage that has been caused to the natural and man-made environment by the instruments of modern living. Now it is up to modern industry to provide ways for alleviating the damage, and it can be done. Sandblasting was considered the efficient method of wiping away the grime until the effects of blasting away brick and stone façades became clearly evident.

The pitted remains of once finely-surfaced brick and cut stone were hardly worth saving. Now there are chemical solutions which will clean much more effectively and leave the texture of a façade intact. They are also environmentally safe to use in other ways.

Sermac Systems is just one of several national firms that use new methods of cleaning. They can handle any kind of masonry structure and have also devised safe and efficient ways of removing paint from wood, metal, and masonry. Only the most delicate façades of terra-cotta ornament are still liable to damage, but progress is being made in this area, too.

Brochure available.

Sermac Industrial Cleaning
P.O. Box 1684
Des Plaines, Ill. 60018
(312) 824-1810

House Inspection Services

Anyone seriously considering the purchase of any kind of house—new or old—should also consider asking an outside expert to evaluate the building's condition. Technical expertise of this sort is especially valuable if the soundness of an old house is in question. Many were built of much better materials than those used today, but maintenance may not have been followed with care. In any case, you do not want to find yourself in a Mr.-Blanding-Builds-His-Dream-House kind of situation, with walls tumbling around you from the time the deed is turned over. If you know a good contractor in the area, you may want to depend on his advice. And there are also restoration experts that can be contacted through local or regional preservation societies. Probably best of all, however, is someone who has been trained to inspect buildings. He could save you a great deal of money.

Guardian National House Inspection, Inc., is a group of such trained inspectors. Unfortunately, the company covers only a five state area—New York, New Jersey, Connecticut, Rhode Island, and Massachusetts. If you live outside this region, you still might want to contact them for advice as to how to find a good inspector. Many of the preservation/restoration services cataloged in the next section of this chapter can also provide professional assistance of this type.

Brochure available.

Guardian National House Inspection, Inc.
Box 31
Pleasantville, N.Y. 10570
(914) 769-6186
or

Guardian National House Inspection, Inc.
Box 115
Orleans, Mass. 02653
(617) 255-6609

Restoration Specialists

The old-house field has its jacks-of-all-trades, men and women who can provide professional advice and work of considerable value. Only a few such individuals or groups were written up in the first Old House Catalogue. Their number, however, has expanded in the past two years, and so has their importance as preservation becomes not only a cause but a full-fledged business. These are the kinds of people who may be able to advise you on preservation law and zoning, on tax benefits and liabilities, on structural work and interior design, and who may even be able to provide many of the materials needed for a project.

Townsend H. Anderson, House Joiner

If you ever become depressed about saving an old house, try to communicate with Townsend Anderson. The only trouble is that you probably will not be able to find him. He will be off in pursuit of another period braced-frame dwelling which can be carefully disassembled to join the three that he now has in storage. Anderson doesn't collect these buildings for the fun of it. He is in the business of reconstructing and restoring them for clients. He also designs and builds braced-frame buildings from new timbers, but, as he puts it, "within the parameters of classical proportion and finish. . . ."

Anderson produces all the interior and exterior millwork needed for his buildings, and this work is accomplished by hand. These materials are also available for customers not involved in one of the complete house projects.

Illustrated here are several examples of his work. The Cape Cod—before and after—was found in Northfield, Vermont, disassembled, moved, and rebuilt in Duxbury, Vermont. The hutch and hanging wall cabinet are found in one of his restored houses. Using new timbers, Anderson constructed the braced-framed barn with attached shed in South Duxbury, Vermont.

41

Catalog available, $1.

Townsend H. Anderson
R.D. 1, Box 44D
Moretown, Vt. 05660
(802) 244-5095

Arch Associates/Stephen Guerrant

This is a professional restoration, rehabilitation, and remodeling architectural firm serving the Chicago area. They can help with the location of restoration materials and provide a real-estate inspection service for a fixed fee.

Arch Associates/Stephen Guerrant
874 Greenbay Rd.
Winnetka, Ill. 60093
(312) 446-7810

A. W. Baker Restorations, Inc.

Anne Baker provides a badly-needed service—consultation *before* a restoration project is begun. She and her colleagues will work out a plan to be followed and, if necessary, will follow up with a local contractor once the project is underway. In addition, the firm is continuing with the business of dismantling fine old structures and the reconstruction of them on more permanent sites. Illustrated is preparation for the relocation of a seventeenth-century Cape and the actual journey itself.

A. W. Baker Restorations, Inc.
670 Drift Rd.
Westport, Mass. 02790
(617) 636-8765

John Conti

Every aspect of a period restoration project can be handled by John Conti—from research work to the supplying of proper period materials. He is skilled in the manner of a master carpenter/builder of old.

John Conti, Restoration Contractor
Box 189
Wagontown, Penn. 19376
(215) 384-0553

Wilbert R. Hasbrouck, FAIA

Bill Hasbrouck has received about every preservation award that can be given—for good reason. His work in the South Prairie Avenue section of Chicago has been of great importance. A visit to Glesner House, H. H. Richardson's greatest gift to Chicago, provides ample evidence that this preservation architect is one of the very best. He directs only the restoration of buildings of significant architectural merit and uses the best trained craftsmen.

Wilbert R. Hasbrouck, FAIA
Historic Resources
711 S. Dearborn
Chicago, Ill. 60605

Historic Boulevard Services

This firm provides a fine line of terra-cotta chimney pots which have been described in the section on fireplaces and heating. The owner, William L. Lavicka, is a consulting engineer with a contracting practice. His specialty is 1880–1900 buildings which require renovation and restoration. For this purpose he maintains a large stock of antique doors, trim, railings, and fireplace mantels.

William L. Lavicka
Historic Boulevard Services
1520 W. Jackson Blvd.
Chicago, Ill. 60607
(312) 829-5562

The House Carpenters

These enterprising individuals blend the best of the old with the new. Their specialty is traditional timber frames of select white pine and oak, hewn or hand planed, with mortise and tenon and dovetail joinery. This type of fine reproduction work is illustrated in the framing shown below.

At the same time, The House Carpenters fabricate and supply materials for the restoration of early homes—shingles and clapboards, doors and windows, paneling and flooring, mouldings and hardware. One of their seventeenth-century leaded sash designs is illustrated here.

Brochure available, $4.

The House Carpenters
Box 217
Shutesbury, Mass. 01072
(413) 253-7020

Housesmiths

As the following four photographs show, Housesmiths is very much in the timber-framing business. Stewart

Elliott and Eugenie Wallas have written a whole book on this traditional subject, and Elliott has just completed a follow-up volume, *The Timber Frame Planning Book*. But they do more than write. They will package a custom pre-cut frame and ship it *anywhere*. If you are thinking of a new house built along old lines, you might want to consider such a braced-frame structure. If so, suggest the Housesmith package to a contracter.

The Timber Framing Book, $9.95.
The Timber Frame Planning Book, $15.

Housesmiths
P.O. Box 416
York, Maine 03909
(207) 363-5551

David Howard, Inc.

This is another firm which specializes in braced-frame structures, and like the others, it works out of the New England area. The frames are of oak and are of the sort most compatible for a period-style home of the Colonial period. The firm does not do reproduction work, but, rather, brings traditional techniques to bear on new house construction.

Brochure available, $4.

David Howard, Inc.
P.O. Box 295
Alstead, N.H. 03602
(603) 835-2213

Howell Construction

Restoration of homes in the Middle Tennessee area has become a major business in recent years, and Howell Construction is one of the leading firms. They bring to any project a professional combination of building skills and design knowledge which is necessary in the preservation field.

Howell Construction
2700 12th Ave. S.
Nashville, Tenn. 37204
(615) 269-5659

International Consultants, Inc.

This is a high-level firm of consulting engineers with impressive experience in major industrial, commercial, and cultural projects. A few of the projects they have undertaken involve study of the restoration or adaptation of an historically significant structure. This is not a service for the individual home owner, but it might be a valuable one for a neighborhood complex.

International Consultants, Inc.
227 S. Ninth St.
Philadelphia, Penn. 19107
(215) 923-8888

Bruce M. Kriviskey, AIP

After serving over ten years with various public and private agencies, Bruce Kriviskey has begun his own consulting practice in urban planning and design, historic preservation, and neighborhood conservation. He is the former executive director of Historic Walker's Point, Inc., in Milwaukee.

Bruce M. Kriviskey, AIP
3048-A N. Shepard Ave.
Milwaukee, Wis. 53211
(414) 332-9073

Old Town Restorations, Inc.

St. Paul, Minnesota's Historic Hill District is the special concern of this consulting firm. They can help Twin Cities residents with advice on financing, historical information, the location of skilled contractors and craftsmen, and, most important, with architectural plans.

Old Town Restorations, Inc.
158 Farrington
St. Paul, Minn.
(612) 224-3857

Preservation Associates, Inc.

Valuable skills predicated on knowledge of antique building methods and architectural design are possessed by the two principals of Preservation Associates. They can custom make hand-riven oak roofing shingles, hewn beams, hand-planed mouldings and trim, doors and windows, and even build reproduction log houses; a photo of one such structure is included here.

Their consulting service is also valuable. They provide an inspection service as well as helpful guidance with historic sites surveys, state and national Register of Historic Places nominations, etc.

Brochure available.

Preservation Associates, Inc.
P.O. Box 202
Sharpsburg, Md. 21782
(301) 432-5466

Preservation Resource Group, Inc.

This organization is primarily an educational group that provides information and training for public and private preservation agencies. They could be of inestimable help in developing an effective local or regional program. PRG also assists private individuals with an evaluation of restoration plans.

Brochure available.

Preservation Resource Group, Inc.
5619 Southampton Dr.
Springfield, Va. 22151
(703) 323-1407

Rambusch

It is hard to imagine a more skilled group of artisans than that brought together at Rambusch. They are capable of creating superb reproductions in stained glass, metal, and wood. Decorative painting and mosaics are done with extreme faithfulness to period style. Among their recent commissions has been the restoration of Boscobel. Consultation, planning, and design are also among the services offered.

Brochure available.

Rambusch
40 W. 13th St.
New York, N.Y. 10011
(212) 675-0400

Restorations, Ltd.

Both minor structural work and major restoration projects will be undertaken by Restorations, Ltd. Attention is given to whatever details are important to doing a good job—whatever the scale. Dating of antique paint, masonry, and wallpaper is another one of the services offered.

Brochure available.

Restorations, Ltd.
Jamestown, R.I. 02835
(401) 423-0756

Restorations Unlimited, Inc.

This is a complete restoration contracting firm that provides advice and help on everything from beams and joists to wallpapers and paints. They have recently taken on a franchise for Rich Craft kitchens, one of the more adaptable of modern designs for period homes.

Restorations Unlimited, Inc.
24 W. Main St.
Elizabethville, Penn. 17023
(717) 362-3477

San Francisco Victoriana

A visit to the headquarters of Victoriana is a bit like making a pilgrimage to Canterbury, Rome, or Jerusalem. The founders started in 1972 to provide their beautiful city with the best possible advice and materials available in the restoration field. After completing several hundred projects, they say there is still much to learn. Undoubtedly there is, but they already know more about Victorian design than the rest of us put together. Victorian hardware, millwork, lighting fixtures, etched glass panels, plaster brackets and medallions—all are available here "with the least amount of compromise in authentic design or materials," as the company correctly states. Restoration projects are only undertaken in the Bay area, but the firm is beginning to reach out to serve the greater, national period materials market.

San Francisco Victoriana
606 Natoma St.
San Francisco, Calif. 94103
(415) 864-5477

The Valentas

The Valentas "live" restoration. You cannot fully appreciate the work of Frank Lloyd Wright or Henry Hobson Richardson without talking with this extraordinarily talented couple and their equally-skilled daughter. Their understanding of and ability to work with fine woods is not to be matched by any cabinetmaker. Glesner House and the Frank Lloyd Wright home and studio in Oak Park, Illinois, are two projects on which they have collaborated. They'd like to help everyone with a sincere interest in good workmanship of the past, but, if you are interested, you will probably have to wait some time for your turn.

The Valentas
2105 S. Austin Blvd.
Cicero, Ill. 60650

Architectural Antiques

Suppliers of what has become known as "architectural antiques" are becoming more numerous each year. It is too bad that businesses of this sort did not start much earlier—when whole sections of urban areas were cleared for "redevelopment." Denver and Atlanta alone could have supplied the rest of the country with an almost endless quantity of stained glass, millwork, hardware, mantels, used brick, and on and on. Today's secondhand building materials dealer has to search out quality goods in every possible nook and cranny. Some come in from England; others are found in depressed neighborhoods and in rural areas of the country that have not become fashionable and "picked over."

Some of the firms listed in the following pages are better known as wrecking companies or salvage yards. In the days when restoration was only a pleasant idea, the search for old-house parts often began here. Many such demolition and salvage wrecking companies still provide true treasures, but their days as suppliers are clearly limited. Except for a very few firms, they are not interested in one-of-a-kind pieces which require special handling.

Architectural Antiques/ L'Architecture Ancienne

This Canadian firm specializes in four main areas: stained-glass windows, with over 1,000 in stock; doors, including 400 of the carved variety; mantels, with at least 250 in stock at all times; and gingerbread millwork—cornices, brackets, and fretwork pieces by the hundreds. Twelve-thousand square feet of warehousing space is also filled with paneling, staircases, pillars, moulding, etc.

Stock is continually changing. If you have something particular in mind, Architectural Antiques will furnish pictures or sketches of what they have on hand.

Architectural Antiques/L'Architecture Ancienne
410 St. Pierre
Montreal, Quebec H2Y 2M2
Canada
(514) 849-3344

Berkeley Architectural Salvage

This is a traditional source of old-house supplies in the San Francisco/Oakland/Berkeley area. No details are available as to the kinds of materials in stock; nonetheless, it is well worth checking out.

Berkeley Architectural Salvage
2750 Adeline
Berkeley, Calif. 94703
(415) 849-2025

The Cellar

Antique building parts of all sorts can be found at The Cellar—newel posts, barn siding, metal fireplaces, entrance doors, wood-burning cookstoves, plaster wall ornaments, pedestal sinks, iron fencing. You name it and The Cellar can probably find it for you. Their direct-mail service can also help you with particular design problems.

Information sheet available.

The Cellar
384 Elgin St.
Ottawa, Ontario 2KP 1N1
Canada
(613) 238-1999

Felicity, Inc.

Located in three Tennessee towns, Felicity specializes in columns and carvings, stained- and cut-glass windows and doors, decorative hardware, mantels, and lighting fixtures.

Felicity, Inc.
600 Eagle Bend Rd.
Clinton, Tenn. 37716
(615) 457-5443

Felicity, Inc.
Cookeville Antique Mall
I-40
Cookeville, Tenn.

Felicity, Inc.
Thieves' Market
4900 Kingston Pike
Knoxville, Tenn. 37902
(615) 584-9641

Gargoyles, Ltd.

This is the Philadelphia area's leading architectural antiques supplier. Gargoyles is a particularly fine place for mantels, doors, lighting fixtures, and ornamental iron. Reproduction materials are also supplied, as are new metal ceilings.

Brochures available.

Gargoyles, Ltd.
512 S. Third St.
Philadelphia, Penn. 19147
(215) 629-1700

Great American Salvage Company, Inc.

This firm has sold primarily to commercial clients, but is now planning to enter the home restoration market. They are experts on lighting and restore the old and fabricate the new along traditional lines.

Great American Salvage Co., Inc.
901 E. Second St.
Little Rock, Ark. 72203
(501) 371-0666

Materials Unlimited

Reynold Lowe is a convert to preservation. A former wrecker, he saw the light when Ann Arbor's old Municipal League building was pulled down to be replaced by a plastic fast-food franchise. To make up for his errant past, he devotes all of his time to three acres of antiques and reclaimed architectural materials. Most of these date from the period 1870–1900, but there are supplies of earlier and later items.

Materials Unlimited
4100 E. Morgan Rd.
Ypsilanti, Mich. 48197
(313) 434-4300

Pat's Antiques, Etc.

You'll have to visit Patrick McCloskey in Texas if you want to know exactly what is available for your old house. He has a 5,000 square foot barn full of beveled stained, and leaded glass, fireplace mantels, light fixtures and doors. At the present time, architectural antiques cannot be shipped from Smithville.

Brochures available with self-addressed, stamped envelope.

Pat's Antiques, Etc.
Highway 71 at Alum Creek
P.O. Box 777
Smithville, Texas 78957
(512) 237-3600

The Renovation Source, Inc.

This is a new company that provides consulting services and materials for the home owner. Some of the supplies are antiques; others are good reproductions.

The Renovation Source, Inc.
3512–14 N. Southport
Chicago, Ill. 60657
(312) 327-1250

Greg Spiess

Good solid antique building materials—windows, mantels, exterior doors—are a specialty here. Greg Spiess will also undertake repair work and custom reproduction.

Greg Spiess
216 E. Washington St.
Joliet, Ill. 60433
(815) 722-5639

Sunrise Salvage

Sunrise is one of those junkyards that any lover of old things can admire. "Junk" it may be to some, but for us, and thousands of residents of the Bay area, Sunrise is a good place in which to spend a Saturday afternoon. They specialize in old tubs and sinks, but can help you out with other materials, too.

Sunrise Salvage
2210 San Pablo Ave.
Berkeley, Calif. 94710
(415) 845-4751

United House Wrecking Co.

This is the place that calls itself a "junkyard with a personality." United House is the granddaddy of the East Coast salvage depots and an extraordinary place to visit. There are more than five acres of materials located within 30,000 square-feet of buildings.

Literature available.

United House Wrecking Co.
328 Selleck St.
Stamford, Conn. 06902
(203) 348-5371

Urban Archaeology

Leon Schecter has been tracking down architectural decoration throughout the New York area during the past few years and beating the wreckers to the punch. He's just opened up his own store full of capitals, gates, keystones, stoves, streetlamps, stained-glass windows, and more.

Urban Archaeology
137 Spring St.
New York, N.Y. 10013
(212) 431-6969

Westlake Architectural Antiques

Carved doors, mantels, chandeliers, stained-glass panels—many of the trappings of the Victorian period can be found at Westlake. We've seen pictures of what parts of Austin *once* looked like, and thank heaven someone is at least recycling its past. On request, this firm will supply pictures and prices of particular kinds of items.

Westlake Architectural Antiques
3315 Westlake Dr.
Austin, Texas 78746
(512) 327-1110

The Wrecking Bar (Atlanta)

Over 12,000 square-feet are devoted to the display of architectural antiques. You name it, and The Wrecking Bar can probably come up with exactly what is needed or with a close match. There are doors and windows of all sorts, ornamental iron fencing, hardware and light-ing fixtures, mantels, pediments and pilasters. Most are American; some are European.

The Wrecking Bar
292 Moreland Ave., N.E.
Atlanta, Ga. 30307
(404) 525-0468

The Wrecking Bar (Dallas)

The founders of the Atlanta supply house moved on to new territory several years ago. This is an excellent source for antique materials of all sorts and living proof that not everyone in Big D is interested only in glass and steel.

Brochure available.

The Wrecking Bar, Inc.
2601 McKinney
Dallas, Texas 75204
(214) 826-1717

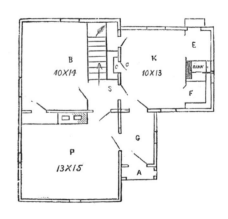

Other Sources of Structural Supplies and Services

Consult the List of Suppliers for addresses.

Paneling/Siding

Dale Carlisle
Craftsman Lumber
Dana-Deck
Driwood Moulding
Guyon
Old World Moulding

Doors

Allwood Door
Castle Burlingame
Simpson Timber
Spanish Pueblo Doors, Inc.

Windows

Blaine Window Hardware
Perkowitz Window Fashions

Shutters

Charles Walker Mfg.

Glass

Ball and Ball
Castle Burlingame
Cooke Art Glass Studio
Genesis Glass Ltd.
J. & R. Lamb Studios
Lead Glass Co.
Morgan Bockius Studios
Rococo Designs
Walton Stained Glass
Whittemore-Durgin Glass

Ceilings

Kenneth Lynch & Sons

Roofing

Celestial Design
Follansbee Steel
L. R. Lloyd
Structural Slate
Vermont Structural Slate

Cleaning

American Building Restoration

Inspection

Arch Associates/Stephen Guerrant
A. W. Baker
National Home Inspection Service of New England
Old House Inspection
Preservation Associates

Restoration Specialists

Bishop's Mill Historical Institute
R. H. Davis
KMH Associates
Jane Kent Rockwell
Raoul Savoie
Townscape
Jay Turnbull
Up Country Enterprises

Supply Houses

Antique Center
The Barn Peope
Castle Burlingame
Cleveland Wrecking
Yours & Mine Antiques

Two-story porch, Morris- Butler House, Indianapolis, Indiana.
Historic American Buildings Survey, 1970.

II   Woodwork & Other Fittings

The making of decorative pieces for exterior and interior use in old houses has to be one of the most satisfying of occupations. From visits to workshops in San Francisco, Chicago, and New York, it seems evident to this writer that the business will never again be a large one, but that the future is bright for those who will learn traditional skills and master the fine art of producing period mouldings and ornamental devices in wood, plaster, stone, or metal.

Most of us are totally unaware of the small details which combine to define the structure of a period interior or exterior. By simply concentrating on specific elements—brackets, cornices, mouldings around doors and windows—a pattern of designs and of their imposition begins to appear. A Federal or Greek Revival house with columns and capitals or a Beaux Arts building embellished with many variations of the classical orders come readily to mind as probably the most prominent building styles which have relied heavily on a revival of sawn, carved, molded, or cast ornamentation of a structural kind. The elements which came into play in the Gothic Revival, Queen Anne, and the Romanesque Revival periods are more simply decorative. On many buildings of the twentieth century, decoration appears to be gratuitous, an attempt to warm up ever so slightly a frozen mass.

Now that the passion for the International Style is being codified in the architectural history books and Philip Johnson's justly famous glass house has been willed to the National Trust, there is the danger that there will be a new sort of revival—a grab-bag kind of camp mixing of traditional motifs. Style will continue to evolve and develop, and there is nothing anyone can do about it. But there is no such thing as "progress" when it comes to aesthetics, to design and its execution. Ornamentation cannot be simply borrowed from one form and transferred to another—with happy results. And what is poured of concrete or molded from fiberglass will hardly begin to approximate that of stone or terra cotta or even solid wood.

Traditional workers in the millwork, metal, and plaster ornamentation fields know that there are appropriate ways to do things and proper forms to follow. They are not without a willingness to try new ideas, to fashion something unique. Few can afford to be choosy. The number of firms which turn out period ornamentation has declined and declined until the last few years. Some didn't make it through the Depression. Decorative architectural elements can never be cost-efficient. But, fortunately, some of the best firms survived and are now being joined by new groups of younger craftsmen who are enthusiastic and dedicated in their work.

Elaborate mouldings are once again being used in interiors of both new and restored houses. The products of such firms as Decorators Supply in Chicago are being shipped from coast to coast. San Francisco Victoriana is offering its first full line of period architectural mouldings on a national basis. This is all to the good, and perhaps we shouldn't be quite so pessimistic about their misuse in kitsch revival interiors of the last decades of the 1900s. What seems monstrous to us now—atmospheric restaurants and boutiques loaded with plywood Victorian fretwork—may be considered merely a novelty or even quite innovative in 2025. There is no reason, however, why period materials should be manhandled in true restoration work. To bring a house back to its proper style is an exercise in careful documentation and imagination. The two approaches should complement each other. With a wide variety of decorative materials available from reputable sources, this kind of work can be accomplished with latitude allowed for personal taste and comfort, as well as for cost.

Wood Supplies

Although the concern of this section is with more than the fiber products suggested by the term "woodwork," a basic knowledge of the various kinds of woods available in the past for decorative architectural use is of real value. Some of these are hardwoods such as oak, cherry, maple, and mahogany. Others are soft varieties like pine or cedar. Pine has always been used in American homes, especially those of an early date. Historically, it has been widely available and easily cut. Supplies of some of the more unusual varieties are noted in the first section of the book. Redwood, an especially durable member of the pine family, became popular after discovery of vast tracts of it in the second half of the nineteenth century.

Hardwoods—always more costly than softwoods— have been traditionally used for decorative rather than structural purposes. There are, of course, exceptions to this general rule. In areas of North America where such woods as ash, cherry, oak, and maple have been plentiful, these have been used for such structural members as flooring, framing, and doors.

The supplies currently available from two firms illustrate the variety of traditional woods that can be used for restoration or reproduction work. From John Harra Wood & Supply: ash, chestnut (wormy), cherry, holly, Honduras mahogany, hard and soft maple, English brown oak, poplar, rosewood, teak, walnut, and others. This firm offers a lumber sample pack which includes ¼″ x 2″ x 6″ specimens of 25 different woods for a price of $18. Any woodworker undertaking a restoration would find this a valuable reference source.

Catalog available, $1.

John Harra Wood & Supply Co.
39 W. 19th St.
New York, N.Y. 10011
(212) 741-0290

David Short's Amherst Wood Working is another source for fine woods: ash, basswood, red birch, butternut, cherry, Honduras mahogany, maple, oak, rosewood, and walnut. Also available are such varieties as Atlantic white cedar, red cedar, yellow pine, and redwood.

Price list available.

Amherst Wood Working
Box 464, Sunderland Rd.
North Amherst, Mass. 01059
(413) 549-2806

Veneers

Veneers are of interest primarily to furniture makers, and Minnesota Woodworkers Supply Company is an excellent source to be consulted. The firm also offers a splendid assortment of inlays which may be called for in fine cabinetmaking. Veneers and inlays, however, can be of use to the home restorer who either does not wish to invest in expensive hardwood lumber or finds that veneer in bands or sheets would be more appropriate for his needs. Minnesota suppies 35 different veneers which vary in width from 4″ to 12″. They are shipped in 36″ lengths. It may be necessary to splice pieces together if you need more width than is available, but lengths over 36″ can be supplied. This firm also offers five basic hardwoods—cherry, walnut, birch, maple, Honduras mahogany, and white oak—if you wish to use only lumber.

Catalog available, $1.

Minnesota Woodworkers Supply Co.
21801 Industrial Blvd.
Rogers, Minn. 55374
(612) 428-4101

Mouldings

These forms are among the most useful materials offered today by manufacturers in the reproduction field. From simple to very complex, mouldings are found in almost every home as cornices, rails, bases, panels, or frames. The "higher" the house style, the more complex these forms become. By fitting one to another, rich and dramatic effects in woodwork were created during the Georgian and the high Victorian periods in domestic architecture.

Mouldings of wood, plaster, metal, and polyurethane are available today. Only the last-named material has no claim on authenticity. Some manufacturers of traditional millwork have suggested that producers of molded synthetic work be excluded from this book on the grounds that it is neither appropriate nor well executed. We believe they are wrong—in at least two cases.

Polyurethane Mouldings

Fypon produces six basic models—two crown dentil mouldings, two dentil mouldings, a surround moulding, and a ceiling moulding—which do not attempt fancy effects. The crown dentils and the ceiling mouldings are available in 16′ lengths; the surround and simple dentil mouldings in 12′. In height, these mouldings vary in size from 1¾″ to 7″. According to the manufacturer, the material can be nailed, drilled, or sawed with field carpenter tools. The mouldings will not rot or warp and can be painted with oil-base or latex paints.

Fypon produces other forms as well, including pediments, mantels, window heads, sunbursts, acorns, brackets, and blocks.

Literature available.

Fypon, Inc.
Box 365, 108 Hill St.
Stewartstown, Penn. 17363
(717) 993-2593

Focal Point is a second major manufacturer making mouldings and other ornamental forms from polymers. Fourteen different mouldings may be examined in kit form. They are based on impressions from traditional wood or plaster models from the past.

Literature available.

Focal Point, Inc.
4870 S. Atlanta Rd.
Smyrna, Ga. 30080
(404) 351-0820

Wood Crown Mouldings

Traditional moulding patterns in wood are available from several manufacturers across the country who supply both retail outlets and individuals buying for themselves. Most of the mouldings are of pressed or embossed wood. KB Moulding is a representative dealer in the field. It offers many different crown mouldings which are of the sort to be used as the crowning or finishing element between wall and ceiling.

Catalog available, 25¢.

KB Moulding, Inc.
508A Larkfield Rd.
East Northport, N.Y. 11731
(516) 368-6009

San Francisco Victoriana's mouldings are of all-heart redwood. The patterns are based on historical models used between the years 1850 and 1920 in the United States. There are six different crown mouldings available, and a large assortment of other kinds which are catalogued later in this woodwork section. It is important to note that the full thickness of nineteenth-century mouldings has been maintained throughout the line. The crown mouldings are recommended for outside use, but presumably can also be employed in rooms of sufficient height.

Catalog available, $1.

San Francisco Victoriana
606 Natoma St.
San Francisco, Calif. 94103
(415) 864-5477

Carved Wood Mouldings

Deeply cut hardwood mouldings are the specialty of Bendix. Many of the designs are contemporary, but some may be useful for a Victorian interior. Bendix also supplies a plain crown moulding with dentils as well as other moulding forms which are covered under separate headings.

Catalog available, $1.

Bendix Mouldings, Inc.
235 Pegasus Ave.
Northvale, N.J. 07647
(201) 767-8888

Cornices

The equivalent of crown mouldings in wood have been produced for hundreds of years in plaster. Decorators Supply is one of the foremost manufacturers of such ornament in the world. The firm has hundreds of different ceiling cornices available, ranging from classical to the modern. Illustrated here, in order of appearance, are: the classic dentil (#1210), Gothic (#3495), Old English (#25114), Elizabethan (#25121), Colonial (#3454), Georgian (#25180), Louis XVI (#25183), and Sullivanesque (#3434).

Catalog available, $1.

Decorators Supply Corp.
3610–12 S. Morgan St.
Chicago, Ill. 60609
(312) 847-6300

Felber Studios specializes·in custom work and in reconstruction of antique plaster. The cornices available from this company are exceptionally accurate copies of the antique. Of particular interest are the Old English or Tudor cornice mouldings which were used in many fine homes of the late nineteenth and early twentieth centuries. Felber has catalogued at least eighteen different styles.

Catalog available.

Felber Studios
110 Ardmore Ave.
Ardmore, Penn. 19003
(215) 642-4710

Casings

The interiors of most doors and windows require at least a simple frame known as a casing. This is a moulding which dresses up any structural opening and renders period interiors a great deal more interesting. Driwood Period Mouldings is one of the major suppliers of such basic woodwork. Illustrated, in order of appearance, are four of many styles available: a simple egg and dart design made up of two mouldings (#2138 and #2137, Assembly CA-7), a one-piece moulding which projects quite far—$2^{3}/_{16}''$ (#2061), a traditional bead design (#2120), and an acanthus pattern (#2108).

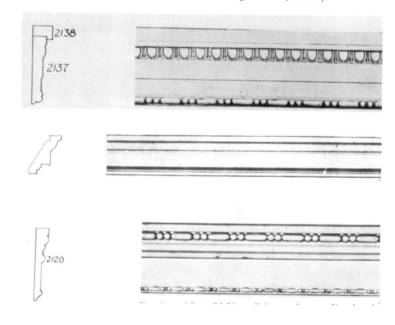

Casings are shipped in random lengths from 4' to 16', but you can request specific lengths. All are stocked in poplar. Work in other woods is done on a custom basis.

Catalog available, $1.

Driwood Moulding Co.
P.O. Box 1729
Florence, S.C. 29503
(803) 662-0541 or 669-2478

Old World casings are slightly more inventive, but no less traditional than those of Driwood. Illustrated are three examples of their work: an egg and dart and flower frieze pattern (#1061), a formal design of geometric patterns (#1042), and a simple casing which makes use of a rope moulding (#1092A). Many of these casings are appropriate for chair rails as well as windows and doors. Poplar is used by Old World, and their random lengths run from 8' to 16'.

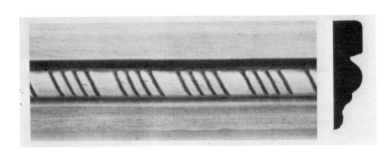

Catalog available.

Old World Moulding
115 Allen Blvd.
Farmingdale, N.Y. 11753
(516) 822-2280

Fretwork Mouldings

Fancy carved and embossed woodwork is frequently found in Victorian homes. This is sometimes termed "gingerbread," a term that refuses to die away. Bendix supplies three different embossed mouldings in hardwood and six overlay mouldings in complicated patterns in birch plywood.

Catalog available, $1.

Bendix Mouldings, Inc.
235 Pegasus Ave.
Northvale, N.J. 07647
(201) 767-8888

Exceptional fretwork panels are available from Victorian Reproductions. These are often used with open cut medallions and spandrils. They are made from oak, a wood especially popular in the late-Victorian period.

Literature available.

Victorian Reproductions
1601 Park Ave. S.
Minneapolis, Minn. 55404
(612) 874-2582

Wainscoting and Baseboard

There is usually no reason to contact a specialty firm for materials of this sort. The paneling of a lower part of a wall is usually no more difficult a job for the average woodworker/carpenter than any other type of panel work. Baseboarding is even simpler and may be only slightly more than a shoe moulding. But there are sometimes special requirements—especially in houses of the late nineteenth century—which call for an expert. The woodwork in a formal Victorian room can consist of as many as five or six components on one wall surface. Each must blend with the other in perfect proportion.

San Francisco Victoriana has mastered the skills and acquired the historical knowledge necessary to help the old-house restorer. In San Francisco alone, this firm has undertaken the restoration of over seventy homes. Their reputation has grown nationally, and they are prepared to provide redwood materials just about wherever they are needed.

There are two basic types of wainscoting available: 54″ tongue and groove (as illustrated in type F) and 72″ batten winscoting. San Francisco Victoriana can supply you with much information regarding these styles—when they were used in the San Francisco area and elsewhere, how they should be assembled and installed, what lengths are available, the number of components, etc.

Baseboards are much simpler in design and consist of no more than two units—a board and a cap. Several different styles are illustrated here from the Victoriana catalog. None extend up the wall more than a foot.

type D Baseboards

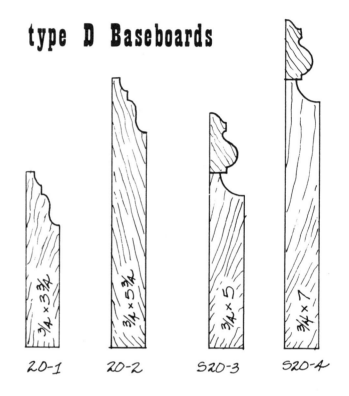

Book of Architectural Mouldings, $1.

San Francisco Victoriana
606 Natoma St.
San Francisco, Calif. 94103
(415) 864-5477

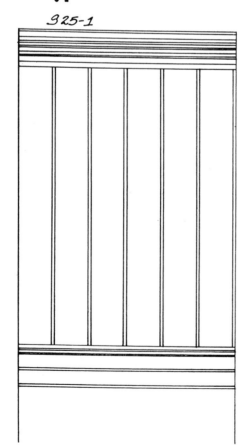

plaster

type F

925-1

Carved Paneling

Paneling itself is dealt with in the first section of this book on structural materials. Although not properly construction work or in any way related to supporting walls, paneling has come to be regarded as an integral part of the basic fabric of a structure in the same manner as lath, or, as a more recent example, sheetrock. This leaves, then, only very special kinds of decorative paneling for consideration. Alan Amerian's hand-carved panels are carefully designed and wrought. Unfortunately, the photograph affords only a dim view of his work. Although rarely encountered in American homes, there is ample historical precedent for the use of

Incised panels and appliqués are other Hallelujah specialties which call for expertise. A sample of an appliqué block is seen at left; a panel at right.

highly decorative woodwork of this sort in homes built from the 1880s until the 1920s.

Amerian Woodcarving
282 San Jose Ave.
San Jose, Calif. 95125
(408) 294-2968

Wood Brackets, Incised Panels, Appliqué, and Corner Blocks

Most of these ornamental devices are sawn or molded and do not involve the considerable amount of time required by hand-carving. Nevertheless, they are out-of-the-ordinary kinds of items which call for skill and patience. Exterior porch and belt course brackets (which can also be used inside) are made of redwood by Hallelujah Redwood. Two of the basic designs are illustrated, the belt course being the simpler of the two.

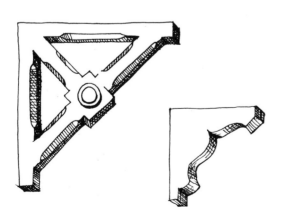

Catalog available, $1.

Hallelujah Redwood Products
39500 Comptche Rd.
Mendocino, Calif. 95460
(707) 937-4410

Corner blocks of various kinds are often found as part of door and window casings from the earliest Victorian buildings to those of the turn of the century. These are one-piece mouldings which incorporate circular patterns as simple as a bull's-eye and as fanciful as a rosette. Woodwork of this sort was standard fare in the 1800s. San Francisco Victoriana has helped us return to it.

Book of Architectural Mouldings available, $1.

San Francisco Victoriana
606 Natoma St.
San Francisco, Calif. 94103
(415) 864-5477

Composition Brackets and Capitals

To examine the catalog that Decorators Supply devotes to these elements is to lose momentarily a sense of time and place. What Kenneth Lynch has achieved in period metalwork, Decorators has more than supplied in wood fiber. Many home owners may have little reason to request such decorative pieces, but these pieces do exist and they are used in churches, theaters, government buildings, and in private residences of considerable scale and elegance. The illustrations can provide only a suggestion of the rich variety of forms and designs offered.

ters, several of which are illustrated. Other architectural antiques firms may be similarly stocked.

Brochures available.

Gargoyles, Ltd.
312 S. Third St.
Philadelphia, Penn. 19147
(215) 629-1700

Very simple new balusters are available through Bendix. The seven stock sizes—from 13″ to 30″ in length, and from 1⅜″ to 2½″ in diameter—are shown here.

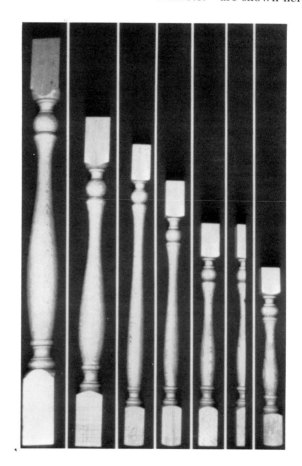

Catalog available, $1.

The Decorators Supply Corp.
3610-12 S. Morgan St.
Chicago, Ill. 60609
(312) 847-6300

Balusters

Turned rails known as balusters or banisters are often the victim of unruly children and shaky adults. These frail reeds are easy enough to split, but very difficult to repair. Gargoyles has a limited supply of antique balus-

Catalog available, $1.

Bendix Mouldings, Inc.
235 Pegasus Ave.
Northvale, N.J. 07647
(201) 767-8888

Metal Ornaments

This is Kenneth Lynch territory. No one can offer more than he, and the best we can do is to illustrate some of the many varieties of brackets and modillions, shells and shields, panel ornaments such as wreaths and garlands, scrolls, crestings, mitres, rosettes, urns and balusters, capitals, drops, and pinnacles. Then there are finials, pediments, eagles, gargoyles and caryatids, bows, festoons, ribbons.

At the same time, we should mention that Lynch can also provide metal mouldings which could be used to great effect with the stamped metal ceilings catalogued in the first section of this book on structural materials.

A book, Architectural Sheet Metal, *cataloguing 2,000 items, is available in paperback, $2.50.*

Kenneth Lynch & Sons
78 Danbury Rd.
Wilton, Conn. 06897
(203) 762-8363

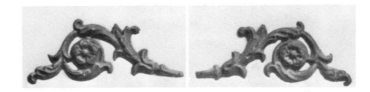

Plaster Ornaments

You've seen these before—on late nineteenth-century buildings in cities throughout the country. They were made of stone or of terra cotta, and many have either been ripped to the ground or fallen victim to pollution. Artist Pat Dunn is making copies in plaster, and you may prefer to keep these indoors. Illustrated is a design termed "Renaissance Man."

Catalog available, $1.50.

Architectural Ornaments
P.O. Box 115
Little Neck, N.Y. 11363
(212) 321-4159

Decorators Supply's plaster ornaments are truly splendid. Their castings are made of hard plaster of Paris which has been reinforced with hemp fiber and steel rods when necessary. As with Kenneth Lynch's products, they are nearly impossible to catalog. Every possible nuance of style appears to be represented—Classical, Gothic, Byzantine, Renaissance, Elizabethan, Tudor, Colonial, Victorian, Art Nouveau and even Art Moderne. There are grilles, rosettes, centers, panels, festoons, shields, wreaths, pineapples, eagles, urns, shells, columns, ribbons, pediments, corner decorations.

Catalog on plaster ornaments available, $1.

The Decorators Supply Corp.
3610–12 S. Morgan St.
Chicago, Ill. 60609
(312) 847-6300

Felber Studios is a more limited, but no less accomplished manufacturer of plaster ornaments. Including the ceilings and cornices, there are over 8,000 models to choose from. That should be enough for anyone. Niches and shells, centers, and cartouches are among their stock offerings.

Catalog available.

Felber Studios
110 Ardmore Ave.
Ardmore, Penn. 19003
(215) MI2-4710

Such different plaster ornaments as rosettes, corbels, and modillions are reproduced by the Larimer Dry Goods Co. There are twenty different rosette styles. The firm also makes available six different cresting styles cast in either iron or aluminum.

Catalog available, $1.

Larimer Dry Goods Co.
Attn.: RLC/RS
P.O. Box 17491 T.A.
Denver, Colo. 80217

In addition to their fine redwood work, San Francisco Victoriana is also a supplier of plaster brackets and centerpieces, including rosettes. Ornamentation of this sort may be needed in any late-Victorian building which has been substantially altered. When ceilings have been lowered or otherwise changed for modern lighting, much of the past may have become obliterated.

Price list available.

San Francisco Victoriana
606 Natoma St.
San Francisco, Calif. 94103
(415) 864-5477

Wood and Wood Fiber Ornamentation

Nearly every supplier of millwork offers some sort of decorative embellishment which will enrich a period interior. Decorators Supply's wood fiber carvings duplicate in large part what is offered in plaster, but those of wood are especially useful for mantels, cabinets, and such architectural details as pediments. Hallelujah

Redwod products offers strips of repeating ornament which would be useful as edging on shelves. San Francisco Victoriana and Driwood Period Mouldings supply plate rail mouldings. Driwood also has window drapery cornices in six different styles; the "Jenny Lind" is illustrated here.

Consult previous entries for addresses or see List of Suppliers.

Other Suppliers of Woodwork Materials

See List of Suppliers for addresses.

Lumber

Bangkok Industries
Castle Burlingame
Albert Constantine & Son
Craftsman Lumber
Harris Manufacturing
MacBeath Hardwood

Veneers

Architectural Paneling
Bangkok Industries
Albert Constantine & Son
Janovic/Plaza
Noel Wise Antiques

Crown Mouldings

Architectural Paneling
Decorators Wholesale Hardware

J. di Christina & Sons
Driwood Moulding
House of Moulding
Old World Moulding
Walter E. Phelps
Preservation Resource Center

Carved Wood Mouldings

Minnesota Woodworkers Supply

Casings

Driwood Moulding
Old World Moulding
San Francisco Victoriana

Wainscoting and Baseboard

Accent Walls
Bendix Mouldings
Castle Burlingame
Craftsman Lumber
Driwood Moulding
Guyon, Inc.
Maurer & Shepherd
Old World Moulding

Balusters/Railings/Spindles

California Wood Turning
Haas Wood and Ivory Works
Hallelujah Redwood Products
Minnesota Woodworkers Supply
Walter E. Phelps
Preservation Resource Center

Metal Cornices

AA Abingdon Ceiling
Barney Brainum-Shanker Steel
Guilfoy Cornice Works

Plaster Ornamentation

Gianetti Studios

Wood and Wood Fibre Ornaments

Bendix Mouldings
K.B. Moulding
Minnesota Woodworkers Supply

Columns and Capitals

Hartmann Sanders
A. F. Schwerd Manufacturing
Western Art Stone

61

III Hardware

Hardware is a fascinating and endless subject to explore. Locks, latches, pulls, and hinges are among the most functional objects in any house and can be among the most decorative. Unless hardware is of a bright, brassy sort, however, few people are going to stop to exclaim over basically utilitarian pieces of metal. Good hardware remains semi-hidden and should blend in with the general style of the dwelling itself.

Quality material lies at the heart of the hardware problem. Today it is difficult to find solid brass, heavy iron, and substantial carved wood fixtures. The best of the metal is hand-forged. The worst is stamped out in a thin manner. Pieces of wood are sometimes little more than composition. Until fairly recently, one could depend on the services of a local hardware supplier, but stores of this type are quickly disappearing to be replaced by supermarkets offering only a limited selection of second-rate materials. If you are fortunate enough to live in an area where a true-to-life hardware dealer can still make a livelihood, by all means strike up a friendship. But what to do in those many places where you are on your own?

Buy through the mail, visit wrecking yards, sift through the junk at secondhand furniture stores, ask antique dealers to help you find old architectural and furniture hardware. There is a surprising amount of stuff "out there." Hardware is less likely to have been thrown away and lost forever than other building supplies. Because of its weight and substance, it is also less likely to have decomposed with age. Rust remover may be all that it takes to make an old piece useful again.

Commercial imitations of period hardware are immensely popular. Most are not worth the metal from which they are formed. As Henry and Ottalie Williams wrote in a pioneer work on restoring old houses, "Labored imita-tion is worse than frank and honest indifference to authenticity." Nevertheless, the "rustic" look in imitations is favored today. This might be, for instance, an iron hinge which has been "aged" by hammering and then painted a jet black. When applied to a door or cabinet, such a bogus antique stands out like the proverbial sore thumb. Once paint began to be used in the interior of a house during the early to mid-eighteenth century, authentic hardware of this sort was painted over. It did not dominate the pieces to which it was attached. This is not true, of course, of doorknobs or knockers of brass or even of some iron latches. Many latches, however, as this writer has discovered in his own house, were routinely painted in the past.

To add insult to injury, hardware appropriate for a Colonial-style dwelling—strap hinges of various sorts, sliding door bolts, Suffolk latches—is frequently used on later-style buildings. Hardware styles kept pace with technology—even in the simple blacksmith's shop—and forms common to one age gave way to "improvements" of another. Thus, the strap hinge was replaced by the H and H-L; the Suffolk latch by Blake's cast-iron model. Only in the deepest recesses of the countryside did practice lag far behind technology.

Until recently no one bothered too much with Victorian reproduction hardware; it was too easily found in junk yards, barns, and attics. Even two years ago, when the first *Old House Catalogue* was published, few reproduction hardware suppliers carried it in their catalogs. Now such quality firms as Ball and Ball, Horton Brasses, and Pfanstiel Hardware devote considerable space to such wares. The use of period hardware is slowly growing more sophisticated. The number of trained metalsmiths is also on the increase. The village blacksmith was deserving of poetic praise. Although his day will never come again, his tradition of good workmanship is worthy of being maintained.

Architectural Hardware

Almost every part of an old house is fitted with some sort of hardware, and many areas contain objects of iron, brass, or bronze which are made by blacksmiths or metalsmiths. A few well-maintained homes may still have examples of the original hardware on doors and windows. In most places, however, locks have been changed, latches removed, and hinges may have rusted away. If old hardware is still in place, every attempt should be made to recondition it. If this fails, a careful reproduction can be installed in its place. A number of suppliers can give you what you need at nominal prices.

Hinges

Hinges in mid-eighteenth-century homes (and on into the 1800s) were usually painted the same color as the door, and were less obtrusive than they are today. Common types include these H and H-L, foliated H, cross garnet, and butterfly hinges. All are offered in various sizes by Newton Millham.

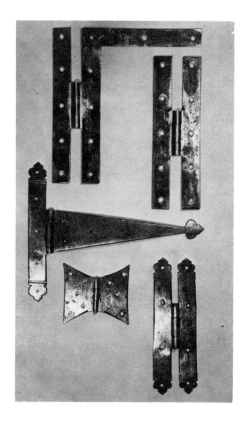

Brochure, $1.

*Newton Millham-Star Forge
672 Drift Rd.
Westport, Mass. 02790
(617) 636-5437*

Nearly everyone would like to find antique strap hinges. It is a relatively easy job to "antique" a reproduction, so be extra careful. The Cellar has some true antiques in stock, and so do other architectural antiques firms. Many originals were made of purer iron than today's reproductions and have resisted rust surprisingly well.

Information sheet available.

*The Cellar
384 Elgin
Ottawa, Ontario
Canada
(613) 238-1999*

Reproduction brass hinges are to be found at Horton Brasses, one of the traditional New England manufacturers of hardware. These should be used only where little stress is likely to occur. Larger iron strap hinges are also available. A 13″ butt type is $13.50 a pair.

Catalog available, $1.25.

*Horton Brasses
P.O. Box 95, Nooks Hill Rd.
Cromwell, Conn. 06416
(203) 635-4400*

Knobs

Various kinds of knobs can be bought separately from locks. Round and oval reproductions in brass and porcelain are available from Baldwin. Pfanstiel's line of new materials is far more ornate and includes some unusual decorative items, including very elaborate handles.

Brochures are available from Baldwin, 50¢.

*Baldwin Hardware
841 Wyomissing Blvd.
Reading, Penn.
(215) 777-7811*

Catalog available, $2.

*H. Pfanstiel Hardware Co.
Jeffersonville, N.Y. 12748
(914) 482-4445*

Antique knobs are still in plentiful supply, especially in the warehouses of such architectural antiques collectors as Materials Unlimited.

*Materials Unlimited
4100 Morgan Rd.
Ypsilanti, Mich. 48197
(313) 434-4300*

Knockers

There is nothing quite so ludicrous as a huge traditional brass knocker on a modern ranch house front door. This practice reminds us that decorative hardware is frequently misused. It is one of those "touches" which seem irresistible to the pretentious.

Large brass knockers of whatever variety are appropriate for only relatively high-style homes of the Colonial or Georgian style. More modest dwellings may have iron knockers. Many late-Victorian structures make use of pulls for mechanical bells.

The ever-popular Federal eagle knocker is cast in bronze by Steve Kayne. It is 8½" x 3¾" and sells for $20. Another bronze piece is in the form of a ring. Without the stud, it can be used as a door pull. It is priced at $12.

Catalogs available, $2.

Steve Kayne
17 Harmon Pl.
Smithtown, N.Y. 11787
(516) 724-3669

Dare we call this a striking object? This unique knocker is worked from polished steel. Robert Griffith will undertake a similar project only on a custom commission basis.

Robert Griffith, Metalsmith
16 S. Main St.
Trucksville, Penn. 18708
(717) 696-2395

A rather unusual knocker is sold by the Victorian supply house of Ritter and Son. It is a kissing couple—one partner on the doorplate, the other on the ring. Their busses can be heard through a closed door. The price is $5.

Catalog available, $1.

Ritter and Son Hardware
46901 Fish Rock Rd.
Anchor Bay (Gualala), Calif. 95445
(707) 884-3363

Latches/Bolts

Door latches of the eighteenth century reflect the creativity of local smiths who performed infinite variations on original English designs. Increasing numbers of very competent metalsmiths are now hammering out their own expressions for the trade in reproductions. The modern smiths are producing hardware which is appropriate for both public buildings and homes. Some of the ware is hand-forged; some is stamped out and then worked. The lore of the latch is rich and complex. Regional differences are considerable, and need to be studied by the serious student.

The bean latch was a common style throughout the Colonies and was still being made in the early 1800s. The illustrated version comes from Newton Millham's Star Forge and can be made in 6, 7, 8, and 9" lengths.

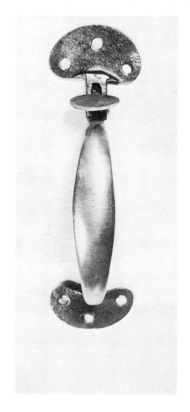

A more sophisticated, and therefore less common, device in the eighteenth century was the spring latch. Millham forges these in several sizes. The oval knob is made of brass.

Generally, thumb latches of an early period were called Suffolk latches, as opposed to Norfolk, and are distinguished by the wide, flattened portions at both ends of the handle called "cusps." Robert Griffith reproduces this early Suffolk for $45.

This backlatch has a locking feature which holds the bar in the notch of the strike. The original piece was made in central Massachusetts in the mid-1700s.

Door bolts provided greater security than latches in Colonial times. The same is true today. But don't be afraid to sacrifice authenticity for safety. If a reproduction is appropriate, Griffith's designs range from very simple to decorative. These examples sell for $25, $35, and $45.

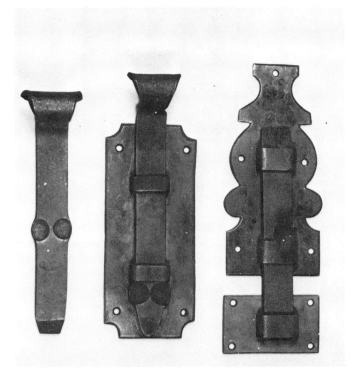

Brochure available, $1.

Newton Millham-Star Forge
672 Drift Rd.
Westport, Mass. 02790
(617) 636-5437

Catalog available, $1.

Robert Griffith, Metalsmith
16 S. Main St.
Trucksville, Penn. 18708
(717) 696-2395

Richard E. Sargent is another accomplished artisan. He produces a thumb latch which has arrowhead-shaped cusps. It's about 7″ long, and its $25 price includes nails and back group.

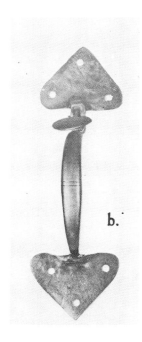

Catalog available, $2.

Richard E. Sargent
Hartland Forge
Box 83
Hartland Four Corners, Vt. 05049
(802) 436-2439

Complete latch sets are available for $13.50 from Horton Brasses. Each piece has a smooth finish and is painted flat black.

Catalog available, $1.25.

Horton Brasses Co.
Box 95, Nooks Hill Rd.
Cromwell, Conn. 06416
(203) 635-4400

Letter Plates

Noel Wise has both a wrought-iron and a solid-brass letter plate. Your choice will probably depend on the door's other hardware. The iron plate is rather ornate and sells for $17.50; the brass is priced at $30.

Catalog available, $1.

Noel Wise Antiques
6503 St. Claude Ave.
Arabi, La. 70032
(504) 279-6896

Locks

There are hundreds, if not thousands, of varieties of locks used in the past, and a goodly number are still kicking around. While other parts of an old house were quickly disposed of, there was a reluctance to toss out something as intricate and useful as a lock. Many antiques dealers stock these quite routinely. And there are reproductions galore.

Outwardly, the brass rim locks produced by Baldwin resemble the Colonial originals from which they were copied. Internally, the locks have been adapted to conform to contemporary security needs. Nevertheless, the locks are still operated with a skeleton key.

5634

Brochures, 50¢.

Baldwin Hardware
841 Wyomissing Blvd.
Reading, Penn. 19603
(215) 777-7811

Sash Lifts

It's a rarity to find a Victorian flush-mounted sash lift without several coats of paint on it. These are removed easily enough. But if the lift itself is missing, you can turn to several manufacturers for a reproduction. Ball and Ball has brass copies 3″ x 1⅝″ for $18.50 each.

Catalog available, $2.

Ball and Ball
463 W. Lincoln Hwy.
Exton, Penn. 19341
(215) 363-7330

Shutter Hardware

Shutter fasteners, or dogs, are utterly simple in function, but our forebears could not resist embellishing them on the forge. The four shown here were fashioned by Newton Millham. They are typical of shutterdogs found from New England down through the Mid-Atlantic states.

Brochure, $1.

Newton Millham-Star Forge
672 Drift Rd.
Westport, Mass. 02790
(617) 636-5437

Snow Guards

Snow guards, snow brakes, snow birds—whatever you choose to call them—perform both decorative and practical functions. They are attractive additions to almost any roof line and serve to break the fall of snow. Architectural antiques dealers usually stock the originals. Kenneth Lynch is surely the leading reproduction manufacturer in the field. His stock includes a score of different designs, such as the classic eagle, 5″ high and 6″ wide. It comes in cast brass, bronze, lead, or iron. According to Mr. Lynch, the iron model is bought mostly by collectors.

Lynch has a special brochure available on all models.

Kenneth Lynch & Sons.
Box 488, 78 Danbury Rd.
Wilton, Conn. 96897
(203) 762-8363

Bathroom Hardware and Fixtures

We remain adamantly opposed to dolling up the bathroom. If you already have a room which is fitted out with antique fixtures that work, keep them in place. They may require some cleaning up, perhaps even a new application of porcelain. Or if the bathroom in your new old house is in complete shambles, you will have to start anew and might as well consider something that fits the general decor. But if you are fortunate enough to have a perfectly fine modern bathroom, leave it as it is, adding only a bit here and there to take away the medicinal look. For some strange reason, the bathroom can become the kitsch-est room in the house, new or old. Perhaps it is our modern tendency to spray away any evidence of natural human functions. In any case, please don't tart up the john with a wicker throne for a toilet or covers for everything in sight.

Toilet Seats

Don't laugh. It can be hard to find a good seat that won't crack or slide away underneath you. The new foam jobs are not to be believed. They are hardly better than the plastic seats which yellow and crack in a wink.

Northwood, New Hampshire, seems to be the wooden toilet seat capital of America. Here you can find two firms—Shepherd Oak Products and Fife's Woodworking & Manufacturing Co.—that specialize in sturdy seats. Those from Fife are available in oak ($39.50), pine ($35), or mahogany ($58). You must specify light or dark in each case. Brass hinges are supplied. Shepherd Oak provides both a regular—illustrated here—

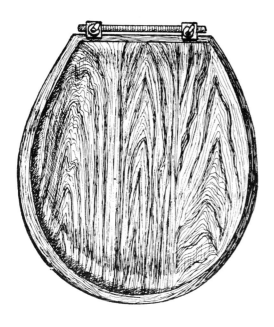

and an elongated seat for $53 and $58, respectively. These are of golden dark oak, and come with brass or chrome hinges and brass mounting screws.

Literature supplied by both firms.

Shepherd Oak Products
P.O. Box 27
Northwood, N.H. 03261
(603) 942-8148

Fife's Woodworking & Mfg. Co.
Rte. 107
Northwood, N.H. 03261
(603) 942-8339

A California firm, Heads Up, also supplies solid oak seats which will fit all standard toilets.

Brochure available.

Heads Up, Inc.
3201 W. MacArthur Blvd.
Santa Ana, Calif. 92704
(714) 549-8903

Toilets

If your bathroom has to be reconstructed, you might want to consider installing a pull chain toilet. Remember, these fixtures are not very silent. But they are efficient. An old-fashioned toilet of this sort will use only two gallons of water a flush, rather than eight. Sunrise Specialty outlets have the new reproductions, and Sunrise Salvage stocks the old originals. The new model #1 has an oak box which is fitted with a copper tank liner and an oak seat fitted to a porcelain base. All the fittings are brass.

Sunrise Specialty provides a brochure and has two showrooms:

Sunrise Specialty
The Galleria
101 Kansas St., Rm. 224
San Francisco, Calif. 94103
(415) 552-4148

Sunrise Specialty
8705 Santa Monica Blvd.
Los Angeles, Calif. 90069
(213) 652-3741

Sunrise Salvage
2210 San Pablo Ave.
Berkeley, Calif. 94710
(415) 845-4751

Restoration and Reincarnation Co. offers a useful service to residents of the San Francisco area. They will re-surface an old toilet, bathtub, sink, or other fixture in your home or apartment. The charge for a toilet is $125 and up; a sink, $100 and up; and a tub, $250 or more. The firm also re-surfaces wall tile.

Literature available.

Restoration & Reincarnation Co.
250 Austin Alley
San Francisco, Calif. 94109
(415) 495-3233

Hardware

The hardware required for an old-style sink may not be any less drippy if it is antique, but it may be more fitting. Without a doubt, paper holders, bars, and rings of wood or solid brass will be sturdier and more attractive than those of plastic or lucite.

Broadway Supply Company features several different lines of bathroom hardware in their "Heritage Collection." In the "Old Dominion Suite" there are solid brass towel bars in three sizes (18, 24, and 30"), a towel ring, and robe hook. The toothbrush and tumbler holder, soap dish, and paper holder are of solid brass and porcelain.

Literature available.

Broadway Supply Company
7421 Broadway
Kansas City, Mo. 64114
(816) 361-3674

Shepherd Oak's basic accessory fixtures are of solid oak and can be too much of a good thing, but they are plain as can be and appear to be indestructible.

Shepherd Oak Products
P.O. Box 27
Northwood, N.H. 03261
(603) 942-8148

The fixtures for sinks, tubs and showers which Sunrise Specialty features are of a very clean, handsome sort. Those for a sink are available in three basic types—widespread, 4" center, or single-hole mixers—and are either all brass or a combination of china and brass.

Brochure available.

Sunrise Specialty
The Galleria
101 Kansas St., Rm. 224
San Francisco, Calif. 94103
(415) 552-4148

Sunrise Specialty
8705 Santa Monica Blvd.
Los Angeles, Calif. 90069
(213) 652-3741

Tubs and Sinks

Most people appreciate a good-sized tub and an amply proportioned wash basin. Those of an antique variety are usually considerably larger than modern versions. This is an especially curious situation when you realize that people are larger today and really do require larger fixtures. Instead, we are being squeezed down.

The National House Inn manufactures three types of cultured marble sinks which date in style from c. 1900—old enough to be interesting. One is a drop-in ($65), a second a corner top with integral bowl ($75), and the third a rectangular top with integral bowl ($95). Illustrated is the self-rimming drop-in model. All bowls measure 14" in diameter.

Literature available.

The National House Inn
102 South Parkview
Marshall, Mich. 49068
(616) 781-7374

Heads Up's Bristol model wall-mounted oak sink with china bowl is an attractive, unfussy fixture. Above it in the illustration can be seen the "Concord" recess mounting medicine cabinet of oak and mirrored glass. The hardware for the sink is your responsibility.

Sunrise Specialty features this oak-rimmed clawfoot antique in their literature. How many others like it exist

today, no one knows. But there are are thousands of standard free-standing tubs to be found in salvage yards and through period architectural antiques specialists. If you are on the West Coast, you might start first with Sunrise. If not, then get in touch with one of a number of firms, including United House Wrecking Co. (Stamford, Conn.), Rotar Services (Dallas, Texas), Cleveland Wrecking Co. (offices across the country), and P & G New & Used Plumbing Supply Co. (Brooklyn, N.Y.). *See* List of Suppliers for addresses.

Furniture Hardware

Proper pulls, escutcheons, latches, hinges or other hardware fittings for furniture are made by both individual craftsmen and large companies. The demand is so great that there is ample room for both stamped and forged pieces. The focus here, however, is on the better handcrafted pieces. In most cases, they do not have to be custom made, but are readily available in various sizes. Until recently, it has been somewhat difficult to find reproduction Victorian ware, but that, too, is now commonly available.

Latches

Colonial period closet and cupboard latches are one specialty of Steve Kayne. There are two basic kinds—pigtail and knob—which are of solid cast brass. They are priced from $3 to $4 a set, depending on the type and on the size (which ranges from 3″ to 7″).

Catalogs available on Colonial hardware, $2.

Ritter & Son offer a Victorian latch set of the sort that would be found on an ice box. Either righthand or lefthand sets are available, and each is made of solid brass and priced at $7.95.

Catalog available, $1.

Pulls/Drops

Ball and Ball has been making traditional William and Mary, Queen Anne, Chippendale, Hepplewhite, and French-style pulls and drops for many, many years. Illustrated is a series of the William and Mary fittings, dated c. 1860 to 1710. All, of course, are "brasses" made of real brass. They vary greatly from style to style in thickness. The hardware for mounting each differs as well.

There are many standard designs to choose from. If you are trying to match a particular type, then Ball and Ball insists that you send them an actual sample: "Whenever copies are required, please send your BEST plate as the sample, since the copies will be cast from it. . . ."

Catalog available, $2.

Ball and Ball
463 W. Lincoln Hwy.
Exton, Penn. 19341
(215) 363-7330

Drops and pulls of various styles, many of them appropriate for high-style French furniture, are available through Noel Wise Antiques. All of the hardware is solid brass and is offered in an antique or polished finish. These are reproduction pieces.

Catalog available, $1.

Noel Wise Antiques
6503 St. Claude Ave.
Arabi, La. 70032
(504) 279-6896

Ritter & Son offers the best cast and stamped late-Victorian dresser pulls that we have seen. They also supply bin pulls. A selection of some of their cast pull designs is illustrated here. They are of solid brass.

Catalog available, $1.

Ritter & Son Hardware
46901 Fish Rock Road
Anchor Bay (Gualala), Calif. 95445
(707) 884-3363

Horton Brasses is one of the last traditional New England hardware manufacturers and supplies many essential needs. Colonial-style pieces are their specialty, but they are also very strong in Victorian hardware of the mid- to late-nineteenth century. Illustrated, in order of appearance, is a Victorian tear drop, a Victorian drawer pull, a Hepplewhite drawer pull, and a Chippendale drawer pull. All are of brass, the tear drop being of wood with a stamped brass back plate.

Catalog available, $1.25.

Horton Brasses
P.O. Box 95, Nooks Hill Rd.
Cromwell, Conn. 06416
(203) 635-4400

Knobs

Knobs of various sorts are useful for cupboards and drawers—antique or otherwise. Much country-style furniture has nothing but plain wood knobs, and, if you need replacements or additions, it might be simpler to ask a local woodworker to make them up. But there are other sorts, too, and you can contact Ball and Ball regarding their supply of original striped brown "Bennington" knobs. These are not reproductions, and the supply is dwindling. Ball and Ball is also a good source for glass, "compression bronze," and china-decorated knobs of the mid- to late 1800s. The reproduction of a "compression bronze" knob of the sort originally made by the Russell and Erwin Company is illustrated here.

Catalog available, $2.

Ball and Ball
463 W. Lincoln Hwy.
Exton, Penn. 19341
(215) 363-7330

Noel Wise Antiques supplies reproductions of stamped hollow and solid-brass knobs which are most suitable for Sheraton and early nineteenth-century pieces. The stamped brass face or rosette of each is very simple, but then most were.

Catalog available, $1.

Noel Wise Antiques
6503 St. Claude Ave.
Arabi, La. 70032
(504) 279-6896

Escutcheons and Roses

An escutcheon is used to frame a lock, and includes a keyhole. A rose is most often fitted to the outside of a cylinder—whether in a door or piece of furniture. Most door or furniture pulls come with roses. But they are available separately from H. Pfanstiel Hardware in quite wide variety. Three of the designs are illustrated here. As the manufacturer points out, "they provide the only effective and inexpensive means of converting old or commercial 'run of the mill' door hardware. These will eliminate the additional expense for carpentry work in plugging the old cylindrical lock hole which was previously a deterrent due to cost." The same principle holds for their use as replacements on furniture.

Catalog available, $2.

H. Pfanstiel Hardware Co., Inc.
Jeffersonville, N.Y. 12748
(914) 482-4445

Escutcheons of all sorts are available from Horton, but the Victorian styles are especially interesting. Several are illustrated, and each has a matching pull.

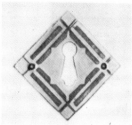

Catalog available, $1.25.

Horton Brasses
P.O. Box 95, Nooks Hill Rd.
Cromwell, Conn. 06416
(203) 635-4400

Hinges

Hinges for such different kinds of furniture as a slant front desk, tall case clock, a butler's tray, and a blanket chest are made by Ball and Ball. Stylistically, there are square, H and H-L, rattail, strap, harpischord, and butterfly hinges. Some are semi-handmade of iron; most are stamped or cast from brass.

Catalog available, $2.

Ball and Ball
463 W. Lincoln Hwy.
Exton, Penn. 19341
(215) 363-7330

Roll-Top Desk Hardware

This is hardware of a very special sort, and Noel Wise Antiques can supply you with special escutcheons of solid brass, the designs of which are illustrated here—

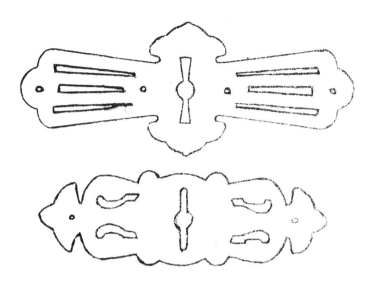

locks, a label holder, and a cast card frame pull. Carved drawer pulls of unfinished walnut are also available.

Catalog available, $1.

Noel Wise Antiques
6503 St. Claude Ave.
Arabi, La. 70032
(504) 279-6896

Kitchen and Miscellaneous Hardware

Blacksmiths and other traditional metalworkers produce a great number of useful objects which are also attractive to the kitchen and other areas of an old house. Some are hand-forged originals which cannot be found in hardware stores.

Utensil and Pot Racks

Racks for the hanging of pots can be made in almost any size by an experienced blacksmith. J. R. Wallin offers two standard models, a round rack ($37) 20″ in diameter and a half-round ($32) which is 25″ wide. He also

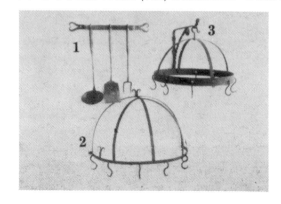

custom makes other sizes and shapes. Illustrated here with the racks is his cooking utensil set ($35).

Catalog available, $2.

Wallin Forge
Rte. 1, Box 65
Sparta, Ky. 41086
(606) 567-7201

Robert Griffith is an accomplished metalsmith and primarily produces pieces of wrought iron. Most of his work is custom order only, including this handsome utensil rack.

Robert Griffith, Metalsmith
16 S. Main St.
Trucksville, Penn. 18708
(717) 696-2395

Trivets

No object is more folksy than a trivet. Those sold in gift shops are usually not worth their weight in iron, if, indeed, they contain any. Robert Griffith's stock trivet is a reproduction of an eighteenth-century wrought-iron Pennsylvania object. It is available in a black forge finish ($40) or polished ($50), as illustrated.

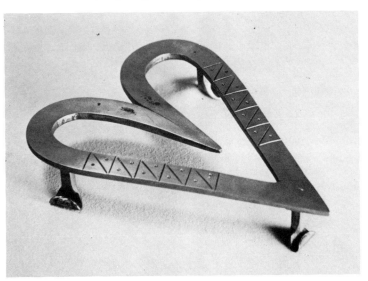

Robert Griffith, Metalsmith
16 S. Main St.
Trucksville, Penn. 18708
(717) 696-2395

Toasters

Newton Millham forges a number of different toaster models, but this is the most interesting. It is based on an eighteenth-century design and holds bread between finely twisted retainers and bent "flowers." When toasted, the bread has an unusual "brand."

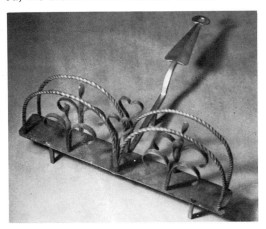

Catalog available.

Newton Millham-Star Forge
672 Drift Rd.
Westport, Mass. 02790
(617) 636-5437

Skewers, Fork, and Spoon

Inventive hand-forged hardware is the specialty of Steve Kayne. He is particularly interested in producing

primitive Colonial pieces which can be used at home or out-of-doors. Illustrated are an eating fork and spoon on a hook rack and six skewers on a holder. The utensils are of the sort carried by soldiers many years ago.

Catalogs available, $2.

Steve Kayne
17 Harmon Pl.
Smithtown, N.Y. 11787
(516) 724-3669

Hooks

These most useful of small objects are produced by almost every blacksmith working today and serve a multitude of purposes. R. Hood & Co. offers a rugged 8″ wall hook for hanging plants ($7.50), a simple 4″ curled hook for attaching to the wall ($2), 5″ beam hooks which are either pointed for driving into the wood or drilled for screwing or nailing ($2.50), and a 4½″ ceiling hook ($2.75) which is flattened at the top for underside attachment. All are hand-forged of iron.

Literature available; send stamped and self-addressed envelope.

R. Hood & Co.
Heritage Village
Meredith, N.H. 03253
(603) 366-2200

Ritter & Son's hat hooks, some illustrated here, are of solid brass. The most interesting are of Victorian design, and all are well fashioned. These range in price from $1.35 to $4.50.

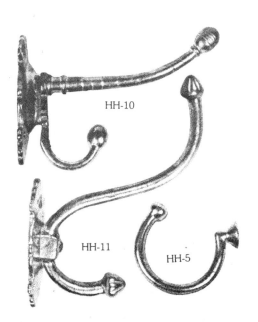

HH-10

HH-11

HH-5

Catalog available, $1.

Ritter & Son Hardware
46901 Fish Rock Road
Anchor Bay (Gualala), Calif. 95445
(707) 884-3363

Among the special hooks made by Steve Kayne are those used to hang a musket or rifle. There is also a hook or spike which can be used for hanging a lantern from a tree or beam, a trammel hook which can be raised and lowered, and a spice hook from which herbs, spices, and tobacco were hung in the barn.

Catalogs available, $2.

Steve Kayne
17 Harmon Pl.
Smithtown, N.Y. 11787
(516) 724-3669

Brackets and Other Hangers

Pete Taggett makes wall hangers of many varieties. Some can be used for plants or lighting fixtures; a few may be appropriate for signs. All are hand-forged iron.

Catalog available, $1.

Pete Taggett
Box 15
Mt. Holly, Vt. 05758
(802) 259-2452

Hand-crafted wrought-iron brackets are available from G. W. Mount, Inc. The plainest are made for shelves and are drilled both for wall mounting and shelf fastening. These reach out either 6, 8, or 12″.

Brochure available.

G. W. Mount, Inc.
P.O. Box 306
576 Leyden Rd.
Greenfield, Mass. 01301
(413) 773-5824

Nails, Keepers, Staples

Illustrated is a wide variety of fasteners made by blacksmith Newton Millham. Hardware of this sort was once a stock item in any hardware or general store. It is too expensive to use extensively, but you may find that it is suitable for replacement purposes here or there.

Catalog available, $1.

Newton Millham-Star Forge

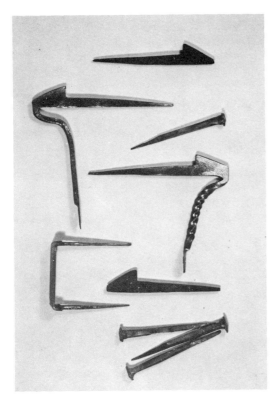

672 Drift Rd.
Westport, Mass. 02790
(617) 636-5437

Don't forget the Tremont Nail Co. This firm was written up extensively in the first *Old House Catalogue* and is the major supplier of old-style cut nails—cut spike, masonry, foundry, common siding, finish, clout, box, hinge, slating—and on and on. The company has been in business since 1819.

Literature available.

Tremont Nail Co.
P.O. Box 111
Wareham, Mass. 02571
(617) 295-0038

Tools

If you've looked through a tool supplier's catalog, you've probably found dozens of handy gadgets for performing tasks you never thought of doing. Did you know that you could get a hand-held tool for turning your own bed springs? Indispensable! But even the strangest devices can often mean the difference between a quality job and a merely adequate one. There are several excellent sources for quality mail-order tools. It might be worthwhile to peruse the catalogs, if only for the fun of it. We wager that you'll wind up buying something that you really needed all along.

For example, Brookstone sells giant rubber bands. They are perfect for clamping together chair legs for glueing, because they don't go limp like cords or cloth straps and they resist slippage on uneven surfaces. Beechwood carpenter's mallets, chamfering spoke shaves, shavehooks, carbide drills for glass, tap and die sets for threading dowels—all have their specific functions and have either proved their worth over generations or have become available through advanced technology.

Catalog available.

The Brookstone Co.
127 Vose Farm Rd.
Peterborough, N.H. 03458
(603) 924-7181

Veneering supplies and all the necessary paraphernalia can be ordered from the Minnesota Woodworker's Supply Company. They have special tools like joint and strip cutters, punches, saws, and rollers. Their upholstery equipment includes a complete collection of necessary and helpful gadgets such as needles, spline chisels, and ripping tools. Minnesota also supplies clamps, hand screws, sanding devices, knives, plug cutters, and dado sets.

Catalog available, $1.

Minnesota Woodworker's Supply Co.
21801 Industrial Blvd.
Rogers, Minn. 55374
(612) 428-4101

Albert Constantine is also big on veneering and offers materials, kits, tools and many how-to books on a variety of crafts. Many of this supplier's tools can be found in any good hardware store, but not so the specialty items.

Catalog available, 50¢.

Albert Constantine and Son, Inc.
2050 Eastchester Rd.
Bronx, N.Y. 10461
(212) 792-1600

Hardware from the Woodcraft Supply Corp. should be of particular interest to carpenters and joiners, because this is such a good source for traditional tools. They have broad axes, hatchets, heads, bark spuds, and peaveys which are essential to log cabin builders. The collection of carving and turning tools is outstanding.

Catalog available, 50¢.

Woodcraft Supply Corp.
313 Montvale Ave.

Woburn, Mass. 01801
1-800-225-1153

What Woodcraft doesn't have for log cabin building, Frog Tool Co. probably does. The two-man saw and the pit saw are just two examples. Frog also offers dozens of full-length books and manuals from carpentry to blacksmithing.

Catalog available, 50¢.

Frog Tool Co., Ltd.
541 N. Franklin St.
Chicago, Ill. 60610
(312) 644-5999

The nineteenth-century format of the Cumberland General Store's catalog is as fetching as the items they sell. The tool sections are especially strong in logging, joinery and blacksmith needs. Anyone seeking basic tools for country living should turn to Cumberland.

Catalog available, $3.

Cumberland General Store
Rte. 3, Box 479
Crossville, Tenn. 38555
(615) 243-0063

Furniture and cabinetmakers might want to take note of the Universal Clamp Company's products. Their mini-clamp treats each joint individually, and this feature eliminates the need for cumbersome pipe clamps. The Porta-Press frame and door jig is lightweight and keeps the work square and flat.

Send large stamped, self-addressed envelope for free information.

Universal Clamp Co.
6905 Cedros Ave.
Van Nuys, Calif. 91405
(213) 780-1015

Other Sources for Hardware

Consult List of Suppliers for addresses.

Architectural

Hinges

Ball and Ball
Broadway Supply
Cohasset Colonials
Robert Griffith
R. Hood & Co.
San Francisco Victoriana
Wallin Forge
Williamsburg Blacksmith

Knobs

Broadway Supply
The Cellar
R. Hood & Co.
Ritter & Son
San Francisco Victoriana

Knockers

Ball and Ball
Horton Brasses
G. W. Mount
Period Furniture Hardware
Pfanstiel Hardware

Latches

Ball and Ball
R. Hood & Co.
Horton Brasses
Steve Kayne

Period Furniture Hardware
Wallin Forge

Letter plates

Baldwin

Locks

Ball and Ball
Folger Adam
Newton Millham
Period Furniture Hardware
San Francisco Victoriana
Noel Wise

Shutter Hardware

Ball and Ball
Steve Kayne
Period Furniture Hardware
Wallin Forge
Wrightsville Hardware

Window Hardware

Blaine Window Hardware
Period Furniture Hardware
Ritter & Son

Bath Hardware

Toilets

Heads Up
P & G New & Used Plumbing Supply

Faucets/Taps and Accessories

Bona
Kohler Co.
Materials Unlimited
Pfanstiel Hardware
P & G New & Used Plumbing Supply

Tubs and Sinks

Broadway Supply Co.
Kohler Co.
Mayfair China
Period Furniture Hardware

Furniture Hardware

Escutcheons and Roses

Period Furniture
Noel Wise

Hinges

Robert Griffith

Horton Brasses
Steve Kayne
Minnesota Woodworkers Supply
Period Furniture Hardware
Richard E. Sargent

Knobs

Horton Brasses
Minnesota Woodworkers Supply
Period Furniture Hardware

Latches

Ball and Ball
Robert Griffith
R. Hood & Son
Horton Brasses
Period Furniture Hardware

Pulls/Drops

Broadway Supply
Albert Constantine & Son
Steve Kayne
Minnesota Woodworkers Supply
Period Furniture Hardware
Pfanstiel Hardware

Roll-Top Desk Hardware

Ball and Ball

Kitchen Hardware

Hooks

Broadway Supply
G. W. Mount
Richard E. Sargent
Pete Taggett

Toasters

Richard E. Sargent

Trivets

Steve Kayne

Utensil and Pot Racks

G. W. Mount
Pete Taggett

Miscellaneous

Nails/Staples

Ball and Ball
Cohasset Colonials
R. Hood & Son
Woodcraft

Raised-panel fireplace wall with "floating" mantel shelf by
Townsend H. Anderson. *See* page 39.

IV   Fireplaces & Heating

Everyone who wants to stop waste in our society—from the destruction of old houses to the leveling of hillsides on which they stand—agrees that energy is at the heart of the problem. Preservationists and environmentalists have a great deal in common, and in no area is this most strikingly illustrated than in heating. A recent Herblock cartoon showed a wreck of a Victorian house with a "for sale" sign outside. The real estate sign noted that the building contained four wood-burning fireplaces and went with an acre of woodland. The offering price *had* been $10,000; slapped over the old price was a new one, $100,000, and beneath this in large block letters was the simple word—"Sold."

Like any good cartoon, the point has been exaggerated, but not to the point of ineffectiveness. Wood can be used at least as a supplementary fuel in many homes. It is an almost infinitely renewable alternative source if used with care in small towns and in the country. Wood-lot management has never been practiced with much care in America, but we are learning quickly that there are ways to maintain a good stand and supply of wood. In those cities where the burning of wood is allowed, its effectiveness and availability is limited. Technology must come to the rescue with new devices that will generate energy from wind power, the sun, and the burning of waste materials.

Many old houses and buildings are already energy efficient. Their exterior walls are thick, and rooms are divided one from another with more than plasterboard. A good growth of trees serves as a windbreak, and the structure itself is positioned in a way that it does not bear the brunt of northwest winds. The building of a house in this manner was a common practice and no one needed a consulting engineer to come up with a plan for saving fuel and money. To site a house properly, to provide it with a cover, to construct it of solid materials which withstand heat loss—these were matters of common sense and experience. To do the same thing today with a new building is a very expensive proposition. Many of the best sites are gone, planting of bushes and trees runs into the thousands of dollars, *real* wood is at a premium. Therefore, we need our old buildings even more than ever before. What was $10,000 ten years ago *may* be approaching the $100,000 level in the late 1970s.

This is not to say that all old houses are as snug as a bug in a rug. Modern forms of insulation provide an extra security blanket. Just a small amount of material blown into an attic floor may save considerably on the winter fuel bill and also serve to keep the floor below cool during the summer. Windows must be kept properly caulked and covered with more than shutters. Some rooms, especially in large and high-ceilinged Victorian structures, should probably be sealed off in the winter and the heat concentrated in those areas where it is of most use.

Anyone who lives in a house or apartment that contains fireplaces will certainly want to use them. Despite all the talk about how inefficient they are in providing heat to a room, this writer's experience is that the temperature may rise as much as 10 degrees in a half hour in a moderately-sized area without the use of any sort of modern gadgets. A cast-iron fireback will help to reflect heat out into the room as will a properly-proportioned firebox or opening. A solid damper is, of course, necessary for proper draft and heat flow.

There are, however, appliances of recent origin which will cut down on heat loss up the chimney. One of these—a special grate—is covered in the following pages. Of course you can always convert your fireplace, as many nineteenth-century Americans did, for a Franklin-type stove. It does seem a shame to do this. Unless your fireplace is already merely a disreputable hole in the wall, think of keeping the fireplace and installing in addition a free-standing stove that can be vented either through the chimney flue or a new outlet.

Wood and coal-burning stoves are all the rage. Antique fixtures once sold for practically nothing as no one could even figure out what to do with them. Now they may bring as much as $2,000. Reproduction stoves are sold everywhere along with newer types of models, some of the best from Scandinavia, which have been engineered to produce more BTU's more efficiently. As with any new field of commercial endeavor, the rip-off artists are at work. Before buying any heating device—merely for warming up a room or for cooking—be sure that it is of solid construction, is safe to use and can be properly installed in the space you have in mind.

The center of focus in many period rooms was the hearth. The appointments and furnishings, therefore, were designed and arranged in relation to this structural "given." It is curious that in the last part of the twentieth century we are again returning to the central concern of keeping warm. If we can keep our old buildings standing, those of us lucky enough to live in them should have no trouble at all.

Antique Mantels

A handsome mantel properly finishes off almost any fireplace. Most mantels will surround the fireplace on three sides and effectively frame it in the manner of a picture, but mantels may also be nothing more than a series of mouldings which form a shallow shelf at the top. More elaborate are those which consist of a series of levels and sculpted projections which form a veritable console. Mantels in old houses may be of wood, quarried stone (such as marble), cast iron, or ornamental plaster. Not every period structure, of course, contains fireplaces which have been framed by a mantel. Some of the earliest fireplace walls are simply paneled room ends.

The supply of "used" or antique mantels is quite good. The mantel is one of the first features of an old house to be saved when demolition is the only prospect in sight. Mantels were also removed in the nineteenth century when fireplace openings were closed up for the installation of stoves. More than one fortunate old-house owner has found these stored in a barn or the attic. Others have found them in wrecking yards or architectural antiques supply houses in their area.

The New York showroom of William Jackson always displays a variety of antique mantels, from early American pine to imported marble. (Do not confuse this friendly company with another of a similar name which boasts the sale of only eighteenth-century mantels for use in estate houses.) William Jackson provides a much wider selection and documents its resources in a handsome brochure. The company has also reproduced many of its fine acquisitions in its own workshops.

Wm. H. Jackson Co.
3 East 47th St.
New York, N.Y. 10017
(212) 753-9400

A growing number of architectural antiques supply houses stock mantels as a matter of course. Gargoyles is a virtual general store. It makes a point of maintaining a variety of styles—from carved Jacobean to Art Nouveau to stately marble mantels.

Gargoyles, Ltd.
512 S. 3rd St.
Philadelphia, Penn. 19147
(215) 629-1700

Materials Unlimited operates a salvage operation with a late-Victorian influence, much of their supply coming from doomed Midwestern sources.

Materials Unlimited
4100 Morgan Rd.
Ypsilanti, Mich. 48197
(313) 434-4300

The Renovation Source is an architectural consulting service that specializes in restoration of pre-1930 buildings. Among its other virtues, it is a good source of mantels.

The Renovation Source, Inc.
3512-14 Southport
Chicago, Ill. 60657
(312) 327-1250

You'll find a regional influence at Old Mansions which is welcome almost anywhere. Most of their mantels come from early New England homes.

Old Mansions Co.
1305 Blue Hill Ave.
Mattapan, Mass. 02126
(617) 296-0737

Westlake is based in Texas and offers some marble pieces which are most appropriate for Victorian homes—wherever they are found.

Westlake Architectural Antiques
3315 Westlake Dr.
Austin, Texas 78746
(512) 327-1110

Victor Carl's focus is limited to fine eighteenth-century French and English mantels with a price range of $600 to $5,000.

Victor Carl Antiques
841 Broadway
New York, N.Y. 10003
(212) 673-8740

The classic Georgian has a 3′ x 4′6″ opening. You must add 15% to its $450 price tag if you prefer oak or walnut.

Reproduction Mantels

Reproduction mantels can be constructed with as much fidelity as the craftsman and his customer choose to indulge. Almost every material used in the past is available today, and a number of firms employ craftsmen who have retained the skills of yesterday. An old-house owner may wish to duplicate the style of a mantel found in several rooms and missing in another. The same style was often used over and over within the same building or even the geographic area in which a woodworker was active. The apartment dweller may need a particular kind of mantel for a living room furnished in a period manner. And even the owner of a new home built with one of the manufactured fireplaces, such as the Heatilator, may decide to tie his modern fireplace into a traditional setting.

Reproduction mantels have been produced for years by Decorators Supply. They not only provide individual customers with any number of different styles, but also supply other dealers with their fine products.

Among the mantels which can be ordered are models in poplar and birch. The one illustrated, the Adam, sells for $410 and is shipped with a prime coat of paint. It has a 3′6″ x 4′3″ opening. Special sizes increase the price by 15%.

Catalog available, 50¢.

Decorators Supply Corporation
36100 S. Morgan St.
Chicago, Ill. 60609
(312) 847-6300

Constructed in what is termed a Williamsburg style, this Readybuilt poplar mantel and paneling combination is 8′ high and 7′6″ wide. Most of Readybuilt's mantels have a 50″ x 37½″ opening. This one sells for a reasonable $430. It is appropriate, of course, for only Colonial-period interiors.

Readybuilt lives up to its name in supplying mantels designed especially to fit metal prefabricated built-in

fireplaces. The model illustrated is 47" wide and the legs can be cut off to accommodate hearth heights less than 39". It is finished in prime white and sells for $87.45.

Catalog, $1.

The Readybuilt Products Co.
P.O. Box 4306
Baltimore, Md. 21223
(301) 233-5833

Alan Amerian executes a number of different styles—Colonial, Federal, Georgian, Greek Revival, and—for the home in a more European style—Louis XV and Italian Renaissance. Each mantel requires skillful carving. Woods such as oak, walnut, cherry, mahogany, bass, and poplar are used. The handsomely-carved piece shown here would dignify any mid-Victorian home.

Brochure available.

Amerian Woodcarving
282 San Jose Ave.
San Jose, Calif. 95125
(408) 294-2968

Fireplace Accessories

Supplies for the fireplace constitute a world of objects distinctly different from any other. Andirons, tools, firebacks, brooms, pots and pans, cranes, tiles for facing, grates, scuttles, bellows, match safes, screens—the list goes on and on. The skills of blacksmiths, foundry craftsmen, brass and copper metalworkers, and other artisans are called for to supply useful and attractive objects. Fortunately, the services of such individuals are widely available. The decorative appeal of fireplace accessories survived even when the necessity for their use ebbed away.

It is unnecessary in a book of this sort to provide souces for many of these very common objects which can be found in hardware and furniture stores and in antique shops. Rather, it is more useful to spotlight some of the high-quality manufacturers and to mention some of their most exceptional products.

The mythical dispensers of charm and beauty are framed in this 30" x 37" iron fireback from Steptoe & Wife. You'll need a fireplace of nearly Olympic proportions to accommodate it. But if the opening is that large, you will need the radiating effect of a cast-iron fireback in order to draw some of the heat into the room.

The "Castle Fire" suggests a medieval setting. You won't have to put it in the hearth of a long and narrow mead hall, however, because it's small enough (18″ wide, 11″ deep) for the most modest fireplace. Both the fireback and the grate are available only from this innovative Canadian firm.

Catalog available, $1.

Steptoe & Wife Antiques Ltd.
3626 Victoria Park Ave.
Willowdale, Ontario M2H 3B2
(416) 497-2989

Common sense dictates that some form of screening separate the fire from the room. Three-panel folding screens are very popular and are usually less expensive than permanently-mounted sliding curtains or recessed screens. But where to find well-made screens? Lemee's, a major supply house of fireplace accessories, sells several with brass tubular trim and handles. The extended width of each is 52″. Prices range from $24 to $109.50.

Keep a match holder near your stove or fireplace. You'll always have a light handy but in a place removed from children's hands. Lemee's has several to choose from. One depicts Venus and Cupid on two receptacles. It is cast iron and has a serrated edge for striking. The price is $4.40.

Although many fireplace accessories are just excess baggage to clutter up living space, some utensils can enhance the enjoyment and usefulness of the hearth. Iron skillets are fairly easy to come by, but kettles of cast iron are not as common. Those from Lemee are not to be confused with the thin models available in gift shops and used as planters. These are kettles and pots that can be hung from a crane or, if footed, kept steady on the fire surface. An eight-quart pot with lid sells for $21.95. A two-quart cast-iron bulge pot with a brass handle is $21.50.

Catalog available, 50¢.

Lemee's Fireplace Equipment
Rte. 28, 815 Bedford St.
Bridgewater, Mass. 02324
(617) 697-2672

Keep the handles of your fireplace tools within easy reach with this brass jamb hook. And the appropriate device for the business end of a poker, tong, and shovel is a tool stone. It is 7″ square, 1½″ thick, and indented and grooved to keep the tools from sliding along the hearth. Both of these items are available from Ball and Ball, a company better known for its furniture and architectural hardware. The jamb hook sells for $21.75 and is one of many models; the stone is unique and is priced at $19.50

Catalog available, $2.

Ball and Ball
463 W. Lincoln Highway
Exton, Penn. 19341
(215) 363-7330

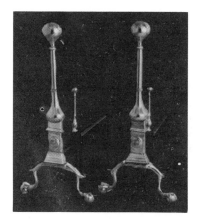

Andirons are as useful as the most modern of fireplace devices and can be found in every possible size and form. If you can't find an antique pair that will look right on the hearth, there are reproductions galore. These 20″ high solid-brass andirons are as handsome as any antique and carry the Historic Newport Reproduction label. They extend 21″. Virginia Metalcrafters makes them, and the price is handsome, too—$200. But, as the firm states about its whole line, "These products are intended for a discriminating clientele who appreciate craftsmanship 100 years behind the times." In this case, and we are grateful, they are about 200 years late.

Catalog available.

Virginia Metalcrafters
1010 E. Main St.
Waynesboro, Va. 22980
(703) 942-8205

As a purveyor of high-quality fireplace equipment since 1827, Wm. H. Jackson offers considerable flexibility when it comes to special needs. This 7″ high brass fender, for example, can be ordered in any length. Early fenders of this sort were imported from England, and American manufacture has always been limited.

Jackson also does custom designs for tile facing. Six-inch square tiles are painted by the firm's own artist. These ceramic pieces range in price from $10 to $14 each. For someone seeking to duplicate or fill in an authentic design, Jackson's expertise is greatly appreciated.

Brochure available.

Wm. H. Jackson Co.
3 East 47th St.
New York, N.Y. 10017
(212) 753-9400

Several different kinds of grates have been devised in recent years that will send out more heat from the hearth. Some are complicated affairs that require closing up the fireplace is some manner and/or installing an electric fan. The Thermograte operates by natural convection only, and the manufacturers claim that it can double the heat output. The principle is a sound and simple one. A standard mild steel unit carries a two-year warranty against burn-out; the stainless steel model is guaranteed for five years. Various sizes are offered. Both models are known as "open grate." The company also makes an enclosed, glass door circulating air model. We suggest that you try the simpler first.

Literature available.

Thermograte Enterprises, Inc.
1639 Terrace Dr.

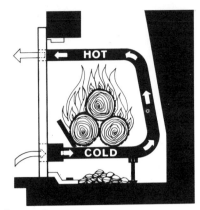

St. Paul, Minn. 55113
(612) 633-1376

Chimney Needs

Most chimneys just require a good cleaning every so often. Birds like to nest in them, and soot and creosote collect in amazing quantities. The danger of a chimney fire is always present, but, if the basic structure is maintained properly, the chance of this kind of misfortune is greatly lessened. Most home owners complain not of the dirt but of the chimney's draw. Some stacks are simply not high enough, and there is little that you can do about it without adding to them. Other chimneys are not topped properly, and a chimney pot or two may be the solution. In any case, call in an expert and don't try to remedy such problems as these yourself unless you are prepared to do the same for others.

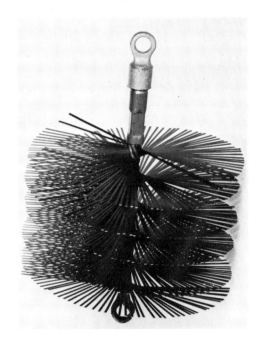

All chimneys need cleaning, but you needn't call on an expert if you can learn to use one of Kristia's chimney brushes from Norway. If you are successful at it, you

86

may have discovered a lucrative new career. These days chimney sweeps are even being written up in *The New York Times*. Kristia's instruction book ($1) lists the names of sweeps across the country. None of them force a pine tree through the chimney or load shotgun shells with rocksalt to blast away the soot. They prefer the Kristia brushes which come in several sizes.

Literature available.

Kristia Associates
343 Forest Ave.
P.O. Box 1118
Portland, Me. 04104
(207) 772-2821

Another enterprising firm, Self-Sufficiency Products, manufactures the brush illustrated here. This is suitable for cleaning out both a fireplace chimney or a metal chimney used for a stove. The tool is priced at $49.95.

Brochure available.

Self-Sufficiency Products
Environmental Manufacturing Corp.
P.O. Box 126
Essex Junction, Vt. 05452

There is more to the chimney pot than aesthetic appeal. It improves the draft and minimizes downdrafts. It also helps keep out the rain. A chimney pot can even be stuck on a non-functioning chimney to improve the roofscape, if that strikes your fancy. Historic Boulevard Services has a line that ranges in price from $37 to $109. The pots are clay and are available in six styles which are designed to fit various needs. They measure 2½ to 3 feet high, weigh 80 to 150 pounds, and are ½″ to 1″ thick.

Brochure available.

Historic Boulevard Services
1520 W. Jackson Blvd.
Chicago, Ill. 60607
(312) 829-5562

Heating Stoves

Even if we don't have winters like that of 1976–77 and 1977–78 during the next few years, oil and gas prices will continue to rise. The sale of free-standing and fireplace stoves will continue to increase. What was once a staple in the cabin has now become a part of the surburban and country home. Those who live in old houses are in a better position to make use of these devices. Older homes have more flues that can be used for venting purposes. Such buildings are also likely to contain more room for appliances of this sort.

The hard sell approach, as we've already observed, is gaining in momentum. Stove shops are becoming as popular as tennis centers, and one competitor is nudging another. As long as the boom is on, you might as well profit from it. More and more of the consumer and home magazines are paying attention to the stampede to wood. Read the literature carefully, and look for Underwriter's Laboratory approval. Above all, make sure that you will have an adequate supply of wood or coal on hand (some stoves will burn both) when the time comes, and that you will have the time to keep the home fires burning.

Today's wood-burning stoves must be as practical as they are good-looking. If you have to choose between these two criteria, by all means opt for the practical. In this case, you have the best of two worlds. Illustrated is a reproduction of the Victorian De Dietrich & Co.

stove. Its ornate exterior surrounds an internal baffling system and draft control for efficiency. An ash removal pan is slung under a full-width firebox. The upper chamber is a heating oven. The top, when lifted off, reveals a burner and warming area. This is model AL-77; six other models are available.

Brochure, free; catalog, 25¢.

The Burning Log (Eastern Office)
P.O. Box 438
Lebanon, N.H. 03766
(603) 448-4360

    or

The Burning Log (Western Office)
P.O. Box 8519
Aspen, Colorado 81611
(303) 925-8968

Like all other Shaker products, the stove is a model of simplicity. In this case, however, simpler may not be better if you're looking for a major rather than supplementary source of heat. It doesn't have a draft control like the more sophisticated designs. If efficiency is not uppermost, then this 20″ high stove will work just fine.

Catalog available, $2.50.

Guild of Shaker Crafts
401 W. Savidge St.
Spring Lake, Mich. 49456
(616) 846-28780

Mohawk's Tempwood II woodstove uses a downdraft principle to achieve an efficient 55,000 BTU/hr. rating. Vents direct air down and around the logs for complete combustion. Since the only access is through the lid on top, ash removal is best left to a vacuum cleaner.

Literature available, including a booklet entitled Wood Energy, *$1.*

Mohawk Industries Inc.
173 Howland Ave.
Adams, Mass. 01220
(413) 743-3648

Le Petit Godin also boasts charm and efficiency. It comes in two sizes, the larger of which generates an estimated 32,000 BTU/hr. when stoked with coal. The gasketed fire door has a mica window and a spin-wheel draft control. The steel body is lined with firebrick and can be loaded through the top. It can also be used with wood. The top, fire door, and base are of enameled cast iron available in several colors—cedar green, sand, brown, and black. All in all, a Victorian beauty of Gallic esprit and dispatch.

Literature available.

Bow and Arrow Imports
14 Arrow St.
Cambridge, Mass. 02138
(617) 354-1459

There are several advantages to parlor stoves from Vermont Castings. A baffling system allows the doors to be removed for viewing the fire without filling the house with smoke. Logs up to 24″ can be loaded from the side or the front in the "Defiant" model. As an airtight stove it develops 55,000 BTU/hr. and can burn from 12 to 14 hours. A thermostat enables a constant temperature to be maintained. The "Defiant" is priced at $545.

The "Vigilant" is smaller than the "Defiant," but shares its efficiency. The top lid opens for loading. The design

of the smoke chamber prevents you from getting a face full of smoke when it's up. An automatic thermostat controls the air supply. These Vermonters have learned to be inventive when it comes to heat. The "Vigilant" is yours for $445.

Catalog available, $1.

Vermont Castings, Inc.
Box 126, Prince St.
Randolph, Vt. 05060
(802) 728-3355

The Fisher design, one of the best known in the heating industry, has a secondary combustion chamber to get the most out of gases released from burning wood. The bi-level top can be used for cooking at two temperatures. The "Baby Bear," shown here, is only 15½″ wide, 29″ long, and accommodates 18″ logs. The construction is of steel plate.

Brochure available.

Fisher Stoves International
P.O. Box 10605
Eugene, Ore. 97440

Many of the newest wood stove designs, like the Schrader, are made from heavy steel plate. This material tolerates a higher temperature than cast iron. Schrader manufactures a compact model with an aluminum alloy door. The maker claims that over 250,000 homes are already being heated with their stoves.

Brochure available.

Schrader Wood Stoves and Fireplaces
724 Water St.
Santa Cruz, Calif. 95060
(408) 425-8125

In an effort to capitalize on utter simplicity, Shenandoah markets a line of "basic" wood stoves like the model R-55 shown here. It is an airtight 18″ diameter steel cylinder lined with firebrick. The air flow is thermostatically controlled.

Brochure available.

Shenandoah Manufacturing Co., Inc.
P.O. Box 839
Harrisonburg, Va. 22801
(703) 434-3838

The folks at All Nighter Stove Works are rightfully proud of the Underwriters Laboratories seal of approval on four of their wood-burners. The heftiest stove, the "Big Mo'," is a firebrick-lined front-loader capable of handling logs up to 30″. There are three other proportionately smaller versions. All are available with an optional electric blower attachment for the hot-air convection system. Another optional feature is the hot-water extraction cylinder which fits around the flue and can supplement an existing hot water heater.

Brochure available.

All Nighter Stove Works, Inc.
80 Commerce St.
Glastonbury, Conn. 06033
(203) 633-3640

Grampa's Wood Stoves specializes in restoring and selling turn-of-the-century wood- and coal-burning ranges and parlor stoves. They use only authentic parts which they will also sell if an adequate description of the part needed accompanies a request.

Parlor stoves such as the "Round Oak" and "Century Oak" are part of Grampa's everchanging inventory.

Literature available.

Grampa's Wood Stoves
P.O. Box 492
Ware, Mass. 01082
(413) 967-6684

Cooking Stoves

Some of the heating stoves described above also serve for simple cooking purposes. A tea kettle or coffee pot was often kept warm on the top of the parlor stove, and perhaps more than one pre-TV dinner was served from the top of a pot belly. Those who have used wood- or coal-burning ranges and ovens swear that they are easy to use and maintain. Most modern housewives or their cooking husbands—in an old house or not—wouldn't want one anywhere near the kitchen. As long as electricity and gas can be obtained at reasonable prices and manufacturers of modern appliances continue to improve their efficiency, there may be little reason to fuss over an old-fashioned model. A stove of this sort is certainly perfect for a summer kitchen or to be used in the country when—as still happens—the lines are down.

The "Victor Jr." cooking range has been re-introduced. Production was halted in 1966 just before "back to nature" and "energy crisis" became household terms. This is a wood-burning cast-iron stove designed to provide even heat throughout or just a hot top surface. Options include a warming oven and a five-gallon water reservoir. Be sure of your wood supply before you depend on this one.

Literature available.

Home and Harvest, Inc.
4407 Westbourne Rd.
Greensboro, N.C. 27401

cooking and heating. Logs are placed so that they burn slowly, like a cigar.

Jotul's kitchen stove (#404) comes with a front grate for firing with coke or coal. It is a little on the small side, but it would be fine for a cabin in the woods or in a summer kitchen.

Book available, $1.

Jotul
Kristia Associates
Box 1118, 343 Forest Ave.
Portland, Me. 04102
(207) 772-2821

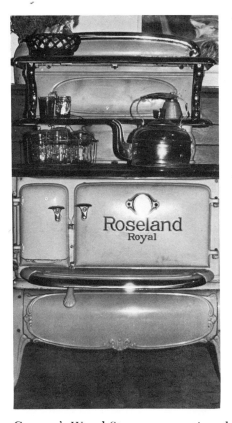

One of the best-known lines of wood stoves comes from Norway, where both wood and frigid weather are common. The "Lumberjack" is a cast-iron stove for

Grampa's Wood Stoves, as mentioned earlier, specializes in the real thing—antique stoves. The imposing "Roseland Royal" looks almost as it did when it left the foundry. The "Home Comfort" is similarly well preserved. A reservoir attached to it keeps water hot for bathing and shaving.

Literature available.

Grampa's Wood Stoves
P.O. Box 492
Ware, Mass. 01082
(413) 967-6684

Stove Accessories

Every one of the stoves described requires installation, and this means stove pipe and other fittings. Requirements are different for each model, and what will be needed at your house could be completely different from what the neighbor down the street needs. You should, however, be able to get most of the necessary materials from a hardware or building supplier. The stove makers themselves will assist you in every way that they can, and various retail outlets may provide installation and servicing.

Jotul is one of the companies that provides expert help in finding appropriate fittings and pipe. Thompson and Anderson, another Maine firm, manufactures pipe and accessories especially for Jotul products. If you have decided on a Jotul, you'll be referred to Thompson and Anderson.

Thompson and Anderson
53 Seavey St.
Westbrook, Me. 04092
(207) 854-2905

The kinds of tools used in stoves differ somewhat from

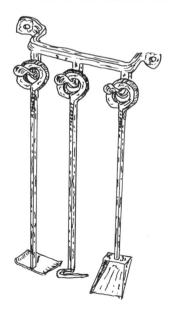

those intended for the fireplace. Again, Jotul has anticipated your needs. Pete Tagget, a blacksmith, has made several handy utensils, and will supply them for Jotul and other stoves. They come in lengths of 24″ and 36″ with either a wall hanger or floor stand in which to hold them.

Pete Taggett
The Blacksmith Shop
P.O. Box 115
Mt. Holly, Vt. 05758

Other Sources for Fireplace and Heating Equipment

Consult the List of Suppliers for addresses.

Mantels/Antique

Architectural Antiques
Castle Burlingame
Eighteenth-Century Co.
Felicity, Inc.
Francis J. Purcell II
Greg Spiess
R. T. Trump & Co.
United House Wrecking
I. M. Wiese
Wrecking Bar

Mantels/New

Architectural Paneling
Black Millwork
European Marble Works
Felber Studios
Focal Point
Fypon
Old World Moulding

Stoves/Heaters

Atlanta Stove Works
Pfanstiel Hardware
Portland Franklin Stove Foundry
Washington Stove Works

Cooking Stoves

Cumberland General Store
Schrader Wood Stoves and Fireplaces
United House Wrecking
Washington Stove Works

Fireplace Accessories

Colonial Williamsburg, Craft House
Cumberland General Store
Robert Griffith
Steve Kayne
Newton Millham
George W. Mount
Period Furniture Hardware
Pete Taggett
Wallin Forge

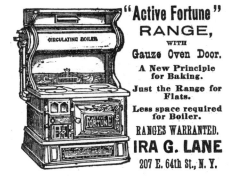

V Floors

One of the features most treasured by admirers of old houses is fine flooring. This may be of oak or pine or even a more exotic wood such as ash or chestnut. Oak was used widely in the Colonies, but the supply became limited and builders turned in the eighteenth century to pine—white in the North and yellow in the South. Like so many other things in an old house, economy and availability determined selection of materials as much as did aesthetic judgment. Oak continued to be used in the West when it was no longer easy to obtain in the East.

The earliest form of flooring was wide-board —from a foot to almost two feet. Not until the nineteenth century did narrow hardwood strip flooring or parquet come into popular use, and then only gradually. Mid-Victorian homes were unlikely to have random-width pine floors, and when remodeling a home (restoration was unthinkable at the time), the Victorians often laid the narrow over the wide and "crude" flooring. The new was easier to maintain and better held carpeting.

Before determining exactly what to do with flooring, the owner of any old house must determine exactly what the base consists of. Has one floor been laid over another? Or is what appears to be a second floor underneath merely a thinner arrangement of boards which closes the joints above? Examination of one small area could well save the restorer much time and effort. Since boards are laid from at least one joist to another, it should be possible to use several square feet of flooring in a room as typical of that remaining elsewhere. In order to do this, the homeowner may have to remove such artificial coverings as linoleum; this is a perfectly permissable operation. No one is likely to complain about the loss of what is almost always a badly-aged synthetic. Although linoleum has its devotees, this is one product of the unnatural past which we can do without.

Once the nature of the original flooring has been determined, the next step is to consider its treatment. Some boards may have to be replaced or pieces of wood relaid. The older the house, the harder it is to accomplish such tasks with success. Antique lumber is becoming more and more rare. Fortunately, the hardware with which it was attached— wooden pegs in many very early floors and hand- or machine-wrought nails on later—is being reproduced today. Attic floors may supply some of the replacement pieces; occasionally lumber from out buildings serves as well if of the proper thickness and wood. It is better to save such weathered wood, however, for more rustic purposes. Patterned wood floors can be much more easily repaired, but the cost is likely to be as great as for those which are earlier and wider.

You will thank your lucky stars if the floors have been covered with wall-to-wall carpeting or some other such material over the years. This will have prevented them from being gouged and scuffed to death. No doubt you will want to remove such a modern excresence as soon as possible, despite what your more "up-to-date" neighbors may think. ("Do you mean to tell me," a prospective home buyer once asked this writer, "that there is no wall-to-wall carpeting? Just these old rugs?") But you must be prepared to live with the past—at least its minor accidents. Great gouges, sagging boards, nasty breaks, etc., must be removed, but if the old floor is to remain, you will have to accept scratches and unevenness. By all means, do *not* have the floors scraped or heavily sanded. This will remove much more that you wish, including the look of age. You might try a stain and linseed oil, and then a light wax (not acrylic) to see how well the surface can "come up" under normal circumstances. Then you may decide that some light sanding with a fine abrasive will be necessary here or there. Of course, if paint has been applied (and not paint of the sort used by home artists of earlier days which may have been original with the floor), you will need to turn to a good remover.

The beauty of an old floor may be enhanced with the use of a fine rug; one complements the other. Orientals of various sorts lead the most desirable list of coverings, but they are not as accurate a period furnishing for most pre-Victorian homes as a rag or hooked rug. A floorcloth or even straw matting may be truer to form. If you wish to be completely (historically) honest, bare floor would have to suffice. This may be fine for a museum, but most home owners will wish to warm up the floor beneath them. A coat of paint can be applied, but, better yet, a stencil design can be drawn. Representative stencil patterns can be bought and, if your ability is limited, even worked by an expert in your own home.

The assumption has been made that most old homes have wood floors. This may not be the case in those of Spanish Colonial design. Here tiles have been used most liberally. Unglazed Mexican tiles are available in most parts of the country. Better ceramic companies can supply you with authentic reproductions of Victorian tiles which are suitable for foyers and kitchens. Marble is always available for those able to pay the price. Slate, too, can be found almost everywhere. Substitutes for these in vinyl should be avoided if at all possible. If it seems the only alternative, then try a solid vinyl which has the thickness, color, and patina of the material it imitates.

Wood Flooring

Good lumber—used (antique) or new—is increasingly hard to find. Anyone who has built a house in the past two years knows how one must struggle to obtain redwood, and even cedar of quality. With a building boom at hand, supplies of solid pine (not merely plywood with a veneer) must be ordered far in advance of the time when it will be needed. Barn siding disappears almost as rapidly as the time taken to bulldoze an old red barn to the ground.

Supplies of old lumber may be found—if you keep looking—in most areas of North America where old houses abound. Reading the classified sections of local newspapers may prove more useful than following the columns of The Old-House Journal *or* Yankee. *A recent issue of one such weekly* The Hunterdon County Democrat *(New Jersey), carried three listings. The word is out: people do want old lumber for new and period homes. Look first, then, close to home. And if you can't find what you need there, start searching farther afield.*

Don't, please, fall for imitations. Floors have to be solid and what is mistakenly used for paneling is, fortunately, not sturdy enough to lie beneath the feet. But there are still ways to be tripped up. For example, some flooring manufacturers produce boards that are already "pegged," that is, they have what looks like a row of pegs stamped on them. You'll know they are not functional, and so will everyone else. Besides, only the very earliest of Colonial houses are likely to have floors that were pegged to the joists rather than nailed.

The atmosphere you wish to create will, of course, dictate the choice of flooring. Too often, the budget is the final arbiter. Wide-pine flooring of more recent vintage might be most appropriate for your project. It can be used—if properly matched—for patching where necessary.

Guyon mills shiplapped pine boards in widths of 6, 8, and 10″. Factory-stained, they run 88¢ per board foot.

You can order wider planks (up to 21″) from Dale Carlisle. He air dries the wood two years and will plane them if requested.

Craftsman Lumber sells pine planks as wide as 24″.

Maurer and Shepherd stock hand-planed, shiplapped pine and oak flooring.

Guyon, Inc.
650 Oak St.
Lititz, Penn. 17543
(717) 626-0225

Dale Carlisle
Rte. 123
Stoddard, N.H. 03464
(603) 446-3937

Craftsman Lumber Co.
Maid St.
Groton, Mass. 01450
(617) 448-6336

Maurer and Shepherd, Joyners
122 Naubuc Ave.
Glastonbury, Conn. 06033
(203) 633-2383

Antique Wood Flooring

Diamond K reclaims hard pine flooring in widths up to 20″. One side of this antique stock is planed so no sanding or waxing is necessary.

Literature Available

Diamond K
130 Buckland Rd.
South Windsor, Conn. 06074
(203) 644-8486

Probably the most sought-after antique flooring is old growth southern yellow pine. The last stands were felled early in this century and used for New England shipbuilding, bridges, and mill construction. The original wood becomes available as the old structures are dismantled. Outfits like The House Carpenters resaw and mill the valuable timber into 13/16″ tongue and groove.

Catalog available, $4.

The House Carpenters
Box 217
Shutesbury, Mass. 01072

Period Pine sells three grades of custom milled planing of southern yellow pine in widths of 4″ to 12″.

Brochure available.
Period Pine
P.O. Box 77052
Atlanta, Ga. 30309
(404) 876-4740

Inlaid Floors

For homes of the Victorian period and beyond, the use of inlaid woods can add distinction to residential foyers, living rooms, libraries, and dining rooms. The Lincoln series from Wood Mosaic is ¾″ tongue-and-groove white or red oak with an antique finish. It sells for $3.65 a square foot and is preassembled in 24″ x 24″ sections.

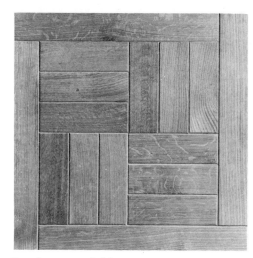

Brochure available.

Wood Mosaic
P.O. Box 21159
Louisville, Ky. 40221
(502) 363-3531

Stairwork and Thresholds

Having selected an appropriate parquet for a restored floor, an equally fitting choice of stairwork is needed. Harris Manufacturing makes standard and custom stair treads and risers in red or white oak, "select" and "better grade." Red oak nosings can be solid or rabbeted and cut to specified length. Thresholds are also red oak and can be as thick as ¾″ and as long as 12′. (Quite a door, that one.)

Catalog available.

Harris Manufacturing Co.
783 E. Walnut St.
Johnson City, Tenn. 37601
(615) 928-3122

Ceramic Tiles

Tiling has always been an expensive way to cover a floor, except in those parts of the Southwest and West where clay products have been widely available. Southern Californians say that Mexico is still the place to go for the widest and most inexpensive assortment of glazed and unglazed tiles, but they are reluctant to give away their sources. As for other forms—Italian, Minton-style Victorian pieces, and the kind of institutional tiles used in the early years of this century—you must be willing to search high and low unless price is no problem. A few of the better salvage/wrecking/architectural antiques outfits may be able to find antique tiles for you.

For the most part, commercially-available American ceramic tiles are exceptionally hideous, or, as Evelyn Waugh might have put it, "sick-making." The palette seems limited to the pastels, and patterns are similarly pale. If you search long enough, however, you may just find a modern pattern in ceramic tile which will enhance your period surroundings. Do-it-yourself kits should be avoided like the plague as the adhesives and grouts supplied are frequently as durable as toothpaste.

Flint and Terra Cotta

A variety of glazed and unglazed "primitive" tiles are available from American Olean. "Flint," in shades of black and brown, and a ruddy "Terra Cotta" have textured surfaces suitable for interior uses. Each can be ordered in several shapes and sizes.

"Murray Quarry Tile" is made from shale and fire clays in seven earth tones. A variety of shapes contributes to individualized patterns. All are ½" thick and are recommended for indoor applications.

Literature available.

American Olean Tile Co.
1000 Cannon Ave.
Lansdale, Penn. 19446
(215) 855-1111

Cerreto Grande and Gascogne

To Europe you may have to go for your tile needs—via an American distributor. The vividness and clarity of ceramic tiles can create startling visual effects. Country Floors imports over 500 tile patterns from many countries. The sunny "Cerreto Grande" is an Italian design. The earthy "Gascogne" pattern is a classic French import.

Catalog available, $2.

Country Floors
300 East 61st Street
New York, N.Y. 10021
(212) 758-7414

Villeroy & Boch

Remember when you could eat out in a gleaming white ceramic-tiled restaurant? Most of these establishments are gone, but the look from the early years of this century is back again. The sanitary glare of white glazed tiles is enlivened with diagonally set squares in this flooring from Villeroy & Boch. It could brighten a residential kitchen and give it a correct period tone.

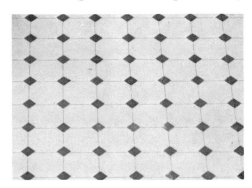

Villeroy & Boch also imports tiles with the early flavor of the Iberian peninsula. These are especially fitting in Spanish Colonial surroundings if Mexican products do not suit your taste.

Literature available.
Villeroy & Boch
912 Riverview Dr.
Totowa, N.J. 07512
(201) 256-7710

Delft for the Hearth

Tiling can also be used in another floor "area"—the hearth of a fireplace. Delft blue tiles have framed such spaces for generations. Typical tile designs are flowers, landscapes, and animals, but anything can be ordered since all patterns are hand-painted. The 4¼" x 4¼" windmill pattern, for example, is $4.75.

Catalog available.

Delft Blue
P.O. Box 103
Ellicott City, Md. 21043
(301) 624-4083

Vinyl Flooring

Yes, we'll admit it. We're prepared to bend a bit on this synthetic. Natural fibers are to be preferred everywhere in an old house, but there have to be compromises. Solid vinyl is one of the acceptable one—if limited in use to those areas of the house such as a kitchen, foyer, or bathroom where traffic is heavy and water sometimes a problem. Specifically excluded, however, is the vinyl asbestos tile which is most often urged on the consumer as a cheaper alternative. It is in every way. It has neither the look nor the wear of quality.

Kentile Solid Vinyl

Kentile makes several handsome solid vinyl patterns which do not strain to be authentic. They are simply attractively designed and worked. None have the real warmth or texture of natural stone or ceramic tile, but they are of appealing colors and are subdued underfoot. One such tile is "Terresque," an approximation of unglazed Mexican tiles, and the second is "Barre Slate," as its name indicates, a reproduction of slate. It comes in four different shades. Both patterns are ⅛" thick. "Terresque" comes in 9" x 9" squares; "Barre Slate" in 12" x 18" pieces.

These very simple patterns are by far the most successful in the Kentile line for the old house. Those which attempt to duplicate marble, brick, parquet, and other more complicated patterns are merely imitative.

Literature available from most flooring dealers.

Kentile Floors
58 Second Ave.
Brooklyn, N.Y. 11215
(212) 768-9500

Stone Materials

The use of natural stone for flooring has been limited in the past and will continue to be the exception in the future. Simply, it costs too much. Stone presents another problem—its unevenness. Only the smoothest quarried rock, such as marble, presents a relatively uniform surface, and it, of course, is the most expensive of all. Stone floors are most often encountered in the basement of old houses, especially in those houses built into a bank. This material may be of the crudest sort such as fieldstone or a semi-smooth sort such as slate. Here, too, one often finds brick, a ceramic material.

Marble Modes

If you can afford real marble for a foyer, by all means indulge yourself. And if you need to replace pieces, these can be found in various colors and patterns. Marble is often used for thresholds, and almost any building supply house can provide this. For more ambitious projects, you may decide to go directly to a quarry or to such a firm as Marble Modes. It has a wide selection of marble in tile form for residential and commercial use. Marble is an excellent investment. Not only is it rich in color and texture, but it is durable and easily maintained. The same thing can not be said for a material which is increasingly used as a substitute—travertine.

Literature available.

Marble Modes, Inc.
15–25 130th St.
College Point, N.Y. 11356
(212) LE 9-1334

Stenciled Floors

From marble to stenciled floors is an enormous leap in style and price. As mentioned in the introduction to this section, stenciling has been applied to wood floors for at least 125 years. It was not a common practice in Colonial America. At that time designs were applied freehand by itinerant decorators. In the nineteenth century stencil artists began to vend their wares. Sometimes the entire floor area was covered with flourishes and geometric patterns and, at others, only a simple border was applied. All of this was done in imitation of high-style interiors which would have contained inlaid flooring and fine carpets. Later in the nineteenth century, floors were even painted in simulation of marble graining.

Stenciled Interiors

S. Tarbox is one of a number of students of the stenciling art and has gathered a considerable collection of historically accurate designs. Custom designing and restoration work is also included in the firm's repertory. *Literature available.*

Stenciled Interiors
Hinman Lane
Southbury, Conn. 06488
(203) 264-8000

Floor Coverings

The covering of floor areas seems a simple task—until you start to do it. The assumption is that some sections of flooring will be left uncovered and that modern "piles" will be eschewed. Something in the shag family has no place in a period interior. The appearance is all wrong, and the maintenance of such rugs has proved to be very difficult. Synthetic fibers do not hold up well in the wash and practically shrivel up if put in a drier. If you must have something soft and fluffy, then consider a sheepskin or other animal fiber.

Orientals are almost always appropriate in formal areas of the house. In the eighteenth century they were rare and most probably were used to cover tables or as wall hangings. Nevertheless, they can be employed without shame by the old-house owner, especially one who lives in a late-Victorian or twentieth-century home. No Persian carpets (Western Turkey) should be used in Colonial homes. These were not introduced in the United States until the 1870s. Most of the Orientals now on the market date from the end of the 1800s and early 1900s. Rugs of this sort are expensive but exceedingly good investments. Dealers in such material are found in every area of North America.

Simpler floor coverings will be used in most areas of an old house. These may be braided, hooked, or stitched rugs made of cotton and/or wool. Sometimes a small percentage of synthetic fiber (10 to 20%) may be mixed in, but not enough to render the rug artificial looking or difficult to maintain. In recent years there has been a virtual renaissance in hand rug making, and the techniques used do not vary that much from those followed in the past. There are also sources for antique rag rugs.

Antique Rag Rugs

You can still get the original antiques at more than affordable prices. The Kelter-Malce partnership has recently sold an 18′ square rug from Connecticut for $550. That's a lot of rug for the dollar. Mr. Malce thinks old rag rugs are still underpriced.

Kelter-Malce
361 Bleecker St.
New York, N.Y. 10014
(212) 989-6760

Ford Museum Hooked Rugs

Designs on homemade hooked rugs were often patterned after motifs on other fabrics such as needlepoint and stencil designs found on chair backs. This is a reproduction from Mountain Rug Mills and is sold through The Henry Ford Museum and Greenfield Village where the original can be found.

A Gothic influence appears in this repetititve pattern also from Mountain Rug Mills and the Michigan museum and historical village.

Catalog available, $2.50.

Henry Ford Museum and Greenfield Village
20900 Oakwood Blvd.
Dearborn, Mich. 48121
(313) 271-1620

Sunflower Rag Rug

Pilgrim's Progress is one good mail-order source for reasonably-priced, versatile, and good-looking rag rugs. Their cotton objects can be custom designed to fit specific needs. The *Sunflower* measures 2′6″ by 4′ and sells for $39.

Catalog available, 75¢.

Pilgrim's Progress, Inc.
Penthouse
50 West 67th St.
New York, N.Y. 10023
(212) 580-3050

All-Wool Rag Rugs

Kay and Ron Loch have retained traditional weaving techniques in their Bucks County shop. They create all-wool rag rugs in any size up to 15′ wide. A typical 8′ x 10′ rug is $295.

Literature available.

Heritage Rugs
Lahaska, Penn. 18931
(215) 794-7229

Throw Rugs

Banjos and fiddles are still more popular than electric guitars in Knott County, Kentucky. Hard times have left life simple, but have not diminished the quality of what talented fingers can create. Local hands also produce charming back-stitched throw rugs in your choice of colors. Custom sizes are available up to 54″ wide. A 2′ x 3′ rug is $20. That illustrated is cotton with cotton/rayon blend pattern thread.

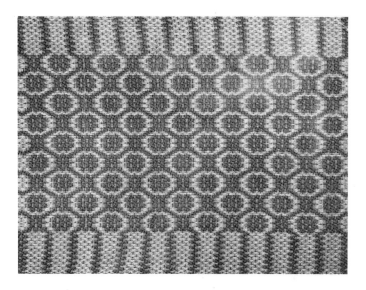

Literature available.

Quicksand Crafts
Vest, Ky. 41772
(606) 785-5230

Strip Rug

This is a sturdy handwoven wool strip rug with a sturdy Irish linen warp and braided ends. It can be made in any size and almost any color. It is sold for $6 a square foot.

Sample available, $2.

Diane Jackson Cole
9 Grove St.
Kennebunk, Me. 04043
(207) 846-5662

Braided Rugs

One of the charms of handcrafting is that when something is finished it is not machine-perfect. Individuality persists in the hit-or-miss designs of braided rugs. Adams and Swett's brochure tells us that their "Country Home" rugs are "handsewn by the wives and families of Japanese rice farmers in their homes." Their best quality rug is priced at $384 for an 8' x 10', and is made of 90% wool. It is suggested that you order a small size first so that you can gauge the quality and appearance.

Literature available.

Adams & Swett
380 Dorchester Avenue
Boston, Mass. 02127
(617) 268-8000

Do-It-Yourself

You can help carry on the Colonial braided rug tradition by doing it yourself. Country Braid House will sell the necessary materials and will even start the first few rows if you want. Or you can buy one already made. Their rugs are wool and are sold either in random colors or as a planned pattern of circular colored bands. Any size is possible. They will be glad to quote a price if you tell them the size and whether you want it round, oval, or long and narrow.

Literature available.

Country Braid House
Clark Rd.
Tilton, N.H. 03276
(603) 286-4511

Braid-Aid markets a complete line of rug braiding and hooking materials, designs, and instructions.

Catalogs available: $1 for book of instructions and patterns, $1 for materials and accessories.

Braid-Aid
466 Washington St.
Pembroke, Mass. 02359
(617) 826-6091

Heirloom Patterns

Although Scandanavia probably gave us the hooked rug, early New England and Canadian designs elevated it to an art of considerable value. Traditional patterns are generally crude floral, animal, or geometric designs. Today the art thrives in craft programs and homes throughout the country. Heirloom Rugs is an especially valuable resource for hundreds of unique patterns. The "Star Diamond" is a charming old guilt pattern and sells for $5. The "Sailcloth Primitive" is a copy of an old rug made by a sailor. The pattern sells for $8.50 and measures 29" x 69"

Catalog of patterns available, $1.

Heirloom Rugs
28 Harlem St.
Rumford, R.I. 02916
(401) 438-5672

Floorcloths

Manufacture of the types of material used in many Colonial homes has just recently been revived. Thanks to the diligent research of historians in the decorative arts, we know much more today about such matters as floorcloths. As has been explained, Orientals and other woven rugs were luxuries that very few people could afford. Even in the best of homes, painted canvas often took the place of textiles on the floor.

Craftswomen

Reproducing an eighteenth-century floorcloth is a time-consuming process. Carol Maicone and Linda La Bove begin with heavy cotton canvas. After each of several coats of hand-mixed paint has been applied and sanded, the surface is ready for the actual design. The pattern is then stenciled and/or painted freehand. The floorcloth then goes through a lengthy varnishing and drying process. The resulting finish is guaranteed for ten years against abrasion and deterioration.

Floorcloths from Craftswomen come in any length and are seamless up to a width of ten feet. Shown here are the "Checkerboard," "Chevron," and "Diamond" designs. The "Tree of Life" is an adaptation of a traditional quilt pattern.

Catalog available.

Craftswomen
Box 715
Doylestown, Penn. 18901
(215) 822-1025

Carpets

While purists in restoration rightfully question the use of Orientals in Colonial-style interiors, they do understand that they, along with such machine-woven carpets as Wiltons, Axminsters, and handwoven needlepoints, have a place in the post-Colonial home. In the 1890s even Sears and Montgomery Ward were offering their versions of Axminster and Brussels carpets. Large rugs or carpets became almost as popular as the widely and cheaply-produced wallpapers of the time. It is not true that the Victorians covered every inch of space in their homes with something, but they did pad out their manses quite comfortably. Severe expanses of wood flooring were not admired then as they are in sophisticated circles today.

Stark Carpets

Decorators and designers have been employing the services of Stark Carpet Corporation for over forty years. Amongst the stock items are these 12' wide Wilton carpets from the Bouclé Collection. A 6¾" stripe border is optional.

JACKS NAVY BLUE
FRENESI NAVY BLUE
MARTINIQUE NATURAL
JACKS HUNTER GREEN | JACKS LIME GREEN
JACKS NATURAL | JACKS TETRE NEGRE | LARGE ROMAIN NAVY BLUE

Boston's recently restored Harrison Gray Otis House, built in 1795, retains much of its original spirit through the use of carefully selected reproduction materials. For the front entry, a velvet cut pile, "Lozenge Directoire," was chosen from Stark.

Literature available. Full catalog available to designers, decorators, and architects, $10.

Stark Carpet Corp.
979 Third Avenue
New York, N.Y. 10022
(212) PL2-9000

Scalamandré Carpets

Through the Victorian period, Wilton carpets were among the most preferred of European imports. Scalamandré is now a major purveyor of these English-made cut-loop pile rugs.

The "Peel" is a mid-Victorian pattern of two colors woven of 80% wool and 20% nylon.

Five colors harmonize in the "Turner," another mid-Victorian reproduction from England.

The term "Axminster" referred originally to the town in England where the rugs were made. By the nineteenth century it came to be used for any British carpet with a "Turkish-knot" weave. Scalamandré offers thirteen patterns in Persian, Turkish, Victorian, and contemporary styles.

Scalamandré's Savannah Collection represents a community's successful effort to preserve a valued past and a manufacturer's dedication to faithfully reproducing it. The "Savannah Parlour" is 100% wool and is available in either cut pile or loop pile. The 100% wool "Savannah Adam," like the "Parlour," is reproduced from the original in the historic city's Werm's House. Both carpets are available with coordinating fabric and wallpaper if so desired.

Literature available. See special list of retail outlets, Appendix A.

Scalamandré
950 Third Avenue
New York, N.Y. 10022
(212) 361-8500

Straw, Sisal, Hemp, Rush, Coir Matting

Natural fibers such as these can be woven into useful and attractive forms for the purpose of covering floors. In Colonial times straw was used in the house and the barn. Without suggesting that you should turn your floors over to mooing creatures, let it be said that mats of various grasses and fibers are just as fitting a flooring material as floorcloths. These were used most frequently in upstairs bedrooms, that is, in less formal areas of the house.

Material of this sort is often sold by very contemporary home furnishing shops. Some flooring suppliers may also have it. It is ironic but true that lovers of simple, primitive things are attracted to old houses of a simpler era and to the most contemporary of structures. Reproduction Shaker furniture can be found in both kinds of homes; so, too, is rush matting.

Conran's

Conran's is a trendy and recent addition to New York. They offer sisal mats which are as natural in the city as they are in the country. Also available is tough coconut coir matting from India at about $9 a yard. Rush tile mats, shown here, are sewn together to make an attract-

ive floor covering. A 3' x 6' section is $10.85. All these things were made from natural grasses and can be wonderfully effective and fitting in a primitive or modern application.

Brochure available, 25¢.

Conran's
The Market at Citicorp Center
160 East 54th St.
New York, N.Y. 10022
(212) 371-2225

Other Sources of Flooring Materials

Consult the List of Suppliers for Addresses.

Wood Flooring

Accent Walls
Amherst Wood-Working
Bangkok Industries
Blair Lumber
Bruce Hardwood
Castle Burlingame

Dana-Deck & Laminates
William J. Erbe
John Harra
Nassau Flooring
New York Flooring
I. Peiser Floors
Simpson Timber
Wagon House
Weird Wood

Wood Flooring/Antique

The Cellar
Eighteenth-Century Co.
Period Pine
Wrecking Bar

Ceramic Flooring

Country Floors
Elon Inc.
Vanderlaan Co.
Western States Stone
Wrecking Bar

Stone Flooring

Delaware Quarries
Materials Unlimited
Structural Slate
Vermont Marble

Hand-Molded Brick

Old Carolina Brick Co.

Stenciling

New York Flooring
Megan Parry
Rambusch Decorating
Wall Stencils by Barbara

Braided, Hooked, and Rag Rugs

S. & C. Huber

Floorcloths

Floorcloths, Inc.

Carpets and Rugs

S. M. Hexter
Charles Jacobsen
Kenmore Carpet
Kent-Costikyan
Rosecore Carpet
F. Schumacher

VI Lighting

Old habits are hard to kick. And in the case of lighting, they are expensive to maintain. We are speaking of the average American's tendency to overlight interior spaces. Despite the energy crisis and the ever-increasing cost of electric power, lights still burn too brightly across the country. The successful use of lighting fixtures in a period interior requires restraint and common sense.

What should be lit? Passageways and stairs, certainly. Artificial light for reading or other close work is often needed during the day as well as at night. Special lights for special requirements—whether it be washing dishes or shaving in the morning—are a must. Closets must be provided with some form of illumination. These are the main "can't do without" areas of modern living. To light a house as it might have been illuminated in the 1750s or 1850s is an exercise in futility and pretense. The conveniences of the electric age allow us to work and rest in relative comfort. We need these improvements to offset the discomforts of the bureaucratic, depersonalized, hectic time in which we live.

Even the utility companies, however, are urging conservation. Bulbs with lower wattage will serve perfectly well and are especially good for period-style interiors. The day may even come when a light bulb will last at least several years rather than a few months. The technology is available to produce them. Expertise is also available for those who can afford to disguise sources of modern illumination. This does not mean wiring a butter churn or coffee mill (Yes, it has been done—all too frequently), but paying the extra dollar for dimmers, batteries, and adapters which adjust the voltage to subdued levels. And since at least the 1920s, light has been used in an indirect manner, boxed in or otherwise hidden in the walls or ceiling. In addition, small spots of a very contemporary design can be used effectively in a period interior.

For most of us, these tricks of the master electrician are too expensive and quite beyond our real needs. Few old houses are "master wired" so that outlets can be opened up with ease almost anywhere. Unless the house is to be rewired, we usually are stuck with the given. Even wires (well-insulated) may have to be exposed here and there. The cost of channeling these into the wall (especially a stone wall) is nearly prohibitive. Since rewiring is beyond the scope of most home remodelers or restorers, careful thought must be given first to exactly what *has* to be lighted electrically. After this had been determined, consideration should be given to appropriate fixtures. There is a fairly plentiful supply of antique fixtures which have been wired for electricity and can be used in Colonial and early Victorian rooms as well as a goodly number of early electric or combination gas and electric fixtures which are appropriate for homes of the 1890–1930 vintage. In addition, one can find a wide assortment of quality reproduction fixtures which may serve the need for light quite admirably. The number of manufacturers of such devices seems to increase each year. It has become more difficult, however, to sort out the good from the bad.

Since the Bicentennial there has been a quickening of the Colonial "fever." The chandelier has become *de rigueur* in the lighting field. Most are used inappropriately. The more elaborate they are, the less plausible they appear in what is the average Colonial-style dwelling, a very simple structure. What lighted Carpenters' Hall in Philadelphia or Faneuil Hall in Boston is probably not the right thing for the Cape Cod on Rural Route 1. Hanging fixtures of wood, tin, and iron are more likely to suit the need for lighting in a dining room or center hall than those of silver, crystal, brass, or even pewter.

Except in Victorian structures fitted for gas

lighting, ceiling fixtures are more likely the exception than the rule. It is better, then, to make use of wall sconces, bracketed lanterns, even picture lights. Combined with carefully arranged table and floor lamps, these wall fixtures will sufficiently light up a period interior. As for lamps, porcelain ginger jars, glass kerosene or oil fixtures, large wooden candlesticks, and toleware columns have long provided handsome bases. The handy home owner can even adapt these himself. Floor lamps are a more difficult problem. The type of wrought-iron candlestand offered in the following pages by Essex Forge (and by other such lighting houses) is one solution. It has been a popular fixture since the early years of electricity and a convenient and appropriate one. There is a decent supply of such lamps in secondhand and antiques shops throughout the country.

Not every light need be an electric one, of course. Gas has had a renaissance in recent years but is becoming increasingly expensive to use. The lowly candle remains available at a relatively low cost. If used with restraint, such tapers provide a muted glow which enhances any well-furnished period interior. If of the dripless variety, they can be employed in hanging fixtures to great effect. Remember only that our pre-electric ancestors used them sparingly because of their cost.

Antique Lighting Fixtures

True period lighting fixtures of an early age are the province of fine antiques dealers and collectors. Rush-lights, crusies, Argand lamps, and Sandwich glass whale oil lamp bases command very high prices. They are not, however, impossible to find or to use. Some of these fixtures can be electrified; others only make sense as candle- or oil-burning vessels. Somewhat easier to locate are the kerosene lamps, gas fixtures, combination gas and electric devices, and early electric fixtures. Some "junk" dealers have specialized in their retrieval from doomed structures and effectively recycled them for new use. Increasingly, however, such later fixtures are being handled by special dealers. In those parts of the

country where Victorian architecture is the norm and does not play second fiddle to Colonial, they are easier to come by.

Jo-El Shop

Bringing an old fixture back to life is often a labor of love. John Beglin sometimes spends more than forty hours rejuvenating a single antique. His Jo-El Shop is crammed with his collection of Victoriana and turn-of-the-century fixtures. Many are gas and early electric lights.

Catalog and other information available, $2.

John A. Beglin
Jo-El Shop
7120 Hawkins Creamery Rd.
Laytonsville, Md. 20760
(301) 253-3951

Yankee Craftsman

Increased interest in the restoration of period homes has encouraged some craftsmen to specialize in renewing old fixtures. The process demands technical and artistic skills as well as a feel for the era that produced the original. Yankee Craftsman offers a restoration service and executes custom designs, too. The firm maintains a sizable stock of antique fixtures. If you are looking for a specific type that they might have, Yankee Craftsman will send a photo and information at no charge. Seen here is one view of the shop and a restored chandelier.

Yankee Craftsman
357 Commonwealth Rd.
Wayland, Mass. 01778
(617) 653-0031

Gargoyles, Ltd.

Much of the Gargoyles, Ltd. collection is original. Most of the pieces date from the nineteenth and early twentieth centuries. This chandelier is solid brass and spans 24".

No catalog as of yet, but brochures are available on specific kinds of items.

Gargoyles, Ltd.
512 South Third St.
Philadelphia, Pa. 19147
(215) 629-1700

The Wrecking Bar

Some of us just have to have the "real thing." In many cases, the original has not been reproduced. The Wrecking Bar has a sizable collection of antique lighting devices, including these sconces, some of which have been electrified.

Literature on particular kinds of items available.

The Wrecking Bar of Atlanta, Inc.
292 Moreland Ave., N.E.
Atlanta, Ga. 30307
(404) 525-0468

John Kruesel

John Kruesel's collection of original devices spans two centuries. He specializes in pieces fueled with whale oil, gas, kerosene, gas/electric combinations, and early electric fixtures.

No catalog available, but please write for information.

John Kruesel
R. R. 4
Rochester, Minn. 55901
(507) 288-5148

Brasslight

Owner Steve Kaniewski prides himself on personal service. If he doesn't have the desired fixture in his collection, he keeps the request on file until he locates it. His specialty is Victoriana. Antiques only, please.

Write for information on various kinds of fixtures.

Stephen Kaniewski
Brasslight
2831 S. 12th St.
Milwaukee, Wis. 53215
(414) 672-0938

London Ventures

Some firms specialize in collecting, restoring, and selling Victorian era fixtures. London Ventures deals strictly with these originals, many of which are of European provenence. All have been electrified and lacquered to preserve their sheen. A new listing of available pieces appears quarterly.

Quarterly catalog, $1
London Ventures Co.
2 Dock Square
Rockport, Mass. 01966
(617) 856-7161

Candleholders

The simplest of lighting fixtures are those which hold and burn candles. Rushlights, of course, are even more venerable, but their use is best left to antiquarians. Although candles have risen in price in recent years (along with everything else), they can still provide an economical means for throwing just the right amount of light on the dinner table and in other places where 20/20 vision is not a prerequisite.

There are a thousand and one ways in which the candle can be held. Antique sticks are still widely available, and there is no reason to recommend the use of reproduction glass, ceramic, pewter, or other antique metal fixtures. Candesticks were produced in all forms for use in the kitchen, living room or parlour, and bedroom. Some can be carried from room to room and are equipped with a wide drip pan. Others are fragile columns which are best left in one place. The candelabra is probably the most romantic of the candle-burning devices, and with its varied numbers of branches can provide a surprising amount of light. Sconces, especially those equipped with reflectors, can also throw off much in the way of candlepower. These wall fixtures are covered in another section of this chapter.

The several candle-burning devices shown here are of the unusual sort not so easily encountered or come by. Each is a traditional form and illustrative of the fine reproduction work which is being done today.

Hanging Candleholders

The candle is an ideal source of light. It consumes itself and leaves no residue, only a stump to be removed. Since the invention of the braided wick in 1825, it has needed little or no tending. The hanging candleholder is also a simple device that lends mobility to a solitary light. Its pleasant curves and twisted shaft were commonplace in the eighteenth century. It can hook over the back of a chair, hang on a hook, or be carried. Robert Griffith is a gifted artisan who creates this and many other pieces at his coal-fired forge. It is priced at $20.

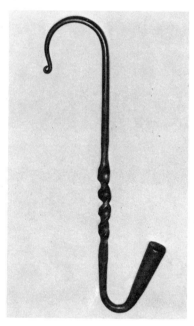

Catalog available, $2.

Robert A Griffith, Metalsmith
16 Main St.
Trucksville, Pa. 18708

Another authentic candleholder is available from the Craft Program of the Henry Ford Museum and Greenfield Village. The metalsmiths there turn out a 9″ model that is identical to a wrought-iron ancestor of 1750.

Catalog available, $2.50.

Henry Ford Museum and Greenfield Village
20900 Oakwood Blvd.
Dearborn, Mich. 48121
(313) 271-1620

Candlestand

One of the more important and affordable improvements in domestic lighting in the eighteenth century was the adjustable candlestand. It often consisted of a tall spindle mounted on a sturdy tripod. Candleholders were affixed to a crosspiece which could be snubbed up and down the spindle to the desired height. A 20″ high table version is crafted by Wallin Forge for $45.

Catalog available, $2; charge deducted from first order.

Wallin Forge
R. R. 1, Box 65
Sparta, Ky. 41086
(606) 567-7201

Chandeliers

Chandeliers, as noted in the introduction to this chapter, are often used for the wrong reason—to make fancy what was originally simple. Handsome fixtures of brass and of silver were used in Colonial America, and a vast majority of them came from the foundries of England. Magnificent fixtues could be found in churches, town halls, and in the homes of the very wealthy. In most homes, however, the chandelier was nothing more than a form of hanging light, and might have been made of wood or tin. Not until the nineteenth century, and well into it, could any sizeable number of people afford to use more elaborate fixtures which made use of crystal or etched glass. The Victorian chandelier can be a very fancy affair. Even the most utilitarian of late nineteenth century gas/electric combinations or electric fixtures display a delightful play of shape and decoration.

Of several or many branches, this form of lighting device is designed to dispel the shadows in a large area of almost any room. Since they are suspended from the ceiling, however, chandeliers must be wired in a special manner. The wire is sometimes carried through a metal shaft (as with many Victorian fixtures), or threaded through a link of chain which is attached to a canopy. In either case, a chandelier requires just the right-sized canopy cover for the outlet and the proper hardware to attach this to the ceiling and the chain or shaft to canopy and outlet.

Since almost any kind of reproduction chandelier is likely to be a major purchase, the buyer is urged to determine his electrical needs very carefully. Length of chain or shaft is also critical. Almost any reproduction, of course, can be made as a candle-burning fixture. With more than a few holders, such a light will provide quite sufficient light for dining.

Gas and Electric Chandeliers

Classic Illumination of San Francisco is a sophisticated manufacturer of honest and handsome Victorian light-

ing fixtures. Their products are offered directly from the firm or through several suppliers listed below.

The years of transition from gas to electricity are captured in gasoliers which have been equipped for the best of both worlds. The Victorian home owner of the period may have impressed his neighbors by flirting with the future but could not fully part with the dependable past. "The Merchant Street" is a four-light gasolier suitable for the proper Victorian parlor.

A lofty hall, bath or kitchen might be the spot for a two-arm electric chandelier, the "National Hotel." It need not be the focal point of a room's symmetry, as might be expected of a multi-branched fixture.

The three-and-three electric/gas combination is typical of Classic Illumination's level of achievement. Each detail reflects the spirit and form of the original. All the work from this firm comes with standard size sockets and modern electrical wiring for easy installation. For the traditionalist, gas pipe fittings are available upon request at no extra cost.

Catalog available, $2.

The Classic Illumination
P.O. Box 5851
San Francisco, Calif. 94101
(415) 527-5106

Classic Illumination fixtures are also available from the following distributors: San Francisco Victoriana, 606 Natoma, San Francisco, Calif. 94103 (415-429-5477) and Victorian Reproductions, 1601 Park Avenue South, Minneapolis, Minn. 55404 (612-338-3636).

Seven-Arm Chandelier

Richard Scofield combines the skills of an artisan and the rigors of a scholar. His lighting fixtures are individually-crafted reproductions. The Period Lighting Fixtures catalog is also a reference source on the origin, selection, and installation of his pieces. Scofield's research has led him to write a book on early American lighting.

Period Lighting's repertoire includes this handsome seven-arm chandelier. Most fixtures can be ordered in pewter, aged tin, and painted finishes. The pewter option is the hand-rubbed result of a careful dipping process. The candle covers are made with real beeswax.

Catalog available, $2.

Period Lighting Fixtures
1 Main St.
Chester, Conn. 06412
(203) 526-3690

Dutch Colonial Chandelier

The Delft influence in Holland, England, and North America has persisted for over three hundred years. Here it is expressed in this elegant solid brass chandelier.

Free brochure.

Dutch Products and Supply Co.
14 S. Main St.
Yardley, Pa. 19067
(215) 493-4873

Six-Arm Chandelier and Billiard Light

The quality tradition of Lester H. Berry has been carried on since the turn of the century. Over the years the firm has imported some of the finest European lighting devices. Their craftsmen have expertly recreated many of these pieces since many countries have restricted export of rare creations. The spirit of the eighteenth-century artisan has been strictly adhered to in these recreations. Each fixture is individually made. All parts are brass castings. The chandelier arms are held to the shaft with pins and are removable. The six-arm brass chandelier illustrated here has been reproduced from a rare French model of the eighteenth century. Unwired, it sells for $631; $48 additional is charged for wiring.

Gentlemen of noble bearing have played billiards in one form or another for centuries. Louis XIV played it for exercise after dinner. Here is a light worthy of the

noble tradition from Lester H. Berry. Note that this is termed a "light" and not a chandelier. It was probably called a chandelier in the eighteenth century; after that time the French adopted the term "lustre."

Catalog available, $3.
Lester H. Berry
1108 Pine St.
Philadelphia, Pa. 19107
(215) 923-2603

Wrought-Iron Chandeliers

Kenneth Lynch's craftsmen can do almost anything with metal. They produce a staggering array of products. Their wrought-iron chandeliers are rugged and unique. This hand-forged example can have as few as six lights or as many as sixteen, depending on its diameter. It can be finished in old iron or half-polished iron.

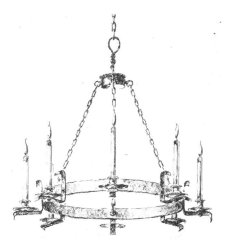

The second linear design can be lengthened to order. Lynch's craftsmen are accustomed to following the specifications of the customer.

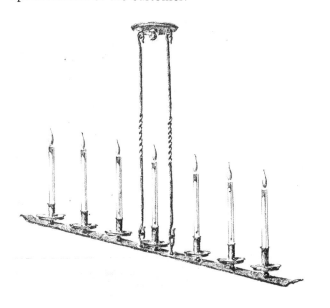

Catalog available, $3.50.

Kenneth Lynch & Sons
78 Danbury Rd.
Wilton, Conn. 06897
(203) 539-0532

Small Hall Chandelier

Wasley Lighting manufactures early American and traditional pieces of other sorts. They have just introduced this compact, handsome model (10″ diameter). You can get it in polished brass, antique brass, or pewter. It is equally appropriate in the dining room, foyer, or parlor. The list price is $101.40.

Catalog available, $2.50.

Wasley Lighting Division
Plainville Industrial Park
Plainville, Conn. 06062
(203) 747-5586

Sunburst Chandelier

Not many interiors are suited for a chandelier this fanciful. It illustrates the temptation facing the home

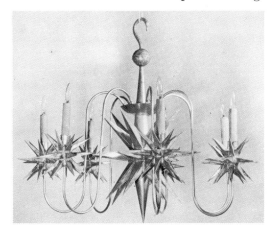

restorer seeking striking but appropriate furnishings. If you have the room in which to display such a dazzling fixture, be our guest. It is available from Gates Moore. The light from seven candles plays delightfully on these painstakingly-wrought sunbursts. The chandelier spreads across 26″ and comes with a ceiling canopy. It sells for $500.

Catalog available, $2.

Gates Moore
River Rd., Silvermine
Norwalk, Conn. 06850
(203) 847-3231

Moravian Tin Chandelier

The Mercer Museum's collection includes a chandelier of primitive Moravian design. Its radiant arms hold six candles. The pierced tin center is a bit like a Revere lantern in design. The chief difference is that the chandelier's light source surrounds the center instead of emanating from it.

Brochure available, 50¢.

The Mercer Museum Shop
Bucks County Historical Society
Pine and Ashland
Doylestown, Pa. 18901
(215) 345-0737

Table Lamps

Table lamps are a dime a dozen. Truly handsome fixtures of this sort are very rare. Frankly we've had it with bean pots and crocks for bases. Another cliché is the candle mold. Why not try something that was intended to hold an electric, gas, oil, or kerosene fixture, or even a candle? Bases for kerosene or whale oil table lamps can be simple or fancy affairs, slender glass sticks with graceful fonts or marble, ormolu, and crystal confections. Shades may be pierced tin, a heavy paper, or luxurious silk. The general style of a room will determine in large part what is appropriate in lamp style. The best rule seems to be: let it be a functioning fixture, not a purely decorative one, and choose a form that is fitting for a lamp.

Among the thousands of models to choose from are such standards as brass desk lamps, "Gone With the Wind" lamps (ironically not introduced until after the Civil War), cut-glass parlor lamps, molded and cut

girandoles, small chamber lamps of glass, tin, pewter, and brass, and various "student" lamps. In most cases, one needn't turn to a reproduction manufacturer to find what you need. For the very special, however, you may choose to contact such a firm as Royal Windyne, Ltd.

Victorian Brass

This distinctive solid brass table lamp could accent a rich Victorian study *and* provide useful light. Royal Windyne sells this and other period styles with accurate reproduction glass shades. A tarnish-preventing lacquer is applied unless you're a traditionalist who would rather buff than switch. The fixture sells for $82.50.

Catalog available.

Royal Windyne Ltd.
Box 6622
Richmond, Va. 23230
(804) 355-5690

Floor Lamps

Floor lamps, as noted in the introduction to this chapter, are old-fashioned fixtures, and most are horrendously designed. There is no reason to go out of your way searching for something you can live with. Floor lamps aren't necessary in most cases, yet they are handy things to have behind a large upholstered chair used for reading. What is termed a "bridge" lamp has been around for years, and may do the trick.

Bridge Lamp

Originally this was a candlestand. Electrified, the 52″ fixture commends itself to lighting up awkward corners and can hover conveniently over the back of an easy chair. The harp moves up and down on the iron spindle and turns a full 360 degrees. It sells for $49.50 from Essex Forge.

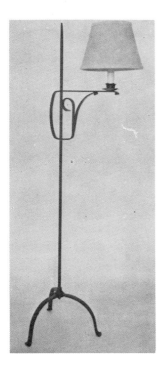

Catalog available, $1.

The Essex Forge
1 Old Dennison Rd.
Essex, Conn. 06426
(203) 767-1808

Hanging Lamps

Hanging lamps are not used as frequently as chandeliers in many period-style homes, but in many ways are more fitting. These are less expensive to buy and to maintain. For a small room, they may present the proper scale. In a narrow hall- or entryway a hanging lamp can provide just the right amount of light. Styles vary greatly—from Colonial period glass globes to late Victorian electric "gasoliers."

Glass Lamp and Smoke Bell

Ball and Ball reproductions hang in Independence Hall, Philadelphia. The brass they use is solid and the glass is off-hand blown lead crystal. The objects copied by the firm are of the sort found in the better homes of late

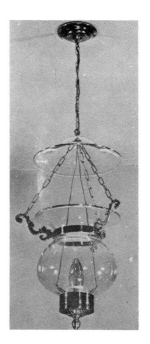

eighteenth and nineteenth-century America. Illustrated here is a pear-shape lamp and smoke bell. There are several different models but all hang on 6″ of chain from a canopy. The fixture is priced at $215.

Catalog available, $2.

Ball and Ball
463 West Lincoln Highway
Exton, Pa. 19341
(215) 363-7330

Oil Lamp

Saturday evening guests might have sat in the glow of this oil lamp as they discussed the shocking news of Lee's surrender at Appomatox. Its wood-polished crys-

tals, colorfully painted decoration, and brass trimmings combine perfectly with the glass font and shade. This classical "Lightyear" interpretation is supplied by the MarLe Company and sells for $405. MarLe is also a manufacturer of other kinds of traditional fixtures which are not part of the "Lightyear" line.

Catalog available, $1.

MarLe Company
170 Summer St.
Stamford, Conn. 06901
(203) 348-2645

Ceiling Canopy

All hanging lanterns, lights, lamps, or chandeliers require an appropriate piece of hardware from which to suspend them. A ceiling canopy is usually provided by the manufacturer along with the fixture. If such is not available, you might consider this model which, like the others, fits a universal ceiling adapter. Although it is of Spanish descent, its hammered look will suit most iron fixtures. It is priced at $4.95.

Catalog available, $1.

Mexico House
Box 970
Del Mar, Calif. 92014

Oil and Kerosene-Burning Lamps

Oil and kerosene-burning lamps are being used today indoors and out. If handled with normal care, there is no reason why such fixtures should not be as safe to use as an electric lamp. A surprising amount of light is given off by many of the models. There are a number of producers of modern and reproduction lamps.

"Northeaster"

The kerosene-burning "Northeaster" is substantially unchanged since the days when whaling fleets rounded Nantucket. It is made on Cape Cod with traditional techniques. Each fixture is solid copper and bears the signature of its maker, John Kopas.

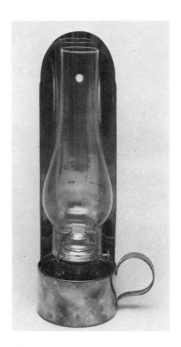

Brochure available.

Copper Antiquities
Cummaquid P.O.
Cummaquid, Mass. 02637
(617) 775-7704

"Mary Light"

The "Mary Light" is a high-quality rendition of the old kerosene-fueled standby. It comes in hand-rubbed solid copper or brass. For the same $39, you can get this lamp wired for electric operation. But why not try the real thing?

118

Catalog available, $2.

Heritage Lanterns
Dept. OH78
Sea Meadows Lane
Yarmouth, Maine 04096
(207) 846-3911

Pottery and Betty Lamps

Until the mid-nineteenth century, hand-thrown pottery lamps were a common fixture in North American homes. The mass production of pressed glass made this labor-intensive piece virtually obsolete. Now interest in traditional crafts is bringing us back to older forms. Sturbridge Yankee Workshop makes a 17″ high fixture which comes with wick and crystal hurricane. The oil reservoir is hand-glazed with black and brown striations. It is priced at $28.50.

The same firm also produces a betty lamp reproduction. The betty was truly a lamp for the people. It made its way from Western Europe to America where it was often crafted by village smiths as an affordable alternative to the more exotic, ornamented fixtures of the gentry. Many of today's reproductions are designed to hold candles instead of oil and a wick. This is the case with Sturbridge's wrought-iron model. It is 7½″ high and sells for $4.95.

A two-year subscription to the Sturbridge Yankee Workshop catalog (quarterly issues) is available for 50¢.

Sturbridge Yankee Workshop
Dept. OHC
Sturbridge, Mass. 01566
(617) 347-7176 or 765-5550

Lamp Brackets

The natural place—and a safe one—for an old lamp may not be the mantle or a shelf. A lamp bracket combines convenience and safety. It can be mounted almost anywhere. A pin on the end of the bracket fits into the wall mount and allows it to pivot. This one is cast iron and comes in raw metal or black finish.

Literature available.

Wrightsville Hardware Co.
N. Front St.
Wrightsville, Pa. 17368
(717) 252-1561

Lanterns

For some reason lanterns seem to be the most popular of lighting forms. These convenient fixtures are often very portable, and they have been carried by soldiers, miners, country doctors, heroes and villains for hundreds of years. Lanterns are most often used today as postlights, and this is a pity. They may be conveniently hung by the door against a wall or suspended from the ceiling. Indoors or out, designed to fend off drafts or the wind, simple to carry or to hang, they provide an attractive and practical alternative means of lighting. Most lanterns—reproduction or antique—have been electrified, but they can be used or altered for the burning of candles.

"The Essex"

Lanterns from The Essex Forge are solid copper. The "Essex," seen here, is one of a pair that frames the entrance to Essex, Connecticut's Griswold Inn. At 21″ high, this lantern can take the measure of any early American doorway. By adding a fourth pane of glass and a collar, its can also perch atop a lampost.

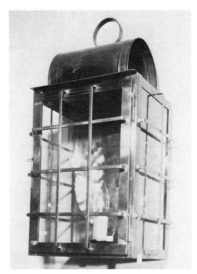

Catalog available, $1.

The Essex Forge
Old Dennison Rd.
Essex, Conn. 06426
(203) 767-1808

"The Castille"

If you are into Spanish Colonial, Mexico House has a striking array of lighting fixtures at reasonable prices. Some are embellished with wrought-iron leaves and curlicues. Here is the "Castille," a 15″ high wall-mounted lamp. It lists for $20.95 or two for $37.

Catalog available, $1.

Mexico House
Box 970
Del Mar, Calif. 92014

Tall Lantern

This tall (18″) lantern can be mounted on a wall and comes in copper or pewterlure, a metal with the satiny sheen of real pewter. We'd rather stick with the copper.

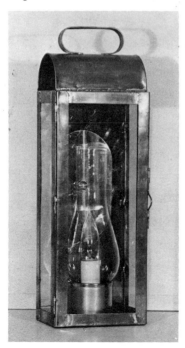

Brochure available.

Copper Antiquities
Cummaquid P.O.
Cummaquid, Mass. 02637
(617) 775-7704

"Wall Huggers"

Many exterior wall-mounted lanterns might also be suitable for indoor use if they were only a little thinner. Newstamp has an attractive line of "wall huggers" that help solve the problem of overextension. Their smallest model is 5¾″ wide and extends only 4¾″ from the wall. It is solid copper and sells for $47.50 in hand-rubbed copper or brass finishes or $42.50 in satin black.

Catalog available, $2.

Newstamp Lighting Co.
227 Bay Rd.
North Easton, Mass. 02356
(617) 238-7071

"Welcome" and "Octagon" Lanterns

A trio of electric candles cast their light through the huge front panel of the "Welcome Lantern." The hous-

ing is tin and is pierced on the sides and front of the hood. It measures 21″ high, 13″ wide, and 7″ deep. The fixture is available in black and sells for $95 if electrified; $80 with candles.

The "Octagon Lantern" is a stately design. The pierced tin top creates a pattern on the ceiling. It comes with two feet of chain and a ceiling canopy. Electrified, it sells for $125.

Catalog available, $1.

Hurley Patentee Lighting
R.D. 7, Box 98A
Kingston, N.Y. 12401
(914) 331-5414

E.G. Washburne Lanterns

The ubiquitous lantern was born out of the need to protect and reflect a source of light. The accommodation of these requirements to period styles has produced

enormous variety and gives them almost universal appeal. E. G. Washburne markets a series of hanging and wall-mounted lanterns of eighteenth-century simplicity. Their copper housings take on a distinguished patina and will weather any storm.

Catalog available.

E. G. Washburne & Co.
85 Andover St., Rte. 114
Danvers, Mass. 01923
(617) 774-3645

"Hanging Lamp with Door"

The lamps from Washington Copper Works share unique features. First of all, many of them would be considered lanterns. More important, an aesthetically pleasing copper conduit houses the wire that enters the socket. A copper bug screen keeps out the moths. Each light is numbered and initialed. Their "Hanging Lamp with Door" is both graceful and practical. Thick copper wire runs diagonally down from each corner for a spiral effect. The lamp/lantern comes is a variety of sizes and prices. The largest, at $170, is 18″ wide and 28″ high.

Catalog available, $1.

The Washington Copper Works
Serge Miller, Proprietor
Washington, Conn. 06793
(703) 868-7527

Postlights

The postlight has become as ubiquitous a modern accessory as the cutely decorated mailbox. Nevertheless, this fixture may be a useful one, especially for the country or suburban house. Beside lighting the way to the door, it provides a cheerful welcome to the night visitor. Lanterns were once hung from posts to accomplish the same aims. In the electric age, the practice has only become more uniform. As an alternative to the flood-lit look of Alcatraz, increasingly common in these security-conscious days, the postlight is definitely to be preferred.

The electrified or gas-lit lantern is the proper form, but globes of various sorts are also historically accurate. The buyer of a post and a light must be conscious of several matters. Make sure that the light is of the right scale for the setting; a tiny or too large lantern will appear ridiculous. Also make sure that both elements are of sturdy construction. Changing bulbs, for instance, can be a hazardous business, especially if you have to lean over a stepladder to perform the operation. Last, be certain that the light is suitable for outdoor use and that it and the post have been properly weatherproofed.

Early Pennsylvania Design

This postlight is a copy of an early Pennsylvania design. The original was made of tinned sheet iron. The reproduction is antiqued solid brass and will surely outlast all of us. It sells for $175.

Brochure available, 75¢.

American Period Lighting Fixtures
The Saltbox
2229 Marietta Pike
Lancaster Pa. 17603
(717) 392-5649

and the following two authorized sales locations: 608 N. Greene St., Greensboro, N.C. 27401 (919-273-8758), and 216 W. Maxwell St., Lexington, Ky. 40508 (606-254-1265).

Welsbach Lighting

Welsbach patented the first of the "Boulevard" series in 1899. It became a standard fixture in American cities. Although the glass type is still available, a vandal resistant model has been developed that has metal or polycarbonate domes and globes. Despite this allowance for contemporary criminal mores, the spirit of the original line has been retained.

Welsbach's free brochure does not do justice to their line of uncatalogued items such as gas burners, chimneys, mantles, glass ware, electric conversion kits and more.

The firm uses a variety of foundry techniques to create durable and attractive posts. Some are spun, tapered, or extruded aluminum, while others are cast in aluminum or iron. One model has an upper section of wood.

Welsbach's pier bases are cast aluminum and are consistent in style with their Victorian heritage. They can be fairly simple or quite ornate.

Literature available.

Welsbach Lighting Inc.
240 Sargent Dr.
New Haven, Conn. 06511
(203) 789-1710

Sconces

Sconces provide the most natural appearance of artificial light. Used with candles, they are truly antique in appearance. But even those wired for electricity can carry the true look of the past. While no reproduction can be "authentic," it can aim toward a convincing verisimilitude. Most sconces are relatively simple fixtures to fashion. And good models are in plentiful supply. Providing for their wiring is a more complicated matter.

Combined Gas and Electric

Gas and electric combinations found their expression in wall sconces as well as chandeliers. Classic Illumination reproduces several fine examples, including one that, when viewed from the front, looks like a sine wave length. One end has an electric socket which points downward. To the other end is affixed a filigreed key and above that is a gas jet. Complementary shade combinations add another another dimension to this solid brass fixture.

Catalog available, $2.

The Classic Illumination
P.O. Box 5851
San Francisco, Calif. 94101
(415) 527-5106

Classic Illumination fixtures are also available from the following distributors: San Francisco Victoriana, 606 Natoma, San Francisco, Calif. 94103 (415-429-5477) and Victorian Reproductions, 1601 Park Avenue South, Minneapolis, Minn. 55404 (612-338-3636).

Williamsburg Sconce

Among Williamsburg's architectural treasures is the Peyton Randolph House. It sits in shaded serenity off the Green. Of particular note are its series of paneled rooms, considered the best in Williamsburg. Hanging from one of these walls is the original dark mahogany sconce from which this reproduction is copied for Williamsburg by Victorius, Inc. The curved glass front slides up for access to the candle. It measures 18″ by 13⅝″ and with this Balister candlestick sells for $273.50.

Catalog available, $4.95.

Colonial Williamsburg
Craft House
Williamsburg, Va. 23185
(804) 229-1000

Brass "Hands"

Whether these heavy cast-brass hands served as inspiration for Bram Stoker is a matter of conjecture. A left and

right hand is available. Each extends 11½″ from a 7″ diameter back plate. You can buy one for $149. A pewter or silver finish is available at additional cost.

Catalog available, $3.

Lester H. Berry
1108 Pine St.
Philadelphia, Pa. 19107
(215) 923-2603

Antique Tin

Antique American tin sconces rarely reveal their age, but it is widely accepted that the ones with circular reflectors are among the oldest. This reproduction has the popular channeled sunburst design. It is an object in the Old Sturbridge Village collection and sells for $18.50.

Catalog available.

Virginia Metalcrafters, Inc.
1010 East Main St.
Waynesboro, Va. 22980
(703) 942-8205

Gates Moore

To the Gates Moore people, electrification of authentic reproductions is an unfortunate necessity—but they make no apologies for their workmanship. The electric wires, for example, are as unobtrusive as possible. No modern bolts or fasteners show in any fixture. All metal parts are bent or crimped with simple hand tools. These

faithful reproductions come in distressed tin, pewter coat, or painted finish. Prices range from $20 for the diamond-shaped sconce to $45 for the twin candle.

Catalog available, $2.

Gates Moore
River Rd., Silvermine
Norwalk, Conn. 06850
(203) 847-3231

Reflector Sconce

Like all Hurley Patentee reproductions, the original of this unusual sconce is a museum-quality piece. The

glass-enclosed reflectors are of antique leaded tin and are framed in wood. Wired, it sells for $70; subtract $10 for candle power.

Catalog available, $1.

Hurley Patentee Lighting
R.D. 7, Box 98A
Kingston, N.Y. 12401
(914) 331-5414

Supplies

True devotees of the art of lighting will find that their need for various supplies and replacement parts is never ending. Almost every reproduction lighting house carries a number of such items in its regular inventory. And even the once-in-a-lifetime home restorer may find that he will need to call on them for help.

Prisms

Crystal prisms have a way of breaking or disappearing over the years. Replacements may be elusive. Luigi Crystal imports several types that range in price from 50¢ to $2.50 each. Styles include pendalogue (tear drop), spear, Colonial, frog, and "U" drop.

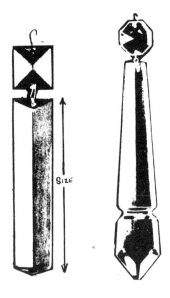

Catalog available, 25¢.

Luigi Crystal
7332 Frankford Ave.
Philadelphia, Pa. 19136
(215) 338-2978

Candle Covers

The Saltbox ("American Period Lighting Fixtures") offers off-white candle covers for electric fixtures in either 4″ or 6″ heights. The drippings add a touch of authenticity.

Catalogue available, 75¢.

American Period Lighting Fixtures
The Saltbox
2229 Marietta Pike
Lancaster, Pa. 17603
(717) 392-5649

and the following two authorized sales locations: 608 N. Greene St., Greensboro, N.C. 27401 (919-273-8758) and 216 W. Maxwell St., Lexington, Ky. 40508 (606-254-1265).

Tiffany Lamp Kits

Tiffany lamps are beautiful luxuries. The originals are stored in museums and prized by lucky collectors. For those of us less fortunate, there are reproductions. Better yet, if we are so inclined and skilled, there are kits. Tiffany's famous Wisteria lampshade, for example, which is now valued at over $33,000, can be bought in kit form for $47.50. Coran-Sholes has just about anything a professional artisan or rank amateur could want. Their kits include all the necessary materials such as precut glass, lead cames, solder, electrical and hanging hardware, *and* complete instructions.

Catalog available, $1.

Coran-Sholes
509 East Second St.
South Boston, Mass. 02127
(617) 268-3780

Gas Shades

Gas shades are often as delicate as flowers. Names like Diamond-Daisy and Snowflake suggest their character. Craftsmen have enhanced their fanciful form with intricate etching, pressing, and frosting. There are so many styles that one can be found to fit the personality of almost any room or its inhabitants. The shades are exact reproductions and range in price from $10 to $15.

Quarterly catalog, $1.

London Ventures Co.
2 Dock Square
Rockport, Mass. 01966
(617) 856-7161

Other Sources of Lighting Fixtures

Consult the List of Suppliers for addresses.

Antique Fixtures

Jerome W. Blum
The Cellar
Florence Maine
Materials Unlimited
Mrs. Eldred Scott
Westlake Architectural Antiques

Candleholders

Baldwin Hardware
Ball and Ball
Lester H. Berry
Historic Charleston Reproductions (Mottahedeh)
Colonial Williamsburg (Virginia Metalcrafters)
Copper Antiquities
Gates Moore
Guild of Shaker Crafts
Hurley Patentee Lighting
Steve Kayne
Mercer Museum Shop
Mexico House
George W. Mount
Period Furniture Hardware
Sturbridge Yankee Workshop
Washington Copper Works
Wasley Lighting

Chandeliers

Alcon Lightcraft Co.
American Period Lighting Fixtures (The Saltbox)
Authentic Designs
Ball and Ball
Colonial Williamsburg (Virginia Metalcrafters)
Copper Antiquities
Essex Forge
Robert Griffith
Heritage Lanterns
Hurley Patentee Lighting
Lightyear (MarLe)
Luigi Crystal
Mexico House
Newstamp Lighting
Packard Lamp Co., Inc.
Period Furniture Hardware
Spanish Villa
William Spencer
William Stewart & Sons
Sturbridge Yankee Workshop
Village Lantern
Wallin Forge
Washington Copper Works

Floor Lamps

Cohasset Colonials
Magnolia Hall
Rainbow Art Glass Corp
Sturbridge Yankee Workshop

Hanging Lamps
(including wall-mounted lamps)

American Period Lighting Fixtures (The Saltbox)
Authentic Designs
Lester H. Berry
Colonial Williamsburg (Virginia Metalcrafters)

Dahlman-Clift Lamps
Essex Forge
Gates Moore
Heritage Lanterns
Hurley Patentee Lighting
Magnolia Hall
Mexico House
Newstamp Lighting
Period Furniture Hardware
Royal Windyne Ltd.
Spanish Villa
William Spencer
Sturbridge Yankee Workshop
Wallin Forge
Washington Copper Works

Oil/Kerosene Lamps

Faire Harbour Boats (Aladdin)
Sturbridge Yankee Workshop
Washington Copper Works
Wasley Lighting

Table Lamps

Classic Illumination
Colonial Williamsburg (Virginia Metalcrafters)
Henry Ford Museum and Greenfield Village (Norman Perry)
Hurley Patentee Lighting
Luigi Crystal
Magnolia Hall
Ephraim Marsh
Mercer Museum Shop
Sturbridge Yankee Workshop
Wasley Lighting

Lanterns

American Period Lighting Fixtures (The Saltbox)
Copper House
Essex Forge
Gates Moore
Heritage Lanterns
Kenneth Lynch & Sons
Mercer Museum Shop
Period Lighting Fixtures
William Stewart & Sons
Sturbridge Yankee Workshop
Village Lantern
Wasley Lighting
Welsbach Lighting

Postlights

American Period Lighting Fixtures (The Saltbox)
Copper House
Gates Moore
Heritage Lanterns
Kenneth Lynch & Sons
Mexico House

Newstamp Lighting
Period Lighting Fixtures
William Spencer
Washington Copper Works
Wasley Lighting

Sconces

American Period Lighting Fixtures (The Saltbox)
Authentic Designs
Ball and Ball
Copper Antiquities
Essex Forge
Heritage Lanterns
Horton Brasses
Mexico House
Newton Millham
Newstamp Lighting
Period Furniture Hardware
Shaker Workshops
Spanish Villa
William Spencer
William Stewart & Sons
Sturbridge Yankee Workshop
Pete Taggett
Wasley Lighting

Supplies

B. &. P. Lamp Supply
Classic Illumination
Colonial Lamp & Supply
Hurley Patentee Lighting
Kenneth Lynch & Sons
Rainbow Art Glass
Welsbach Lighting

ELECTRIC LIGHT AND COMBINATION GAS FIXTURES.

MANUFACTURED

By

EDISON GENERAL ELECTRIC CO.

Fixture & Decorative Bronze Dept.

"Chinoiserie Tree Cotton Print," Brunschwig & Fils, The
Winterthur Collection (#7237.04).

VII Fabrics

Fabric coverings are useful as well as decorative materials for the old house. Not only can they enhance a period interior and give it character, but they can help to insulate the inside from the outside elements and hide that which is not particularly attractive. The Victorians used to paper everything over. Today we have the nuisance of adhesive papers that successfully simulate just about everything *except* the intended material, and provide neither protection nor aesthetic value. Fabrics, too, can be an "easy way out" to a particular decorating dilemma. "Cover it" may seem the best advice at the time when you discover that a window sash is rotting away or that the previous owner has changed the height of one window of a series so that it no longer matches the others. But try to make structural improvements first. Fabrics should properly enhance whatever they cover whether it be furniture, a wall, or a window. Now that we have a wealth of reproduction historical textiles at hand, there is no reason why they should not be given the prominence that a budget will allow for.

A return to natural fiber materials is underway. This is a welcome change from the emphasis on synthetics which supposedly offered permanent pleats and colors. Cotton is back "in" again as is wool. Prices that once seemed grossly inflated for natural fabrics are being matched in artificial materials. Such synthetics can be mixed with natural fibers in a truly useful way; the stretched-out, shiny look of double-knit, however, is best left back in the recent past along with the yellowish rayon of the '50s and '60s. Claims of durability were misleading, and the cleaning of chemically-produced fibers was often a mystery that not even the best dry cleaner could solve. The best argument for natural fabrics is their natural look and texture. When mixed with similar natural building marials and furnishings, they not only seem to be right and fitting, they *are* right and fitting.

Fabrics are used primarily for window hangings and for upholstery. In both cases the past has much to recommend. Summer and winter curtains, slip covers and upholstery—these again make sense. Winter curtains were of a heavy sort that served to protect the room from cold. In the summer, sheer organdy or lace or thin cotton filtered out some light, but generally allowed for the flow of air. Slip covers had a cooling effect and protected furniture from the dirt and dust of the warm season. In winter, heavier upholstery material provided a welcome soft and warm cushion. It may not be possible to provide a double set of materials for all rooms in the house, but thought should be given to using two sets of curtains in at least the kitchen, if not the living room. Over the long run, such materials will more than pay for themselves. They will, of course, last twice as long as something which is used all year round.

Reproduction fabrics based on documents found in old homes and museums have been popular for many years. Their number continues to increase with demand. Less exact copies known as "adaptations" are also encountered. The diligent research will find that there is probably at least one reproduction fabric for each year of the period from 1700 to 1850. That is, if your house dates from 1838, you can find a material that was either introduced or was popularly used that year. This is not to say that you should use such a fabric, but merely to point out what a big and exacting business the reproduction of historic fabrics has become. Fabrics, however well manufactured, do not last more than several generations before they begin to disintegrate. Antique textiles can be purchased today, but most have to be used so gingerly that they might as well be framed and displayed as the antiques they are.

The most important recent change in the reproduction fabric business has been the new emphasis on Victorian-period materials. Although we tend to forget or ignore this fact, most of American building dates from the mid- to late-nineteenth century. Boston and Charleston have many more Victorian structures than Colonial. So, too, did Williamsburg and Philadelphia's Society Hill before these buildings were torn to the ground. San Francisco may lavish more love on its Victorian buildings than any other American city, but similar houses exist from coast to coast, and fortunately they are being discovered.

There are not many shortcuts available to the buyer of good period fabrics. Some are sold only through interior designers and the decorating departments of large retail outlets. For those who can afford to follow such paths, the way is relatively easy. Professional help and advice is always the best investment. The alternative is to seek out the increasing number of fabric lines which are sold both through design services and other retail outlets. The persistent and intelligent shopper may even find that very appropriate textiles may be found in surplus or remnant stores. The most fortunate buyer of all is the one who possesses not only the energy to track down good material, but the skill with which to upholster or to work it up at home into curtains, slip covers, hangings, etc.

Curtain and Drapery Materials

Four natural fibers—cotton, wool, silk, and flax—provide the best of materials for window, wall, and bed hangings. All of these basic fibers are often combined with man-made fibers such as rayon polyester. Some curtain material, of course, is totally synthetic, and the majority of such textiles is unsuitable for use in period interiors. The initial expense of a synthetic may be less, but now even this advantage is disappearing with the great advance in basic petrochemical costs. In any case, synthetics are not good long-term investments. On the simplest level, compare a feather pillow with one filled with polyurethane foam after several years of use. The former, if properly cared for, will puff up and remain useful; the foam-rubber filling will have begun its process of disintegration, and you may find that something resembling shredded wheat is all that remains between you and the mattress.

Fabrics are available in a bewildering variety of patterns, materials, and finishes. Fabric lines, like those of wallpaper, are in a constant state of change. For this reason, it is well worth checking remnant outlets in your area; discontinued items may be of considerable interest and value to you. Matching fabrics and papers are still popular. In many cases, however, use of one pattern at the windows and the same in upholstery, bed hangings, etc., can amount to overkill. Although it may be proper to make use of one good fabric in several different ways (our ancestors were similarly economical), it is questionable whether the design motif should be carried out in a paper identical to the fabric selected. Slightly different but coordinated patterns may be the best approach.

Suppliers and manufacturers are listed in alphabetical order.

Laura Ashley

Traditional patterns found in Welsh patchwork quilts and other Victorian fabrics form the country look favored by this design and manufacturing firm located in Wales. The cotton fabrics are mainly small prints with floral or geometric designs. They are just being introduced in North America.

Laura Ashley, Inc.
714 Madison Ave.
New York, N.Y. 10021

Brunschwig & Fils

A glazed chintz is a tightly-woven cotton fabric that has been given a high finish through weaving or through the addition of resins. "Antibes" (#17147.00) is reproduced exactly as designed by Jean-Ulric Tournier in Alsace, France, c. 1845. The document itself is to be found in the Musée Historique de Tissus in Mulhouse. The original was block printed; the reproduction has been hand-screen printed, and is available in six color combinations.

A second glazed chintz, "China Dream" (#6637.01), is appropriately based on watered silk bed hangings in the White and Gold Room at the Henry Francis du Pont Winterthur Museum. The original French pattern is dated 1775–1800. Also 100% cotton, the adaptation is available in the original cream color and four other shades.

Crewel embroidery has been popular for many years and was once one of the simpler ways to decorate woolen material. "Indigo Crewel" (#7328.04) is a hand-screen printed adaptation of an eighteenth-century American curtain panel in wool needlework. The original is found in the Hampton Room of the Winterthur Museum. The effect of hand-embroidery can never be exactly duplicated in a printed fabric, but this design, worked in 57% linen and 43% cotton, is quite effective. The original colors are blue shades and these and four other colorways are offered.

Brunschwig & Fils fabrics are sold through interior designers and decorating services of department stores. Consult appendixes A and B for further information on these sources. Further information may be secured from:

Brunschwig & Fils, Inc.
979 Third Ave.
New York, N.Y. 10022
(212) 838-7878

S. M. Hexter

Eighteenth-century floral patterns from England and France are among the most traditional of designs. They are suitable for elegant interiors of that time *and* of the twentieth century. "Aldbury" is a 100% cotton screen print introduced for the first time in 1977 and is based on an English document. It is available in six different

color combinations: crimson and Canton blue, Nanking blue and camel, sorrel and plum, carmine and copper, burnt umber and stone, and Kent grey and wheat.

"Sylvia" is a glazed chintz developed from drawings found in the antique sketchbooks of Oberkampf, and was originally produced in the factory at Jouy, France, during the mid-eighteenth century. It is offered in biscuit and Canton blue, canary and platinum, peach-bloom and cayenne, white and crimson, and ivory and blue.

"Aesop's Fable" is typical of the documentary prints in cotton popular in America during the early 1800s. Hexter's rendition is based on original material found in the archives of the Henry Ford Museum and is available in spice, Canton blue, raisin, loganberry, and black.

The kind of prints used in French provincial country houses are not that different from those found in rural America during the nineteenth century. "Emilie" is an aptly-named 100% cotton fabric that evokes pastoral simplicity and is offered in nine different colors: brick, blueberry, eggplant, navy, cherry, flagstone blue, cocoa, country blue, and gingersnap.

Water lilies are a motif which occur frequently in printed textiles of the late 1800s. "1889" is based on a French document of that year and is a most appropriate 100% cotton design for any Victorian interior which reflects a passion for things Oriental and aesthetic. There are nine shades available: cinnabar, pewter, peachbloom, mauve, powder blue, tender taupe, sand beige, celadon, and cornsilk.

The luscious peonies of the "Wyndham" screen print would be welcome in any home where there is a love for the naturalistic and floral. In contrast to the florals of the mid-eighteenth century, this fabric is alive with sharply rendered realistic detail. It is based on an English design and is offered in gem blue and coral, navy blue and moonbeam, espresso and pink, umbre and beach, and forest green and blush.

Hexter has showrooms in New York, Atlanta, Boston, Chicago, Cincinnati, Dallas, Denver, Detroit, Honolulu, Los Angeles, Miami, Minneapolis, Philadelphia, Phoenix, Portland, San Francisco, Seattle, St. Louis, Toronto, and London, England, or may be contacted at:

S. M. Hexter Co.
2800 Superior Ave.
Cleveland, Ohio 44114
(216) 696-0146

Old Stone Mill

"Baroda" is typical of the designs from India which were brought to America in the eighteenth-century via England. This is an adaptation from a fragment which survived the wear and tear of the years.

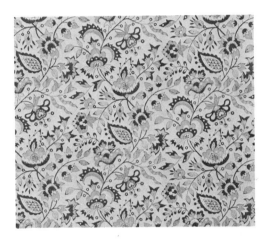

"Mademoiselle" is reproduced from an original block-printed toile de Jouy manufactured at the famous French *manufacture royale* from the mid-1700s to the early nineteenth century. This factory was a source for a number of wealthy Americans of the period.

Scalamandré

Do not let Scalamandré's reputation for expensive quality frighten you away. There are fabrics here of real value and substance which will not break your pocketbook. And there are many about which you (and I) can dream or view—in the White House and other important historic mansions from coast to coast. All of the fabrics are sold through decorating departments or interior designers; and by consulting the information contained in appendices A and B, you may find that using a middleman is not such a difficult task as it may appear to be.

A cotton "Monk's Cloth" (#4010) is one of the reasonably-priced materials which Scalamandré has to offer. It is, of course, the solid pattern formed by a weaver. It can be dyed in one of many colors, and such material is most appropriate for curtains in a simple country interior.

"Coverlet Damask" (#7699-1), another 100% cotton, is also a simple material and uses only one color. It does not have the richness associated with jacquard-woven fabrics such as damasks, but the pattern is a pleasing one and not inappropriate.

Toiles of French origin were used in Colonial and early nineteenth-century homes in America. The fabric illustrated (#6708-1) is a copy of one used in the Betty Lewis bedroom at Kenmore, Fredericksburg, Virginia. It is of one color and of 100% cotton.

The "Directoire Toile" print (#6423) is a more complicated pattern made with two screens. It is representative of fabrics used in the early 1800s in fine homes up and down the East Coast. It is 100% cotton.

134

Italian Renaissance designs of great complexity and beauty slowly made their way in the New World. This is a silk damask (#97178) which was designed by Franco Scalamandré and used for draperies in the State Dining Room of the White House. It is a mixture of gold and cream and has to be custom-ordered.

less than White House surroundings. It is a design adapted from the boiserie effect achieved in the first floor library ceiling of Werms House.

A wallpaper in the Sorrell-Weed House in Savannah was the source for this documentary design in the Adams or Federal style. "Sorrel-Weed House" (#6450), part of the Historic Savannah Collection, is made of 100% duck cotton.

Scalamandré
950 Third Ave.
New York, N.Y. 10022
(212) 361-8500

"Werms House Diamond" (#6446) from Scalamandré's new Historic Savannah Collection is a geometric glazed cotton chintz of the sort that would have been used in

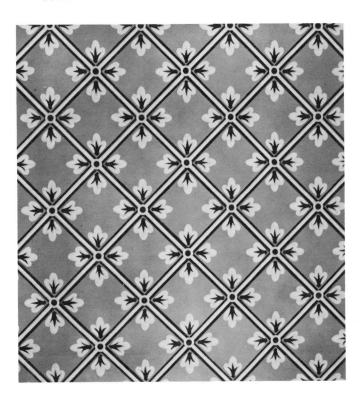

Schumacher

To many, the name Schumacher is only slightly less forbidding than that of Scalamandre. The initiated, however, realize that the firm has been associated with Colonial Williamsburg and many fine other historical institutions for some years and is really quite approachable. As with other high quality fabric manufacturers, there is a considerable variety of materials available in a wide price range. Many of the Schumacher fabrics can be found in retail outlets throughout North America.

"Phillipsburg Manor Resist" (#65555) is from the Sleepy Hollow Collection and is typical of the one-color patterns produced in the Colonies by primitive craftsmen during the early to mid-eighteenth century. The term

"Raleigh Tavern" (#178160 series), "Williamsburg Liner Stripe" (#63110 series), and "Pleasures of the Farm" (#50428) are from the Colonial Williamsburg collection of documented reproductions. These are seen, respectively, from top to bottom. The first is a "resist" block print in 70% linen and 30% cotton; the second, 100% cotton; and the third, a pastoral scene of 100% cotton.

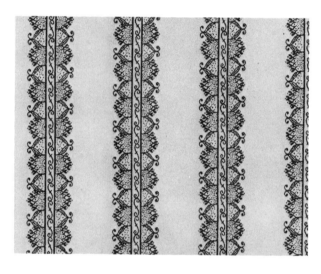

"Van Cortlandt-Honey Comb Floral" (#65512) is another traditional Hudson Valley fabric included in the Sleepy Hollow Collection. Of 66% linen and 34% cotton, it has the weight and the texture of homespun; the design, however, is a great deal more sophisticated as, indeed, were the patroons of New York State.

A shiny glazed 100% cotton—"Peplum Liner" (#67570) —might have been found in a late Colonial or an early 1800s interior. It is from the Smithsonian Institution Collection.

"Noailles (#64874) is yet another glazed 100% cotton print and is part of the Historic Newport Collection. As befits the social graces of this important seaport city, this is a particularly graceful and delicate design. It has been worked in several colors.

Few of Schumacher's fabrics are clearly designated for use in Victorian interiors, but many can be so utilized. Designer John Hargreaves has provided a new translation of a turn-of-the-century Tiffany-style brocade design in 100% cotton. "Topiary" (#69870 series) is a rich, colorful pattern of unusual interest. It is available in deep spruce, Braque brown, dove gray, shadow peach, and cathedral blue.

"Lagos" (#69830 series) is an adaptation of an eighteenth-century Portuguese design by Virginia Bowen, A.S.I.D., in 100% linen. Complex effects of this sort were employed in all the late-Victorian decorative arts—from wall and floor tiles to wallpapers to fabrics. The colors are also typical of the earthy tones favored at the time. Schumacher has given them Portuguese names: Algarve coral and sage, Tagus blue and brass, Oporto slate and brick, Litoral turquoise and beige, Portugal terra cotta and smoke, Marinha green and yellow.

"Ardebil" (#69890) is inspired by an antique Persian rug and is printed on "union" linen cloth and cotton. The design is that of Ruth Strachan Cole, A.S.I.D., and would have excited the interest of decorators in the 1880s and '90s. The colors are deep shades of the sort used in rugs from the Middle East.

F. Schumacher & Co.
939 Third Ave.
New York, N.Y. 10022
(212) 644-5943

Silk Surplus

Residents of the New York City area are fortunate in having three outlets of Silk Surplus to visit. Close-outs and fabrics which are termed "off-colors" are available here along with a large quality line made for sale only in these stores. Many famous names, including Scalamandré, can be found. Business is simply cash and carry. Silk Surplus is one good reason for making a trip to the Big Apple and its environs.

Silk Surplus
223 E. 58th St.
New York, N.Y. 10022
(212) 753-6511

Silk Surplus
843 Lexington Ave.
New York, N.Y. 10021
(212) 879-4708

Silk Surplus
449 Old Country Rd.
Westbury, N.Y. 11590
(516) 997-7469

Albert Van Luit

Almost all of Van Luit's fabrics are highly-colored dramatic prints of cotton or linen. Many would be suitable for mid- to late-Victorian interiors in which floral designs were not at all uncommon. The most interesting fabrics are those in the "Initial Collection," and the dyes used for the colors are obviously extremely receptive to the fibers that form their ground. "Merivale Lane," a 100% cotton, is just one of these colorful fabrics.

Catalog available, 50¢.

Albert Van Luit & Co.
4000 Chevy Chase Dr.
Los Angeles, Calif. 90039
(213) 245-5106

Watts & Co.

Watts' fabrics are of museum quality and in design are a continuation of work begun by the founders of the company during the Victorian era. These reflect tremendous interest in and understanding of Gothic Revival taste. Thomas Garner was the designer of "Gothic," which Watts has recently reproduced in rose and in blue

subtle colors. It is an English floral design and has been named after one of the early merchants of Boston, Horace Draper.

"Fiske Stencil" (#682061) is based on a traditional stencil design. Colors are soft and the pattern is rendered in the somewhat off-hand fashion expected of stencil art. Both this fabric and that illustrated below it, "Village Strip" (#681221), are of 100% cotton. Each is recommended for use in early to mid-nineteenth century interiors.

silk. The high altar frontal at St. Thomas Church, New York, is suitably adorned with a second Watts' fabric, "Gainford," illustrated here below "Gothic." A very special manufacturer for very special needs.

Catalog available, $2.

Watts & Co. Ltd.
7 Tufton St.
Westminster, London
SWlP 3QB England

Waverly

To move from Watts to Waverly is to return to the world in which we all live today, and as the photographs illustrate, the fabrics provide an atmosphere which combines good taste with good sense.

The Old Sturbridge Village Collection provides both interest and quality for the old-house buyer. "Draper Chintz" (#684621) is a glazed 100% cotton of muted,

"French Paisley" (#683972) is also included in the Sturbridge group and is a 100% glazed cotton. Subdued it is not, but paisleys with very exuberant colors and lively patterns were popular from the 1850s on. Queen Victoria even draped a paisley shawl around her royal shoulders.

Waverly Fabrics
58 W 40th St.
New York, N.Y. 10018
(212) 644-5900

Upholstery Fabrics

Material used for covering furniture is of necessity of heavier weight and weave. Printed cottons can be used, but are best reserved for slip covers. Combinations of cotton and linen provide more durability, and pure wool probably the most of all. There are, of course, damasks, brocades, and velvets which are more complicated weaves and are therefore better material for upholstery—regardless of the base fiber used. 100% silk appears on only the finest pieces of period furniture. Horsehair was commonly used in the Victorian era and can be supplied today by many upholsterers or fabric manufacturers.

In recent years upholstery fabrics have been routinely covered with a protective synthetic covering. This is better than slip covering the furniture in sheets of clear vinyl, but these modern chemical shields against spills may make cleaning a fabric more difficult. Drinks will roll off, but dirt and food will inevitably find their way to the surface. Natural, untreated fibers can be cleaned of such "debris," but fibers which have been coated with a repellent lose their elasticity and endurance.

Ephraim Marsh

The company's business is primarily furniture, but it does supply hand-worked India crewel. Designs are stitched in wool against a hand-woven cotton ground. Four patterns are available—"Tree of Life, Floral," "Tree of Life with Bird," "Shalamar," and "Floral." Crewel embroidery for upholstery became popular during the eighteenth century and was later superseded by more precise and complicated forms of needlework.

Ephraim Marsh Co.
Box 266
Concord, N.C. 28025
(704) 782-0814

Scalamandré

"Song of India" (#96356) crewel is made in that country of 50% cotton and 50% wool. It is a higher grade of material than that generally available from American supply houses and therefore of more lasting quality.

Resist designs can also be used for upholstery purposes. "French Resist" (#6410) is an adaptation from a document in the Metropolitan Museum's textile collection and is made of 44% linen and 56% cotton. Not as primitive in appearance as the Colonial American designs, it might be used in both late Colonial and early Victorian interiors. The material comes in seven different colors.

Linen made in Belgium (#L-13) has the nubby, substantial texture which flatters country-style furniture. It is also a material well-suited for simple curtains in either contemporary or early Colonial interiors. Scalamandré imports a basic natural and white cloth which will serve several purposes.

The "Amsterdam" novelty stripe (#9638) is an even stronger weave of 15% cotton and 84% linen which is made in Belgium. Although it features a small flower design, the overall effect is one of formality and neatness that would be suitable for relatively high-style American Federal furniture.

"Flowers of India" appears handmade because of the uneven lines of the contiguous octagonal shapes. This is, however, machine-made material from India of 60% cotton and 40% wool and is available with coordinate border strips. Despite its intentional irregularities, the quite systematic design can be used in the manner of high-style needlework.

Scalamandré is famous for its 100% silk and combination silk upholstery materials which have been used in the White House and in other famous buildings. "French Empire Medallion" (#97347) is a damask of 31% silk and 69% cotton made at their Long Island City plant. The design is most appropriate for early- to mid-nineteenth-century interiors.

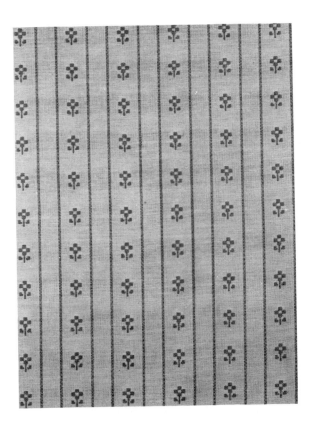

Reproduction of a Scotch ingrain wool fabric is extraordinarily difficult and expensive. "William Morris Bird" (#97373) was woven on Scalamandré's Scotch ingrain loom especially for the William Morris Society. Most fabric reproductions can be manufactured at less cost than the originals would be today, but, in this case, it would have been easier to start completely anew. The material *could* be used for small upholstery purposes but more than likely no one will really want this ruined by contact with the human body. It really belongs on the wall with other fine compositions.

Schumacher's fabrics provide a constant source of materials for professional upholsterers and furniture craftsmen. The range of designs is unusually broad, and most are widely available.

"Stencil Flowers" (#66624) is a Colonial Williamsburg adaptation of a traditional eighteenth-century design. It is woven of 66% linen and 34% cotton.

Some fabrics can be reversed with good effect. "Sunnyside Floral" (#35356) is one of these. It is a very handsome 100% cotton of considerable weight and texture. "Sunnyside" was Washington Irving's home and the fabric is part of Schumacher's Sleepy Hollow Restoration Collection. So, too, is "Sunnyside Stripe" (#35400), seen below. The pattern is that found in ticking, but the effect is of an elegant formal cloth.

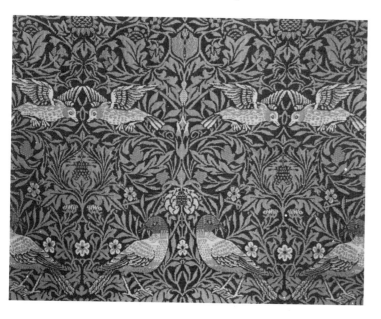

Consult appendices A and B for further information regarding outlets for Scalamandré products, or contact:

Scalamandré Silks, Inc.
950 Third Ave.
New York, N.Y. 10022
(212) 361-8500

Schumacher

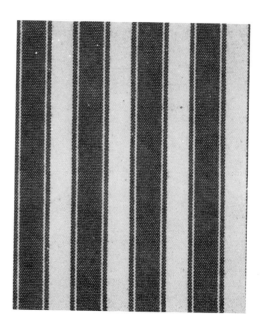

"Marseilles" (#36334) from the South Street Seaport Museum Collection, is an even more formal stripe, perfect for many period rooms of the 1800s.

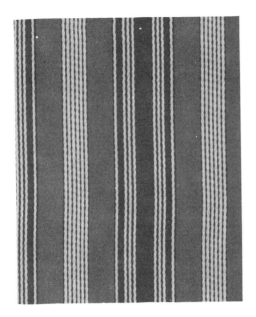

Schumacher fabrics can be seen in showrooms around the country and are sold through numerous retail outlets. For further information, contact:

F. Schumacher & Co.
939 Third Ave.
New York, N.Y. 10018
(212) 644-5900

Trimmings

These are the little extras that can insure successful use of period window handings and upholstery. They are especially important for a high-style interior whether that be Georgian Colonial, Federal, Greek Revival, or Victorian.

Stroheim & Romann

This major supplier of fabric trimmings imports over fifty-three designs from Italy. These have to be hand-woven, a meticulous kind of work that calls for nimble fingers and steel nerves.

The firm's products are distributed throughout North America. For further information regarding sources, contact:

Stroheim & Romann
155 East 56th St.
New York, N.Y. 10022
(212) 691-0700

Scalamandré

Handmade trimmings and tiebacks are produced in America, too—primarily at this firm's Long Island City plant. Illustrated in the following two photographs are braid, gimp, tassels, fringes, and frogs. These by no means exhaust the Scalamandré repertoire.

Available through interior design firms and decorating departments. For further information, contact:

Scalamandré Silks, Inc.
950 Third Ave.
New York, N.Y. 10022
(212) 361-8500

Raw Materials

The weaving and printing of fabrics is not only the concern of large-scale manufacturers. Increasingly, small companies of craftsmen have established themselves in this field. Since they are masters of the arts of spinning, dyeing, and weaving—and, frequently of block printing—they understand full well what went into the production of textiles one- or two-hundred years ago. Old-house devotees fortunate enough to have the leisure time and talent to pursue any or all phases of clothmaking may want to contact one or more of the following suppliers of materials.

Hearthside

This firm is best known for its quilting supplies and calicoes. It also supplies 100% virgin wool, grown and spun at Christopher Sheep Farm in New England. This is available in natural undyed shades or in heather tones.

Catalog and sample cards available.

Hearthside Mail Order
Box 127
West Newbury, Vt. 05085

Mercer Museum Shop

Homespun flax for the making of linen cloth is offered at $1.25 a hank.

Mercer Museum Shop
Bucks County Historical Society
Pine and Ashland Sts.
Doylestown, Penn. 18901
(215) 345-0737

S. & C. Huber

The S. & C. Huber farm is a "center for early country arts." Here one can take classes in spinning, weaving, stenciling, quilting, braiding, paper-making, and needlepoint. Other "country" craft skills are also developed in one-day workshops. All the tools and materials needed for such activities are also available, and these may be ordered by mail. Huber stocks various fibers for spinning, weaving, and dyeing—wool, flax, cotton, silk cocoons, camel's down, and hair. The same yarns—already spun—are available, or you can purchase the woven fabrics. These you can have them dye for you or you may buy the dyes and do it yourself. All the dyes are natural and of vegetable composition with the exception of the cochineal bug.

Catalog available, 50¢.

S. & C. Huber, Accoutrements
82 Plants Dam Rd.
East Lyme, Conn. 06333
(203) 739-0772

Sunflower Studio

Constance La Lena is an exceptional weaver and dyer of yard goods and period clothing. We are not in the practice of reprinting our suppliers' literature, but there is only one way of doing justice to the Sunflower Studio work. Illustrated is an insert from the catalog, giving a

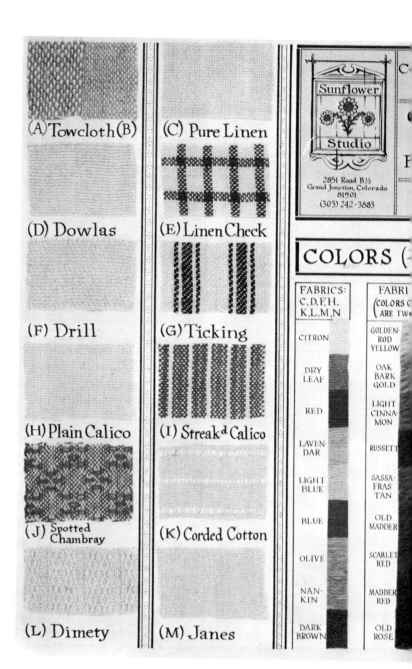

complete rundown of the fabrics available and the colors in which they can be dyed—if so desired. Unfortunately, we cannot reproduce this in color.

Swatches of the actual cloth may be ordered at 35¢ each or 3 for $1. The price is automatically credited to any order.

Catalog available, $2.

Constance La Lena
Sunflower Studio
2851 Road B½
Grand Junction, Colo. 81501
(303) 242-3883

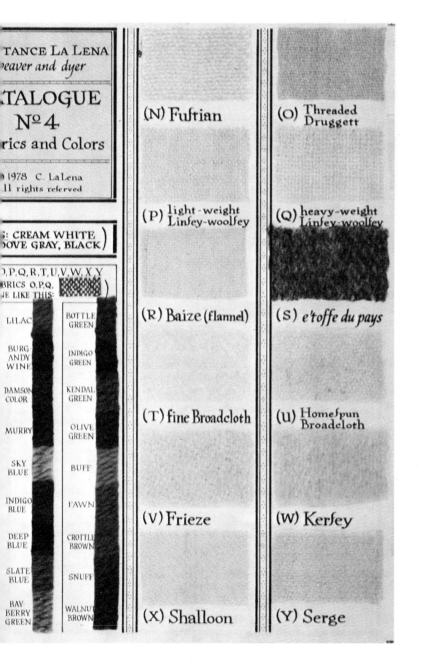

Ready-Mades and Kits

Ready-made curtains, throws, quilts, blankets, and wall hangings are a godsend if sent from a divinely-inspired person. The run-of-the-mill standard items found in many fabric or craft shops may suit some purposes, but are often not of the proper cut or material for period use. It may not be necessary, however, to special-order or have custom-made "standard" items from another era. There are craftsmen who can do the job for you as part of their daily routine. Of course if you are at all talented, you may decide to work on your own patterns and weaves.

Braid-Aid

Although best known for their rug braiding and hooking supplies, Braid-Aid also stocks crewel embroidery and needlepoint accessories and kits. These are handy for making chair seats, footstool and piano bench covers, and bell pulls.

Catalog available, $1.

Braid-Aid
466 Washington St.
Pembroke, Mass. 02359
(617) 826-6091

Carol Brown

If you can't make your way to Putney, Vermont—a trip well worth making—then write to Carol Brown who stocks Irish tweeds and other natural fiber fabrics. Her principal supplier is Avoca Handweavers, a firm known for its rare and beautiful wools. Bedspreads and wall hangings can be made to almost any size. But there are also cottons by the yard. Samples can be sent if you make a specific request.

Carol Brown
Putney, Vt. 05346
(802) 387-5875

Cohasset Colonials

Curtains in two styles—Brewster and Boston—are made of special plain woven fabrics or printed cottons from Waverly. The curtains are simple panels which may be hung from wide tabs (Brewster style) or from brass rings on rods (Boston style).

Decorator packs of 25 fabric samples are available for $4, with this charge credited to orders of $10 or more. General catalog available, 50¢.

145

Cohasset Colonials
Cohasset, Mass.
(617) 383-0110

Diane Jackson Cole

Handweaving of a special sort is undertaken by Diane Jackson Cole. A 100% virgin wool coverlet, illustrated here, is one of two stock items, and it is available in a range of color blends at $200 for a twin size, $250 for a

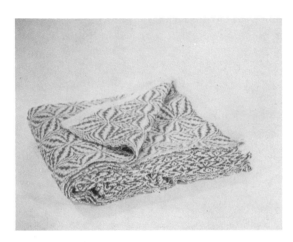

double, and $300 for king. A sample of fabric and color choice will be sent for a charge of $2. Once you have seen the work, you will understand why it is so special.

Diane Jackson Cole
9 Grove St.
Kennebunk, Me. 04043
(207) 457-1289

Country Curtains

This well-known firm has not let success go to its head. Most of their work is done in a mill overlooking the Housatonic and is not jobbed out to others. New additions are made to the basic line from time to time. A tab curtain of cotton and polyester with a wild rose stripe is one such new feature. These are available in varying

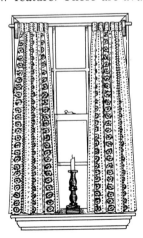

lengths—25, 30, 36, 45, 54, 63, 72, and 81 inches (lengths include the tabs). Prices range from $11 a pair to $17.50.

Catalog available.

Country Curtains
Stockbridge, Mass. 01262
(413) 298-5565

The Designing Woman

Drapery treatments of all periods are the specialty of this St. Louis custom design studio. Standard designs are not available. If you are interested in what they might be able to do, be sure to write precisely regarding your requirements.

The Designing Woman
705 Rivermont Dr.
St. Louis, Mo. 63137
(314) 869-5362

Down Home Comforts

Comforters, featherbeds, and covers for both are carefully crafted by this firm to your specifications. Down and feathers are used exclusively in the products, and good cotton fabrics are standard. Bed and special pillows are also available. And if you can find a way of getting old comforters, featherbeds, and pillows to Vermont, they will remake them for you.

Down Home Comforts
P.O. Box 281
West Brattleboro, Vt.
(802) 348-7944

Gurian's

Gurian's is truly the crewel king, as its literature proclaims. In addition to the many patterns of yard goods available, there are also finished crewel chair seats and backs as well as pillows, bedspreads, and tablecloths.

Brochure and one swatch, 50¢.

Gurian's
276 Fifth Ave.
New York, N.Y. 10001
(212) MU9-9696

The Pilgrim's Progress

Two Elizabethan designs—"Strawberry and Acorn Vine" and "Tree of Life"—are available in crewelwork kits. These are adaptations from embroidery designs found in the collection of the Folger Shakespeare Library. The kits contain 100% Persian wool yarns, hand-printed linen, needle, and instructions. The historical background of the design is also explained. The 18" x 18" squares are suitable for stool and chair covers.

Brochures available.

The Pilgrim's Progress
Penthouse
50 W. 67th St.
New York, N.Y. 10023
(212) 580-3050

Quicksand Crafts

Handwoven bedspreads are one specialty of this Appalachian concern. Split corners are included for poster beds, and corner-"pleat" inserts are available for beds with standard frames. The spreads are woven of a natural-colored mercerized cotton with an ivory pattern.

Literature available.

Quicksand Crafts
Vest, Ky. 41772
(606) 785-5230

Jane Kent Rockwell

Custom-made period draperies and bed hangings are expertly produced by Jane Kent Rockwell in her interior decoration shop. She can also assist with other fabric designs, wallpapers, hardware, lighting fixtures, and decorative plasterwork.

Jane Kent Rockwell, Interior Decorations
48-52 Lincoln St.
Exeter, N.H. 03833
(603) 778-0406

Southern Highland Handicraft Guild

Coverlets, quilts, and knotted and fringe trimmings are among the traditional crafts worked by members of the Southern Highland Handicraft Guild.

Brief literature available.

Southern Highland Handicraft Guild
P.O. Box 9545
Asheville, N.C. 28805
(704) 298-7928

Other Suppliers of Fabric Materials

Consult List of Suppliers for complete addresses.

Curtain/Drapery Materials

Bailey and Griffin
Barclay Fabrics
Norton Blumenthal
Carol Brown
China Seas
Clarence House
Connaissance Fabrics
A. L. Diament
S. & C. Huber
Lee/Jofa
Stroheim & Romann
Richard E. Thibaut

Upholstery Materials

China Seas
Clarence House
Gurian's
S.M. Hexter
Lee/Jofa
Stroheim & Romann

Trimmings

Barclay Fabrics
Bergamo Fabrics
Norton Blumenthal
Clarence House
Conso Products
F. Schumacher
Standard Trimmings
Tolland Fabrics

Ready-Made Materials

Appalachian Fireside Crafts
Constance Carol
Colonial Williamsburg (Bates)
Homespun Weavers
Mather's
Museum of Fine Arts Shop, Boston
New Hampshire Blankets
Quaker Lace Co.

VIII   Paints & Papers

Materials that add decorative appeal to a surface and also help to protect it are widely available from many sources. More and more documented papers and paints, as well as period stencil patterns, are emerging each year. Research into and duplication of such late nineteenth-century materials as Lincrusta Walton—a composition paper based on linseed oil—Japanese "leather paper," and "ingrain" paper are well underway, and soon these, too, will be commercially available. The main problem facing the home restorer, then, is not a dearth of suitable materials, but how to choose from among the wealth of patterns and textures being offered.

Any old house will have been painted or papered several times, perhaps many times. An honest restoration will aim for exact or close duplication of materials from a particular period. If your house dates from the 1820s, for instance, you may decide to return it to that simple era and not a later one. This means that you will probably have to bypass the layers of Victorian decoration in search of the first decorative scheme. Layer upon layer of wallpaper may have to be removed (and carefully preserved, *at least* in fragment form) until you come to some semblance of the true age. The same process is required for discovering original paint colors—methodical chipping away of coat after coat, and—if possible, an analysis of each layer. There are several books which will aid you in this time-consuming but potentially rewarding work, and these are listed in the bibliography.

Most people will have neither the time nor the money, and probably not the inclination, to pursue such meticulous detective work. Their interest is in an approximation of a period style. Just what period to choose—if an old house is, indeed, an antique one—will be determined by the general stylistic characteristics of the structure itself. If a house from the 1870s is predominantly in the Second Empire mansard architectural style, it would make sense to consider panel sets or "fresco papers" of French inspiration for a front parlor. On the other hand, the walls of the parlor in a high-style Queen Anne residence of the same decade might have been covered in the latest William Morris or other complicated English-style print. Rather than vertical panels, the walls would be divided into three horizontal sections: a frieze above, filler below, and dado below the level of a chair rail, with each of the three sections separated from the others by a border.

Well-printed multi-color papers can be a very expensive acquisition. Fortunately, these are better made today than they were twenty-five or one-hundred years ago. Although the use of synthetic coatings is discouraged in other areas of restoration, here such a chemical process is welcomed. Adhesives are also improved, but must be used with care on certain kinds of materials. It is good to keep in mind the fact that wallpapers of the past were often cheaply manufactured and sold. Covering a surface was often no more expensive than painting it. Unless you are attempting a precise restoration job, there is no more need to bear the heavy expense of custom papers or limited-edition work than there was a century ago. Appropriate designs of every period are available at moderate cost. In the following pages, we have attempted to list only documented papers. Designs based on motifs found on porcelain, furniture, or other materials not akin to wallpaper have been excluded.

Application of paint is now the easiest way to radically change the appearance of an interior or exterior space. There are various sorts available from primitive skimmed milk mixtures and lead-based oils to modern latex and alkyd. It is difficult to recommend one rather than another. How they are to be used will determine the appropriate medium.

Paint colors are a somewhat simpler matter than wallpaper patterns. Even the major manufacturers have recognized the need for historical shades. What is fitting in New England, however, may not be right in North Carolina or Utah. Definite regional characteristics have developed over the years, and these are most marked in the oldest of the old homes. When mixing of paints was a matter of combining locally available mineral pigments, a great deal was left to chance. Not until the late nineteenth century and the introduction of manufacturers' books with paint chips did any sort of uniformity in colors begin to emerge.

The tendency to overemphasize color contrasts—particularly on the exterior of a building—is a problem of the 1960s when the whole world seemed to explode in psychedelic shades. At this time many highly ornamented Victorian houses were given a two or three-tone job that offends the eye only a decade later. There has been some move away from this practice since. More and more home owners are following the advice of such a critic as Gervase Wheeler, who wrote in 1855: "Cornices, window dressings, verandah mouldings, etc., might be made more prominent by coloring them a shade darker than the main building, although *this step must be taken with great caution so as not to divide the house by stripes, or produce too marked a line of contrast*"(italics added for emphasis).

Stenciling is an appealing and popular way of decorating a surface whether it be a wall or a floor. Designs of this sort can be transferred to paper or directly to the surface itself. A small number of historical homes in America contain examples of such work, and the remnants are to be treasured and, if worn, carefully restored. For the most part, original stencil decoration was applied from the early to mid-nineteenth century, and not during the Colonial period. At that time, freehand painted decoration—murals, friezes—was more common. This took the place of prohibitively expensive imported Chinese and scenic papers. In the late nineteenth century, painted rather than stenciled decoration again became popular. Ironically, this was not because of its cheapness, but rather because artists could embellish structural details more lavishly with paint than could be done with paper. Even many Victorian home owners who could afford marble and fine woods chose instead to have walls marbleized and grained.

Paints

It is not economically feasible to reproduce paint chips in a book of this sort. Hopefully, the evocative names of many of the hues offered for sale in thousands of outlets across the country will be sufficient to stir up interest. There are many variations of such standard shades as Penn Red, Federal Blue, and Bayberry Green in the lexicon of paints appropriate for Colonial-style buildings; special colors for Victorian houses are much more limited, and their manufacture has not been systematized to any degree. Not even San Francisco claims to have a paint manufacturer specializing in Victorian colors. Some of the following listings, however, may provide leads in this regard.

These listings by no means exhaust the supply of manufacturers. Such firms as Devoe (Historic Charleston), Finnaren & Haley (Historic Philadelphia colors), Glidden-Durkee, Cohasset Colonials, Pittsburgh Paints, Martin-Senour (Williamsburg), and the Guild of Shaker Crafts are covered in the first Old House Catalogue. These are listed at the end of this chapter under "Paints" and the interested person can either contact the company directly or check with one of his area paint suppliers.

Munsell Color Notation System

Before choosing a period paint color, you may want to do some basic research on the colors used at different periods in your own home. As explained in the introduction, this can be a complicated and time-consuming procedure. But it is one of the aspects of old-house restoration which is most challenging and rewarding. Familiarity with and use of the Munsell Color notation system would be of great help. Samples found throughout the house can be compared with the chips found in the Munsell Book of Color available in either glossy finish ($400) or matte finish ($325). The book is made up of 40 constant hue charts bound in 2 ring binders and the chips are removable. With the proper color codes noted (each hue is given its own color notation), a painter (or you yourself) can have proper paints mixed.

For those of us who neither need nor want to make such a large investment, Munsell can provide custom color standards when one submits a sample to them. The cost of this technical service varies and fees are quoted on request.

Brochure available.

Munsell Color
2441 N. Calvert St.
Baltimore, Md. 21218
(301) 243-2171

Old-Fashioned Milk Paints

Milk paint has been made for hundreds of years and may have been applied in your house in the eighteenth or nineteenth century. It is available again today from the Old-Fashioned Milk Paint Co. There are eight colors—Barn Red, Pumpkin, Mustard, Bayberry, Lexington Green, Soldier Blue, Oyster White, and Pitch Black—available in pints, quarts, or gallons. These are powdered paints made from milk products and mineral fillers to which water will have to be added. The paints are most often used for furniture and adhere especially well to wood surfaces, but they can be used for plaster walls as well. The makers suggest that a linseed or lemon oil be used lightly over the surface after painting, a procedure which will give depth and eliminate any chalky look.

Brochure and color card available.

The Old-Fashioned Milk Paint Co.
Box 222
Groton, Mass. 01450
(617) 448-6336

Fuller-O'Brien has a full range of historical colors appropriate for Colonial or Victorian-style homes in the East, South, Middle West, or West, and these are included in what is known as the "Heritage Color Collection." Their paints are especially popular in the San Francisco area. The "Colonial" colors do not differ significantly from those available from other companies, but among the later period shades are Santa Fe Tan, Arizona Tan, Oregon Pass, Sutter's Mill, Prairie, and Yankee Gold—all variations on earthy browns; Donner Pass, Iron Kettle, Pony Express, and Gold Rush—subtle grays; and Spanish Pink and Colony Buff—soft pink browns. Despite their "Western"-sounding names, such shades might well be appropriate for Victorian exteriors or interiors wherever they may be found.

The company has a number of brochures available on its products. That on the "Heritage Color Collection" includes color chips and is free. There are more ambitious decorating guides which also may be ordered for a nominal cost. For further information, contact the nearest office of The O'Brien Corporation:

450 East Grand Ave.
South San Francisco, Calif. 94080

2001 West Washington Ave.
South Bend, Ind. 46634

P.O. Box 864
Brunswick, Ga. 31520

Ox-Line

Ox-Line colors are of the vibrant sort favored by many decorators working in a contemporary vein; some are quite appropriate for period uses. These are deep, rich colors available in low lustre, semi-gloss, and high-gloss finishes in latex. In many ways, they reproduce the look of early lead-based oils. Among the colors possible for interior use are Old Pewter, Oyster White, Pongee, Williamsburg Red, Beaver Brown, True Blue, and Yew Green.

Brochure available with color chips.

Ox-Line
Lehman Bros. Corp.
115 Jackson Ave.
Jersey City, N.J. 07304
(201) 434-1882

Turco

Turco's line of buttermilk paints are already mixed with water. There are eight colors to choose from—a mixing white, Raw Muslin, Blueberry, Brick Dust, Azurite, Green Olive, Golden Ochre, and Raw Umber. These are suitable for furniture or structural purposes, although, as with any milk-based paint, adhesion may be a problem unless the surface is properly prepared. The company's oil base finish, lead-free paints are extremely handsome mixtures. Their use, along with the buttermilk, is suitable only for Colonial period sytles. There are two basic lines—"Old Sturbridge" reproduction colors and "Old Colonial." Both offer superb quality and value.

Free brochures with color chips.

Turco Coatings Incorporated
Wheatland & Mellon Sts.
Phoenixville, Penn. 19460
(215) 933-7758

Pratt & Lambert

Pratt & Lambert's "Calibrated Color" system may yield just the right shade for a mid- to late-Victorian period interior. The firm's "Permalize" house and trim finish line can also be "calibrated" to furnish you with a proper exterior paint. There are eight hundred and eighty colors available for almost every possible kind of use. Historic Denver, the nation's largest community preservation group, has used Pratt & Lambert paints for some of their preservation projects.

Literature available from local dealers, or contact:

Pratt & Lambert
625 Washington
Carlstadt, N.J. 07072
(201) 935-6200

Stains/Varnishes

Staining would seem to be a simple matter—even more so than painting—but proper work requires knowledge of woods and of suitable shades for historical structures. The use of a stain and/or varnish is to enhance and protect the natural qualities of the material and not to hide its imperfections or disguise its inferiority. Nothing seems worse than the application of dark oak and mahogany stains on pine, even though you may discover that "it was done in the past." Mistakes were made then, too. The Victorians were especially good at imitating various grains. It is a mistake, however, to consider the second half of the nineteenth century as one of gloomy, dark coloring. Oak may not be your favorite wood, but it can have a true golden glow to it. Mahogany and rosewood should be prized for their durability and natural beauty. Anyone fortunate enough to live in a home containing redwood will appreciate its extraordinary strength; it is almost impervious to disease. But all woods have to be cared for and given some sort of protective coating. This may be merely a stain such as a weathering oil, often used with cedar. Oiling and then waxing wood is one of the earliest known procedures for preservation. It can work as well on walls as it does on flooring. Regular stains, however, will still be necessary for at least touch-ups and for replacement woods.

California Redwood

The California Redwood Association has prepared a very useful data sheet (number 4B1-1) on redwood exterior finishes—from bleaching oil to paint to light-bodied stains. Paint, of course, is the most commonly used finish for period houses of the sort found up and down the West Coast. But there is no reason why stains of a soft effect can not be as successfully used as period paint colors. The Association also has available two other data sheets entitled "Brand List of Redwood Exterior Finishes" (4B1-2) and "Redwood Interior Finishes" (4B2-1).

California Redwood Association
617 Montgomery St.
San Francisco, Calif. 94111

Cabot

Cabot stains are known for their quality. The "Old Virginia Tints," solid color stains, are particularly useful products for the period home. These oil-base finishes were developed originally for use on shingles and shakes but are just as appropriate and effective with siding, clapboards, and other rough-sawed wood. There are some extremely attractive shades available— Cavalier Gray, Sequoia Red, Powhattan Red, Spruce Blue, Highland Rose, Sagebrush Gray, Coast Guard Gray, Cordovan Brown—which would melt the heart of the preservation purist. Such stains can be used over previously painted surfaces and, according to the manufacturer, will provide much more protection than a similar color paint. There are, of course, other Cabot stains, including the three-in-one stain wax, the stain wax, the transparent stain, and semi-transparent and creosote stains.

Brochures with color samples available.

Samuel Cabot, Inc.
1 Union St.
Boston, Mass. 02108
(617) 723-7740

Martin-Senour

Martin-Senour also produces full-color exterior wood stains which find use on period structures. Their alkyd stains are preferable to those of latex for use on siding because of greater durability.

Brochure on exterior wood stains available from local dealers.

Martin-Senour Co.
1370 Ontario Ave., N.W.
Cleveland, Ohio 44113
(216) 566-3140

Turco

Turco supplies paste wood stains and a clear paste varnish for interior use, especially for furniture. The stains are available in eight wood shades which closely approximate those found in aged lumber. None give that glossy polyurethane look which can spoil even the best reproduction and destroy an antique.

Card with samples available.

Turco Coatings, Inc.

Wheatland & Mellon Streets
Phoenixville, Penn. 19460
(215) 033-7758

Painted Decoration/Stenciling

Freehand decoration has become immensely popular in recent years. Much of it, unfortunately, is badly executed. It is neither inventive nor striking, but rather smacks of cuteness. Stencil patterns are often similarly cliché "artistic" touches. No amount of new decoration of this sort can possibly make up for sagging floors, weakened walls, or just plain ugly woodwork. New painted decoration of any sort should be used sparingly—even in Victorian homes where ceilings, cornices, and walls may have sported festoons of flowers and prancing nymphs. In the eighteenth century and earlier, wall murals and designs painted on floors often took the place of more expensive papers and carpets. If these have survived over the years, they have acquired a mellow patina of age. Their preservation is important and requires the services of a true art conservator. Stenciled patterns of the early to mid-nineteenth century may have also acquired antique status. There are experts on the proper handling of such motifs, a few of which are listed below. Wall and ceiling decoration of the late-Victorian period should also command respect, and there are those who can touch it up, repaint lost motifs, and give it a new lease on a longer life with the use of modern materials.

Stenciled Interiors

Sandra Tarbox is a Connecticut artist and expert on American stenciling. Both original stencil designs suited to the fancy of a home owner or one of a number of historically faithful patterns can be applied to any area of the house where they are deemed appropriate. Frescoes and fireboards are also included in her specialized work.

Ms. Tarbox's modus operandi, according to a recent issue of *American Preservation*, does not differ that much from the itinerant artists of the nineteenth century: "I get a call from someone working on a restoration project. I go. I stay until I'm finished. . . . The people pay me room and board and a pittance, and then I leave."

The cost is only $2 to $5 a foot, not very much for an artist who has studied her subject with as much care as has this one.

Brochure available, 50¢.

Stenciled Interiors
Hinman Lane
Southbury, Conn. 06488
(203) 264-8000

Megan Parry

Megan Parry is another such dedicated person. She has written a book, *Stenciling* (Van Nostrand Reinhold, 1977, $12.95) which handsomely documents her skill and knowledge. Many of her designs are modern and not suitable for period interiors, but she is perfectly capable of working in a traditional manner with documented patterns. And she is willing to travel. She will also provide material for the homebody who wants to do it himself.

Catalog of designs and price list, $1.

Megan Parry
1727 Spruce
Boulder, Colo. 80302
(303) 444-2724

Stencil Specialty Co.

For the home craftsman/artist who has the ability to execute fine work, there are some basic tools which will come in handy for the purpose of wood graining. These are rollers, combs, and grainers of good construction. Also available from the Stencil Specialty Co. are pouncing wheels which are useful to cut stencil patterns.

Literature available.

Stencil Specialty Co.
377 Ocean Ave.
Jersey City, N.J. 07305
(201) 333-3634

D. B. Wiggins

D. B. Wiggins is an itinerant artist who will paint, plaster, and stencil period interiors. Jack-of-all-trades of this sort were common in the glory days of stenciling. He works by day or by contract.

D. B. Wiggins
Hale Rd.
Tilton, N.H. 03276
(603) 286-3046

Thomas Bisesti

Tom Bisesti is a talented and enthusiastic painter of murals. He both restores and executes elaborate designs. Most of his work has been done in Victorian-period dwellings, and he enjoys working in tempera or in oil. New work may be done directly on plaster or on canvas which is then glued to a surface. European craftsmen who executed such painting in the late nineteenth century have long since disappeared from the scene. It is good to know that their skills have not been lost completely.

Thomas A. Bisesti
409 Oakland St.
Springfield, Mass. 01108
(413) 739-4583

Papers

Thanks to technology introduced in the mid-1800s, wallpapers of an almost infinite variety have been produced over the past 130 years. The quality of these papers has varied greatly as has their price. Simple designs produced on high-speed presses are much less expensive than the hand-screened or blocked prints. Every extra bit of handwork means that much more in labor costs. In-between in price are the papers which are run on smaller presses and involve three or four colors and more subtle designs than those printed on high-speed equipment. More time can be taken on a slower press to check color registration and proper inking.

As has been mentioned earlier, wallpapers were scarce in Colonial times because most had to be imported. This is not to say that Colonial-style homes built at a later time did not make use of such materials—imported or domestically-produced. With the end of the Revolution, the trade in fine papers from England and France steadily increased. By the mid-nineteenth century, domestically-produced papers were to be found in many American homes. Most were run off on steam-powered presses with cylinders carrying raised printing surfaces. This machinery was improved almost every year, and, in the last decades of the nineteenth century, wallpaper was being used for everything from ceilings to baseboards. To redecorate then was to repaper.

Manufacturers of fine reproduction papers and of designs appropriate for period interiors are not difficult to find. Even the papers produced by such firms as Schumacher, Scalamandré, and Brunschwig & Fils, which are sold primarily through interior designers, can be found in the decorating departments of major department stores, and good paint and building supply outlets will offer a good supply of pattern books which can be consulted. The problem, once again, is one of selection, and even the most experienced interior designer will admit to having difficulty from time to time on this score. There is so much that is offered and worthy of

consideration. Only if you are seeking to duplicate an antique paper will you find that your choices are limited. There are at least a thousand such documented papers available, and one of these might perfectly match the one you are seeking. If not, your only alternative will have to be custom work, an assignment that any one of several firms will be glad to undertake for a set minimum amount of material. The cost, of course, will be terribly high.

Exact reproductions of antique papers are usually commissioned only by museums or historical home associations. There is no reason why we cannot also use them if they are indeed appropriate for our purposes, and a number of manufacturers have been licensed to produce historically-accurate papers. Some of these are noted in the following listings. But don't forget the more common "undocumented" papers or adaptations of traditional designs. Whether they will "work" or not depends entirely on their intrinsic quality and suitability.

Producers of wallpapers and some of their designs that may serve your needs—documented or not—are given in alphabetical order.

Laura Ashley, Inc.

This is a firm based in Carno, Wales, which is known for its textiles. It is now planning to open an outlet in New York which will offer wallpapers as well. The traditional designs are simple country-style geometrics and florals. Colors are soft and pleasing.

Laura Ashley, Inc.
714 Madison Ave.
New York, N.Y. 10021

Bassett & Vollum, Inc.

George M. Funke is a talented antiquarian and craftsman who has done much to bring Galena, Illinois, alive with the spirit that it knew in the days of its most famous citizen—Ulysses S. Grant. His home, "Orrin-Smith," is open for private tours by prearrangement, and it is here that some fine papers and other antique materials are on display. Illustrated are three rooms from the house.

Bassett & Vollum once acted as the United States representative of a prestigious French wallpaper firm that was forced to destroy its wood blocks during the Second World War and afterward did not resume operation. The American distributor was given permission, however, to reproduce the French papers, and the bedroom pictured here contains a Louis Philippe design border which was part of the original collection. The striped paper is one of Funke's original designs which blends handsomely with the border.

The walls of a small front parlor or reception room are covered with another of Funke's designs, and it is called, naturally, "Medal of Honor," since the primary design element is a repeating design of Napoleonic medals. The third room—the drawing room—is papered with a border frieze, side wallpaper, and base in a reproduction of an original hand-blocked document found in Versailles, France. The original design is thought to date from 1840–50, and that of the unusual frieze features an American Indian chief with full headdress.

Bassett & Vollum, Inc.
217 N. Main St.
Galena, Ill. 61036
(815) 777-2460

Brunschwig & Fils

Brunschwig & Fils has supplied some of the leading museums in the country with the best in reproduction wallpapers. These are manufactured overseas and are among the higher-priced papers available for period restorations. Sometimes, however, there is no possible substitute for precisely rendered reproduction work.

"Reveillon Tulips" (#1159.06) is a reproduction of an eighteenth-century block-printed design from the French workshop of Reveillon. It is now available as a screen print in the original reds and greens on blue. There are also four other color combinations or "colorways" available. A high-style design of exceptional beauty, it would be appropriate for a similarly sumptuous Georgian-period town house or country mansion.

"Maize" (#1139.06) is a mannered, but naturalistic, design which features corn ears, tassels, and the swan of the Empress Josephine. The reproduction has been made from an early nineteenth-century French block-printed document and was originally colored in shades of gray or *grisaille*. Four other color combinations are available. This is a simply superb paper for a Federal or Adams-style American interior of elegant restraint and lines.

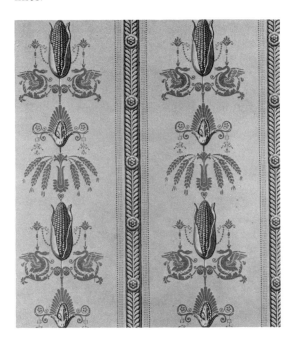

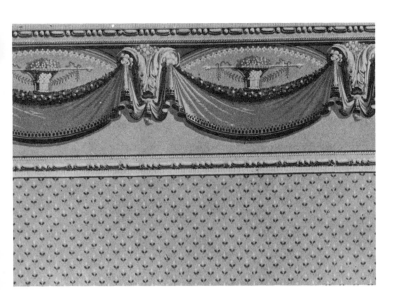

Another well-chosen design for a late eighteenth and early nineteenth-century interior would be the "Alexandria Frieze and Side Wall" (#1151.06). The term "side wall" is used to describe the larger section of paper below the cornice frieze. The original colors are a

striking blue and white; five other combinations have also been printed. The side wall has an accompanying border that can be used as a simple stripe, as a dado, or to frame a door.

Owners of Victorian homes will welcome the "Bosphore Border" and companion side wall of scattered pink clover (#1154.06 for border, #1153.06 for "Bosphore Semis" side wall). The original red and green block-printed border of knotted swags, fringe, and tassels is brilliantly colored in the Napoleon III style, c. 1870, and so is the reproduction. A smaller border of tassel fringe (#1155.06) may also be ordered.

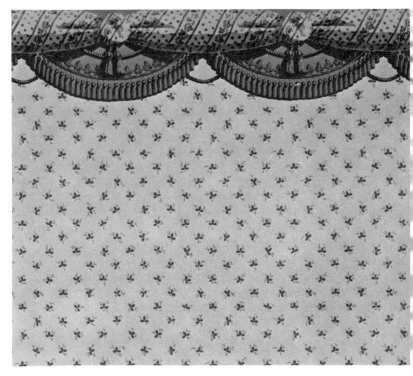

For further information regarding Brunschwig & Fils papers, see Appendix A and B, or contact:

Brunschwig & Fils, Inc.
979 Third Ave.
New York, N.Y. 10022
(212) 838-7878

Cole & Son

This firm is one of the imaginative English manufacturers of late nineteenth-century designs—a very high period, indeed, in wallpaper design. They are able to reproduce these designs from original blocks.

Cole has traditionally supplied dignified, tasteful wallpapers a bit less frenzied than those designed by

William Morris and his colleagues. This company is a superb source for borders and friezes of a delicate sort. A splendid example of a satin-ribbon border is seen in the frontispiece photograph to this section on paints and papers. Cole also produces gold and white borders appropriate for Greek Revival interiors, trompe l'oeil borders, and quite exprensive hand-painted borders of wild English flowers such as "Wild Rose" and "Rose & Pansy."

Cole and Son (Wallpapers), Ltd.
P.O. Box 4BU
18 Mortimer St.
London W1A 4BU
England

S. M. Hexter

The kind of research necessary to produce historically-accurate reproduction papers has been diligently and imaginatively done by the staff at Hexter. Some of their papers are based on documents at the Henry Ford Museum and Greenfield Village; others are adapted from designs found in Europe and the Far East.

Many of the earliest papers brought to America incorporated designs from the Far East. "Calcutta" and "Ceylon" are two companion designs included in Hexter's "West Winds Collection" of wall coverings and related fabrics. "Ceylon" is seen to the left with "Calcutta" on the right and lower left wall. These papers are pre-trimmed, pre-pasted, and strippable vinyl and are available in four colors—brick, yellow, sunset, and blue-peach.

Two other highly decorative papers of Far Eastern design origin are the "Balinesian Garden" and "Balinesian Wave"; the former is also seen in a companion fabric while the Wave is well-suited for border use. Both designs are produced in blue/beige, taupe, green, and "sunrise."

Hexter has showrooms in New York, Atlanta, Boston, Chicago, Cincinnati, Dallas, Denver, Detroit, Honolulu, Los Angeles, Miami, Minneapolis, Philadelphia, Phoenix, Portland, San Francisco, Seattle, St. Louis, Toronto, and London, England, or may be contacted at:

S. M. Hexter Co.
2800 Superior Ave.
Cleveland, Ohio 44114
(216) 696-0146

Jones & Erwin

"American Fancy" will delight anyone who admires the quality of early stencil designs. This is a copy of an early wallpaper removed from an abandoned house in Maine. The original color is blue on white; the reproduction paper comes in seven other colorings as well.

The company produces good copies of William Morris prints. Seen at left is "Poppy," c. 1881; center, "Bruges," c. 1888; and right, "Sunflower," c. 1879.

"Portsmouth Pineapple" has been named in honor of the carved pineapple design to be found on doorways in that old New Hampshire city. A copy of the original paper, c. 1810, was found on a hatbox. (Objects of this sort were often covered in papers). Its vigor and strong colors (rust-pink pineapples and dark green leaves on a blue-green background) is evidence that not all early nineteenth-century designs were of a restrained neo-classical sort. Jones & Erwin has copied the document in its original colors and in five other combinations.

Jones & Erwin, Inc.
232 E. 59th St.
New York, N.Y. 10022
(212) 759-3706

Open Pacific Graphics

Open Pacific Graphics is an innovative restoration and custom wallpaper firm that has supplied materials for historical projects in British Columbia and California and in private homes. Their 150 designs—dating from 1860 to 1910—are reproduced by the silk screen process and are available in rolls of 36 square feet which are usually produced 20″ wide x 20′ long. Prices for these range from $20 (for one color) to $60 a roll (for eight colors); an exceptional bargain, we think, for Victorian-period papers. They are not vinyl, but may be given a protective finish. And they are not pre-pasted but must be hung in the traditional manner.

A similar swirled design, but one that suggests stenciling, is that illustrated below and used in the Hale House restoration, Los Angeles. It is called "Palm."

Reproduction Art Nouveau wallpaper designs are extremely difficult to find, but Open Pacific Graphics offers this example and others.

More traditional Victorian papers are the "Craigflower Manor," c. 1860, seen at left, and a floral panel with roses and decorative oval, seen at right.

Sample patterns sent on request; full sample book, $40.

Open Pacific Graphics
#43 Market Square
Victoria, British Columbia
Canada
(604) 388-5233

Reed "Early American Homes"

Documented papers from American homes dating from 1707 to 1880 form the basis of the Reed, Ltd. collection. Most of these are of English or French origin and many reflect the taste of the wealthy.

The building that served as Washington's Headquarters at Valley Forge is a simple, sober fieldstone building typical of those to be found in rural areas of the Delaware Valley. It is by no means a mansion and has been sparely furnished by curators of the National Park Service. The upstairs sitting room, used by Martha Washington when she visited the camp, is papered with a simple design featuring sprigs of greenery in diamond outlines on a vellum ground. It is a pleasant and airy design for such a cold, sparse interior.

The Faulkner House in Acton, Massachusetts, is a 1707 Colonial of traditional style and was once part of a complex of mills and farmland. It is a rather grand house for its time, and in the mid-eighteenth century the bed chamber over the garrison room was papered in an English hand-block design featuring connecting medallions of classical figures in charcoal and white on a stone-grey ground. This has been expertly reproduced

by Reed from samples. The same paper was also originally used in the House of Seven Gables, Salem.

The entire "Early American Homes" line has been researched and documented by Charles S. Freeman, A.S.I.D.

The complete line of historic papers is fully illustrated in a booklet, "Early American Homes," $4.50; the firm also has available a free brochure.

Reed Wallcoverings
550 Pharr Rd.
Atlanta, Ga. 30318
(404) 873-6363

Sanderson and Sons, Ltd.

This firm is yet another English manufacturer of Victorian and Edwardian papers, and probably the best known of all. Papers can be printed from the original blocks used in the past, and, therefore, are really much more than "reproductions."

Sanderson and Sons is *the* source for Morris papers, most of which are available in at least two color combinations. Among the designs of William and May Morris are: "Chrysanthemum," "Horn Poppy," "Bruges," "Bachelor's Button," "Sunflower," "Fritillary," "Net," "Willow," "Poppy," "Borage," "Pink and Rose," "Bird and Anemone," 'Marigold," and Honeysuckle." Sanderson can also supply an earlier design by Owen Jones, "Ewan," and such early twentieth-century patterns as "Teazel" designed by C. F. A. Voysey, and a deco paper, "Decco-Nova," adapted from a design by William Odell.

All of these papers are part of the "Heritage Collection" and are hand-printed. They must be hand-trimmed before hanging.

Arthur Sanderson & Sons, Ltd.
Berners St.
London W1A 2JE
England

Saxon Paint and Home Care Centers

Wallpapers designed for use in Adler & Sullivan's great 1887 Auditorium Theater in Chicago were reproduced several years ago in a limited run of 400 bolts. Each bolt is equal to 1½ rolls or 49 square feet; this measures out to 7 running yards by a 28-inch width.

The two geometric papers which reflect so superbly the architectural firm's mastery of structural form are "Spi-

ral" and "Oak Leaf." All proceeds from their sale are donated to the Illinois Arts Council Foundation.

For further information regarding availability of the papers, write:

ArchiCenter
111 South Dearborn
Chicago, Ill. 60603
(312) 782-1776

Scalamandré

Scalamandré has more than earned its reputation as the premier American supplier of quality documented papers for museums, historical associations, and private individuals who have had the foresight and good fortune to invest in what is a complex and expensive restoration undertaking. Scalamandré, as with some other high-quality manufacturers, sells only through interior designers and decorating departments in major retail outlets. In this respect, the reader will find the appendixes concerning these two areas particularly helpful if trying to track down Scalamandre materials.

The firm has recently introduced its Historic Savannah Collection of papers and fabrics. These date from the first half of the nineteenth century and considerably enlarge Scalamandré's offerings in post-Colonial period styles. "Savannah Fleur de Lis" is just one of the papers and is an interpretation of the French symbol. The document was found in Savannah, but the design was originally used in the Vander Horst House, Kiawah Island, South Carolina.

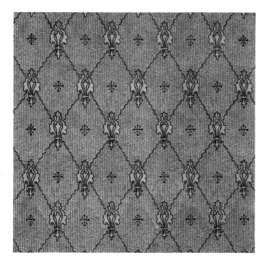

The Werms House is one of Savannah's best, and it is here that this elegant border (#81087) with floral sprigs was found. It has been reproduced just as it was. A coordinating fabric (#6428) transposes the same small groups of flowers into an allover pattern with a stripe motif.

Papers made for the recent restoration of the Barton House (Ranching Heritage Center) at Texas Tech University in Lubbock amply illustrate the variety of Victorian materials that Scalamandré has available. Only in the past ten years have wallpaper manufacturers given serious study to the later Victorian period, and their work in documenting eighteenth- and early nineteenth-century papers has provided them with the research know-how and tools for technical analysis which are a necessity for accurate reproduction. Illustrated in the order of their appearance are: #8115-1, a floral botanical design in shades of purple and green against a brown striped ground which has the appearance of stenciling; #8110-1, soft pink and white morning glories with white flowers and vines in shades of green against either light beige or resist areas of silver; #81104-1, a remarkably heavy Art Nouveau design in two shades of brown which gives the appearance of a Japanese "leather paper."

Information regarding prices and availability of papers is best secured from interior design firms or decorating departments of major stores listed in Appendix B. If further information is needed, contact:

*Scalamandré
950 Third Ave.
New York, N.Y. 10022
(212) 361-8500*

F. Schumacher

Schumacher offers considerable variety to the consumer—both in price and in design. Although best known for its textiles, the firm has available striking and useful papers. One of these was used on the cover of the first *Old House Catalogue* and requests for information about it were received by this writer. It is a simple, inexpensive print (#2825) known as "Amherst" and is part of the Mayflower Legacy Collection II. It is available in several colors, barn red being one of the most suitable for Colonial-style interiors.

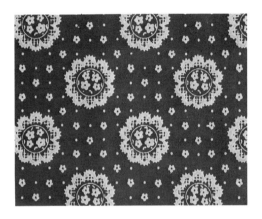

"Truro" is another simple print (#2852) which might be used to handsome effect in a foyer, stairwell, or other small area. It is from the Gramercy Park Collection VIII and can be found in an ultramarine ground with red and white flowers. Both this paper and "Amherst" can be ordered through any well-equipped paint and paper store.

"French Damask" (Side wall #555-161, Group B) is a Warner Wallcovering available through Schumacher and is part of The Art Institute of Chicago Collection. It is pre-pasted and has a vinyl acrylic coating. Papers based on damask designs were used for many, many years to simulate high-style fashion.

"Chrysanthemum" (#5309A) is from the Pierre Frey Collection, Paris, and is a particularly suitable paper for homes of the 1880s and '90s which may have been influenced by what was known as the "Anglo-Japanese" style. This is a much more regular design than many produced at the time, but it is typical of the naturalistic Oriental exuberance which was translated in both fabrics and papers. Schumacher also manufactures a 100% cotton glazed fabric of the same design.

For further information regarding Schumacher papers, you may contact your local wallpaper outlet, a design firm or department, or Schumacher itself.

*F. Schumacher & Co.
939 Third Ave.
New York, N.Y. 10022
(212) 644-5900*

Thomas Strahan Company

The Strahan firm will soon be celebrating 100 years of fine craftsmanship. Since the beginning, the emphasis has been on reproduction of traditional American wall coverings. Since the company is located in the Boston area, there is a definite New England flavor to its products which in no way detracts from their usefulness in other parts of the country.

"Ipswich" was uncovered when the Ross House of Ipswich, Massachusetts, was torn down in 1933. The original was probably a French paper and it depicts America, in the figure of Washington, celebrating the victory over the British in the Revolution; Britannia weeps at left.

The "Samuel Sargent Chintz" comes from the Sargent-Robinson Homestead in Gloucester, Massachusetts. Although the house itself dates from c. 1690, the paper was probably first used in the mid-eighteenth century.

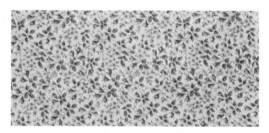

An old Newport, Rhode Island, mansion once used by Washington as headquarters contained this scenic paper. It is known as "Rochambeau" because Washington received the French military commander at this spot in July of 1780. The vignettes are thought to be of Spanish strolling players, the forerunners of modern circus performers.

Strahan papers are widely available through dealers across the country.

Thomas Strahan Co.
121 Webster Ave.
Chelsea, Mass. 02150
(617) 884-6220

Albert Van Luit & Co.

The Van Luit papers are exceptionally luxurious renderings of high-style designs. Many of these are of Oriental inspiration and could be suitable for late Victorian interiors. Other wall coverings are more traditional patterns which originated in eighteenth-century France or England.

"Campagne" is a scenic paper, a pleasant pastoral of the sort that became popular in the second half of the eighteenth-century and again during the Colonial Revival period of 1890–1930. Scenics, as they are called, are most often used in an entrance hall or in a dining room where they will not be hidden by heavy furniture.

A silk wall covering at the Palace of Versailles provided the inspiration for this fanciful pattern. A few extremely well-off Colonists may have used watered silks on their walls; most people turned to papers which cost a great deal less.

"Indienne" is a copy of a printed cotton imported by one of the East India companies in the eighteenth century. Here it is seen used in a contemporary kitchen, and it greatly softens the starkly modern and utilitarian lines. Certainly it could be used in other areas of almost any period house—with restraint. As is apparent, a little goes a long way.

Van Luit wall coverings are available from retailers and interior designers from coast to coast.

Various catalogs available, each 50¢.

Albert Van Luit & Co.
4000 Chevy Chase Dr.
Los Angeles, Calif. 90039
(213) 245-5106

Watts & Co.

This English firm is best known for its ecclesiastical furnishings, but according to *The Times* of London, they "also have a marvelous collection of Victorian designs for wallpaper and fabric, which are still printed by hand from the original carved pear wood blocks." Some of these designs were created by architect Augustus Pugin and are in the best tradition of the Victorian Gothic revival style. Some of Pugin's designs, thought to be lost, were rediscovered in 1975 and added to the Watts selections.

"Pugin Triad" is one of the rediscovered papers, a very felicitous composition which was recently used in a Victorian arts exhibition held at the Delaware Art Museum. Papers are produced by using specially-mixed colors which are then blocked on to the paper by hand and allowed to dry naturally before proceeding with another blocking. The minimum order for any of the Watts papers is 10 rolls. A roll measures 11 yards long and 21" wide. Delivery (not including shipping) takes three months from receipt of order.

The patterns "Birds" and "Pear" appear to be just as imaginative as those of William Morris. Such extravagant compositions will have to be used with great care, but undoubtedly will dramatically set off any surface they adorn.

Brochure describing and showing available patterns, $2.

Watts & Co., Ltd.
7 Tufton St., Westminster
London, SW1P 3QB
England

SOLD UNDER GUARANTEE.
Composed of only the Most Costly and
Finest Materials.
ACTUAL COST LESS THAN $1.25 PER GAL.

Other Suppliers of Paints, Papers, and Stains

Consult the List of Suppliers for addresses.

Paints

Ameritone Paint
Cohasset Colonials
Devoe
Finnaren & Haley
Glidden-Durkee
Guild of Shaker Crafts
Janovic/Plaza
Kwal Paints
Maine Line Paints
Miss Kitty's Keeping Room Kolors
Benjamin Moore
Pittsburgh Paints
Sherwin-Williams

Stains and Varnishes

H. Behlen & Bros.
Cohasset Colonials
Gaston Wood Finishes
Glidden-Durkee

Painting, Decorating and Stenciling Services

Craftswomen
Pamela S. Friend
John L. Seekamp
Wall Stencils by Barbara
Roy Wingate

Papers

Birge Co.
Louis W. Bowen
Clarence House
Inez Croom
Jack Denst Designs
A. L. Diament
Katzenbach & Warren
Last's Paint & Wallpaper
Old Stone Mill
Nancy McClelland
Richard E. Thibaut
Waterhouse Wall Hangings

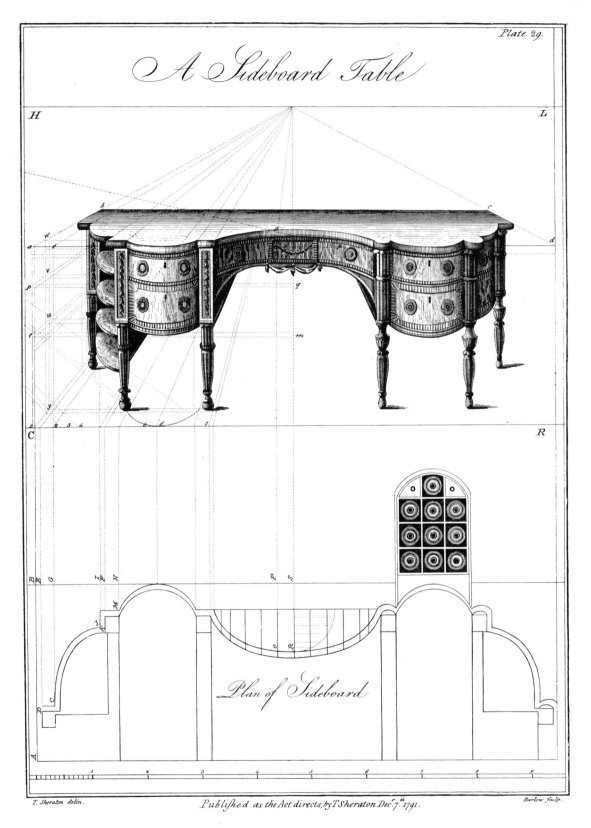

A Sideboard Table

Plate. 29.

Plan of Sideboard

T. Sheraton delin.

Published as the Act directs, by T. Sheraton Dec.ʳ 7.ᵗʰ 1791.

Barlow sculp.

Plate LVIII, Thomas Sheraton, *The Cabinet-Maker and Up-holsterer's Drawing-Book*, London, c. 1793.

IX Furniture

Proper and imaginative furnishing of any period interior—whether it be found in a house or apartment—requires the utmost in patience and resourcefulness. This is not merely a matter of decoration. Rather, it is an exercise in design, in bringing together utility and aesthetic appeal. The basic structural character of the space itself will determine to a large extent the kinds of furnishings that will be fitting. There is no sense, for example, in cramming a low-ceilinged salt box with massive high-style furniture. Similarly, a late-Victorian Queen Anne residence can look rather preposterous if filled with primitive pine pieces from the Colonial period.

Whatever period appearance is called for, the guiding rule in selection of furnishings must be quality. Objects should not only be useful ones, but those which are of sound construction and which make proper use of woods, fabrics, and metals. Furnishing an interior should not be a chance to "show-off" with spectacular effects but, rather, an opportunity to provide a pleasing space for living which appears natural or fitting. Very little furniture of modern making—whatever the period style—will meet these requirements, as they partake of a construction and finish which is singularly graceless and lacking in proper proportions. Mass-produced furniture is today, for the most part, a mere shadow of a more substantial past and carries only the veneer of age. It is stamped out in assembly-line fashion, and sugar-coated with stains, varnish, and even plastic lamination. The end result is schlock of the first order. This writer's objection is not to the use of furniture of modern manufacture per se, but to that which is produced and packaged in an inappropriate manner, and often at a higher cost than the antique. Whatever you buy should not only be of correct design (and this can be checked easily enough by referring to models available in books and museums), but hopefully be of antique "potential."

The same rules of preservation which apply to buildings are appropriate for furnishings of such dwellings. Therefore, it is to the antiques and used furniture markets that one should first turn for materials. This can be a lifelong search and a rewarding activity. By no means does such old furniture have to be more expensive than new. Great objects will always be the passion of the privileged investor/collector. Simpler pieces—of which there are millions to be found—can be added to family heirlooms at relatively low cost. Despite the current fad for the "antique," most Americans will continue to choose the new and shiny and throw out the old. For members of the old house counterculture, this sad situation is a happy one.

Let's face it; *all* kinds of furniture are expensive today. It may not be possible to completely furnish a home in "old" pieces of the same style. Indeed it may not be desirable to do so. Only model rooms in historic houses or museums may be frozen in a particular time frame. In the best of such institutions, there has been an attempt in recent years to introduce a feeling for the movement of time and style by mixing complementary but different pieces representative of two or three generations of people.

Furniture craftsmen are on the increase. These are cabinetmakers who understand and practice the fine art of designing, shaping, joining, and finishing graceful objects. Many work alone; others have joined together in workshops; a few form the backbone of such reproduction furniture firms as Baker and Kittinger. They are to be found everywhere in North America, and this section of *The Second Old House Catalogue* can only provide a tiny sampling of their products. These are experts and their time and the materials they work with are very valuable. Accordingly, the prices they must charge are high. The average old-house owner will use their services infrequently, especially if he has a good eye for antique or "used" furniture. For certain basic types of furniture which are given heavy use—beds, chairs, even tables—and for replacement reproductions which can not be found elsewhere, today's craftsmen provide a most useful service. Customers stung by the high price of the bill will at least have the comfort of knowing that they have bought something which will appreciate in value rather than deteriorate with age.

Beds

Comfortable and properly-sized antique beds are difficult to find. Nothing is worth a sleepless night spent in the throes of a constricting frame and lumpen mattress. There are dealers who specialize in old beds, and such objects can be restored if not remodeled. But it may not be worth the effort and expense required to adapt the past to present needs, especially if this means providing for several members of the household. Of all the pieces of furniture we live with, beds are the most physically used and abused. And since most of us are considerably larger than our ancestors, we may need to call on the services of reproduction craftsmen or manufacturers.

Brass Beds

The Bedpost offers a dazzling array of brass beds suitable for Victorian interiors, and most of them are available in the standard sizes. A double bed with headboard and footboard ranges in price from $444 to over $1,100. All are solid brass. Mattresses and box springs are not included. The firm will also custom design a king or queen-size bed in brass.

If you already have a brass bed and are looking for post caps, finials, cannonballs, or tubing, the Bedpost has quite a selection. Number 15 is $6.50; number 1 is $10.

Literature available.

The Bedpost
R.D. 1, Box 155
Pen Argyl, Penn. 18072
(215) 588-3824

The company has three retail outlets (in Montgomeryville, Zionsville, and Bangor, Penn., but all correspondence should be addressed to the Penn Argyl address.
dress.

Rope Beds

A tradition of furniture-making began with the founding of Bishop Hill, Illinois, in the 1840s. Swedish pietists settled on the edge of the prairie frontier and built a prosperous community on faith and hard work. At first, their handiwork reflected the simplicity of their religious observances. Unlike the Shakers, however, these new Americans found that some ornamentation made their work more saleable. The settlers were finally absorbed by the great All-American melting pot, but their tradition of good workmanship has been continued by craftsmen such as Lehlan Murray. He has been commissioned by the State of Illinois to make eight cannonball rope beds for the restoration of Bishop Hill's Bjorklund Hotel. A standard single mattress will fit its maple frame. The bed can be delivered to your door for $1,160.

Lehlan Murray
Box 18
Bishop Hill, Ill. 61419

168

"Rice Bed"

Historic Charleston Reproductions introduced its new "Rice Bed" in 1977, and it is made by Baker. It derives its name from the delicate carving of rice stalks on the posts, symbolizing the important place of the rice trade in eighteenth-century Charleston. Baker has faithfully reproduced this mahogany bed which was given as a gift to a new bride at Middleton Place House. It measures 64″ wide x 87¾″ deep x 91¾″ high and is available through select retail outlets. Be forewarned; it is expensive, and has to be.

Further information is available, along with a catalog, $4, from,

Historic Charleston Reproductions
51 Meeting St.
Charleston, S.C. 29401
(803) 723-1623

Field and Pencil-Post Beds

The influence of Thomas Sheraton was considerable at the turn of the eighteenth century. The turned posts of this field bed by the craftsmen from the Country Bed Shop are available in maple or cherry. Other options include a canopy frame, box spring brackets or rope, a variety of headboard styles, and varying sizes. The bed sells for $580 as illustrated here.

Country Bed Shop also offers a pencil-post bedstead of a style that made its appearance in the seventeenth century. Its fine, attenuated lines make it the utmost in simplicity. It is priced at $550 but is sold with a number of options such as four different lower post styles, which may raise the price.

Catalog available, $2.

Country Bed Shop
Box 222
Groton, Mass. 01450
(617) 448-6336

Low-Post Bed

Cabinetmaker Thomas Moser makes a low-post bed which is 33″ to the top of the headboard. As illustrated, it is a straightforward design of handsome proportions. The twin size (39″ wide x 74″ long) sells for $385; full size (54″ wide x 74″ long), $422; and queen, (60″ wide x 80″ long), $473. Rollers are an additional $20.

169

Catalog available, $2.

Thos. Moser, Cabinet Makers
Cobb's Bridge Road
New Gloucester, Maine 04260
(207) 926-4446

Chairs

When it comes to chairs, as with beds, there can be little compromise. We need solid, well-balanced, and comfortable objects on which to sit. Whether the activity is reading a book or dining, one wants to rest with ease and not with the fear of splintering underneath. Unfortunately, many antique chairs are not only unstable, they are downright backbreaking. Some may have been designed with shorter people or less bulk in mind. Antique chairs are to be preferred in the home if they do fulfill our real needs. Many can be reconditioned (joints strengthened, seats replaced, upholstery redone and even frames rebuilt), and every attempt should be made to reuse the old. But when your patience is at an end, consider turning to one of many fine reproduction chair makers. Some can also expertly reproduce a chair that is missing from a set.

Queen Anne Armchair

The ancestor of this Queen Anne armchair was made in Philadelphia in the mid-eighteenth century. Its ample seat and downward curving arms make it extremely comfortable. Master craftsman Robert Whitley has reproduced the original in every detail. This gifted artist has achieved considerable renown for his competence in the field. Many of his commissions have been to reproduce pieces for incomplete antique sets.

Brochure, $1.

The Robert Whitley Studio
Laurel Road
Solebury, Penn. 18963
(215) 297-8452

Ladder-Back Chair

Over 2,000 Appalachian craftsmen are represented and served by the non-profit Southern Highland Handicraft Guild. The organization maintains high quality standards and markets through its own merchandising program. This ladder-back chair is produced by a Guild craftsman who has lost none of his ancestral skills.

The Guild operates four retail stores—in Asheville and Blowing Rock, North Carolina, and Bristol, Virginia—where a wide variety of products are displayed. It also sponsors annual Craftsman's Fairs in Asheville, and Gatlinburg, Tennessee. For information on these outlets and the fairs, contact the Guild headquarters.

Brief literature available.

Southern Highland Handicraft Guild
P.O. Box 9545
Asheville, N.C. 28805
(704) 298-7928

Bow-Back and Pressback Chairs

Chairs suitable for use in the dining room or kitchen of a Victorian-period home are in the process of being "rediscovered." Some supply of real antiques is still available at moderate prices, and secondhand stores are a good place to start looking. If you are not successful, you might want to consider the many models produced by American Woodcarving.

The bow-back has retained its popularity through the years. An unfinished chair costs $43; finished, it sells for $55.

The more ornamental pressback features turned members and a carved back. You can get it for $86 unfinished or $106 for a finished piece.

Literature available.

American Woodcarving
282 San Jose Ave.
San Jose, Calif. 95125

Corset Back Armchair

The students and master craftsmen at Berea College must meet high standards of quality. They specialize in careful early American and Colonial reproductions. Each piece is made from select or better walnut, cherry, or mahogany.

The "Corset Back Armchair" is descended from the provincial French *chaise a capucine*, a simple open-back chair found in monastic dwellings in the seventeenth century. The seat is available in corn shuck or Sudan grass. The chair is priced at $235 in mahogany or walnut; $220 in cherry. Berea also produces an armless model of the same form which sells for $195 in cherry and $210 in mahogany or walnut.

Catalog available.

Berea College
Student Craft Industries
Berea, Ky. 40404
(609) 986-9341

Swivel Armchair

Unlike many mass-producers of furniture, Ephraim Marsh does not go in for atmospheric photographs and slick promotional copy. The company sells a full line of eighteenth and nineteenth-century style furniture at very reasonable prices. No one claims that they are "authentic" reproductions. But they are honest, and that is more important since only an antique can be authentic.

The swivel armchair could be found, at one time or another, in every office in the country. Now it's not as common, and, if you can't find such a desk chair in a secondhand store, Marsh can help you out. The seat height and reclining tension are adjustable. This one is $128.

Catalog available, $1.

Ephraim Marsh Co.
Box 266
Concord, N.C. 28025
(704) 782-0814

Continuous Armchair

Thomas Moser's "continuous armchair" is a comfort to sit in and a pleasure to view. The sturdy turned legs are made of rock maple and the spindles are white ash. The

continuous arm and leg supports are fashioned from cherry. Mechanical and design patents are pending on this unique chair—an antique for the future. It is sold for $240.

Catalog available, $2.

Thos. Moser, Cabinet Makers
Cobb's Bridge Rd.
New Gloucester, Maine 04260
(207) 926-4446

Morris Chair

This is William Morris's century-old response to what he thought was the shoddy machine-made furniture of his day. A lot of it *was* shoddy, but this isn't. The Morris chair is a solid and eminently functional reproduction from Greystone Upholstery, and available only from them. It is made of grained oak and available in five

different finishes. The back reclines to four different positions, and the standard upholstery is either a synthetic "homespun" or Naugahyde. Better yet, send them your own upholstery fabric and they will perform the work at no extra charge.

Flyer available.

Greystone Upholstery Corp.
502 Clewell St.
Fountain Hill, Penn. 18015
(215) 691-0140

Cafe Chair and M Chair

Michael Thonet is best remembered for his bentwood rocker (*see* section on rockers), but his greatest success came when he designed this cafe chair for the mass market. Since 1876 it has sold over 50 million copies. The only real change has been in the seat, which is now available in padded vinyl in addition to natural cane or veneer.

The Thonet firm is also responsible for the introduction of Mies van der Rohe's "M Chair" (c. 1930). One of the first to utilize the natural resilience of steel in furniture design, Mies's designs are as appropriate for homes of the 1920s or '30s as they are for the most contemporary apartment of today. These are designs which have become antique in the best sense of that word.

Further information regarding Thonet chairs may be supplied by designers and decorators. *See* list of AISD chapters, Appendix B.

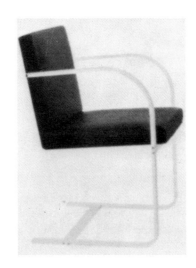

Rockers

The rocker provides a very simple human pleasure—sitting and gently moving to one's own rhythm. It is a homely pleasure, and one that has appealed to the down-home in all of us. Presidents—including Lincoln, Kennedy, and Carter—have enjoyed rocking away troubles. It is a movement from childhood and, often, of old age. No home is truly a castle without one of these chairs with curved runners. There are hundreds of varieties from the historic Boston rockers of the mid-nineteenth century to the weird contraptions on platforms invented by mad Victorians and updated in the twentieth century by kitsch purveyors. For our taste, the simpler the better. Be sure that what you get is sturdy; the pitching movement can create problems for the energetic of all ages.

Brumby Rocker

Jimmy Carter has made the Brumby rocker famous. Five new oak rockers were delivered to the White House last year and are finding good use on the Truman balcony. The chair has been around for over a century and is noted for its balance and superb rock. The handwoven seat and back make the rocker cool and comfortable. Carol Melson, whose husband revived the

Brumby works in 1972, is quoted in *The New York Times*: "Reproduction is not a term I would use. It's really a continuation of a broken production, a continuation from where they left off 30 years ago, using the same craftsmen, the same design and the same machines."

The demand is great for these new "antiques," but you may be able to convince the firm to make one for you—at $208—by contacting their retail outlet.

Literature available.

The Rocker Shop
1421 White Circle, N.W.
P.O. Box 12
Marietta, Ga. 30061
(404) 427-2618

Gliding Rocker

A more complicated rocker—a gliding one—is made by Ephraim Marsh. It moves on a platform in a smooth, easy fashion, and is less cumbersome than many of its Victorian cousins. The wood is maple, and the chair itself weighs 55 lbs. You won't want to move it around from room to room, but at least you'll know that it won't rock away.

Catalog available, $1.

Ephraim Marsh Co.
Box 266
Concord, N.C. 28025
(704) 782-0814

Goose Neck Rocker

Berea's craftsmen produce an unusual goose neck rocker with a caned seat. The spindles and front legs are turned, and the tall caned back is contoured. Back and seat are connected by downward sloping, looped arms. It sells for $465 in mahogany or walnut; $425 in cherry.

Catalog available.

Berea College
Student Craft Industries
Berea, Ky. 40404
(606) 986-9341

Bentwood Rocker

The bentwood rocker is perhaps the most elaborate expression of Michael Thonet's experiments with steam-bent beechwood. This is imported by Thonet and is available in several colors. It features a natural cane seat and back.

Further information regarding the Thonet rocker may be supplied by designers and decorators. *See* list of AISD chapters, Appendix B. Also refer to the listing for Cafe and M chairs for addresses of the company's showrooms.

Chests/Boxes

Long, low wooden chests are perfect for storing many things—from blankets to firewood. The fine antique pieces such as Pennsylvania-German decorated chests and the Pilgrim Century chests of New England have long since departed the common man's scene; these are now prized and priceless objects. Simple storage chests or boxes of nineteenth-century manufacture remain to be found, but because of their utility, the supply is diminishing rapidly. Some persons have turned to old trunks and cases as an alternative. As attractive as some of these containers may be, they really belong in a storage room and not at the foot of the bed or beside the hearth.

Wood Box

Guyon, Inc. makes a Pennsylvania wood box which is just over 4' wide and 22" high. It is not too big for other uses such as a toy box or hope chest. The box is made of pine appropriately enough and has a hinged lid at the top.

Literature available, $2.

Guyon, Inc.
65 Oak St.
Lititz, Penn. 17543
(717) 626-0225

Blanket Chest

This is a mahogany blanket chest which may someday become a treasured heirloom. Its builder, Craig Nutt, began his career restoring antiques and now recreates them with traditional techniques. The chest measures 30" x 18" x 18". Not only are the joints hand-dovetailed, but all the hardware—including lock and key—is made by hand.

Literature available.

Craig Nutt Fine Wood Works
2308 Sixth St.
Tuscaloosa, Ala. 35401
(205) 759-3142

Cupboards/Cabinets

As with chests, these useful pieces of furniture are being put up for sale one day and sold the next. When houses were without large closets, furniture of this sort was highly valued for practical purposes. Again today, with housing costs sky-rocketing and space at a premium, cupboards and cabinets are being viewed with a renewed interest. The antiques market should be searched diligently before turning to the reproduction craftsmen.

Storage Cupboard and Cabinet

At a height of 74″, this tin cupboard from Bittersweet can hold a lot of tin goods. Handcrafted of pine, all the joints are mortise and tenon to assure maximum strength.

Whether or not you preserve your own jams and jellies or put up other canned goods, you can probably find many uses for this handsome storage cabinet. It stands 45″ x 23″ x14″ and is made of pine.

Brochure available, 25¢.

Bittersweet
P.O. Box 5
Riverton, Vt. 05668
(802) 485-8562

Open Cupboard

Charles Thibeau of the Country Bed Shop has designed and will make this handmade open cupboard. It is a copy of an eighteenth-century New England piece. The cupboard measures 12″ x 32″ x 68″ and is fashioned from pine.

Catalog available, $2.

Country Bed Shop
Box 222
Groton, Mass. 01450
(617) 448-6336

Pie Safe

Pie safes are "hot items" in the country antiques market these days, and you will be lucky to find one at all. If you don't want to take time to search for the absolutely real thing, Old Timey Furniture Co. can help you. It would take a good day or two to fill this pie safe with fresh baked goods, and a big, hungry family to empty it. But, then, it is also useful—with punched tin paneled doors for ventilation—for preserves and canned goods. The wood is pine. The measurements are 78" x 36" x 13".

Literature available, $1.50.

Old Timey Furniture Co.
Smithfield, N.C. 27577
(919) 965-6555

Tables

The need for a table becomes evident when you reach out in thin air to deposit a book or are left holding a precarious dinner plate at an informal buffet supper. No one seems to have enough tables, at least of the right size. Purchase of something as large as a reproduction dining table or even one for the kitchen is not strongly recommended. A trestle table is included in the listings; the price of this sort of primitive piece has become prohibitive in the antiques market. Most kinds of tables, however, can be purchased more cheaply "used" than new. You wouldn't want to disgrace your dining room with one of the period "sets" manufactured by hundreds of second-rate concerns that claim to produce authentic reproductions. For the most part, these are clunky designs which are fashioned from nameless woods. Only the brand name of the plastic lamination used on the top is announced with pride.

But there are good reproductions of smaller pieces for those who need them.

Lyre Table

Magnolia Hall is renowned for Victorian reproduction furniture. The two-drawer mahogany lyre table, shown here, is claimed to be the manufacturer's best-selling end table. It has a carved lyre base and an urn on the stretcher. The marble top is 18" x 14". It sells for $189.95. Have you priced the real thing lately? If so, you may decide to shop down South.

Subscription to three illustrated catalogs published each year, $1.

Magnolia Hall
726 Andover
Atlanta, Ga. 30327
(404) 256-4747

End Table

Lehlan Murray of the Bishop Hill restoration in Illinois has fashioned this simple table of white spruce. It can be delivered to you for $200. It would be suitable for use almost anywhere in the house.

Lehlan Murray
Box 18
Bishop Hill, Ill. 61419

Side Table

Brian Considine draws many of his design ideas from Shaker sources. The inspiration for this side table in

maple and pine, a common combination of woods, is a Shaker prototype. Considine also makes a similar table with turned legs. The measurements of the top are 24″ x 19″.

Literature available.

Brian Considine, Cabinet Maker
Post Mills, Vt. 05058

Candlestand

This cherry candlestand or "round stand" is a particularly fine rendition from The Guild of Shaker Crafts. It

is just a shade over 2′ tall; the top's diameter is 16″. Used alongside an easy chair, it will easily carry a small lamp. You can, of course, use it simply with a candlestick. The price is $65.

Catalog available, $2.50.

Guild of Shaker Crafts
401 W. Savidge
Spring Lake, Mich. 49456
(616) 846-2870

Pie-Crust Table

A Philadelphia Chippendale pie-crust table is a valuable antique; Craig Nutt makes a very fine reproduction. A table of this sort was found only in the most elegant home and was used for the serving of tea. The reproduction's carved mahogany top tilts and revolves on a "birdcage" mechanism and is supported by a claw-footed tripod. This 28½″ diameter table sells for $700

but its size, and presumably its price, can be scaled down if requested.

Literature available.

Craig Nutt Fine Wood Works
2308 Sixth St.
Tuscaloosa, Ala. 35401
(205) 759-3142

Ice Cream Parlor Furniture

Not since the 1920s has oak and wrought-iron ice cream parlor furniture been so popular. Crown of Fairhope is one of several companies that supply a set of two chairs and a table for $$99.50. These are shipped in "knock-down" condition and the supplier claims that they can be assembled in minutes. Stools, bought in sets of two, are $22.50 each.

Catalog available, $1.

Crown of Fairhope
P.O. Drawer G
Fairhope, Ala. 36532
(205) 928-2300

Pedestal Base

Pedestals for tables intended for indoor or outdoor use are often very difficult to find. Objects as varied as old sewing machine bases and washstands have been used as substitutes. Here is the real thing, a nineteenth-

century cast-iron base as used in cafes throughout the world. It is coated with a zinc chromate primer and a second coating of rust-inhibitive coloring. The price is $73.

Brochure available.

Santa Cruz Foundry
P.O. Box 831, 738 Chestnut St.
Santa Cruz, Calif. 95060

Trestle Table

Reproductions of trestle tables have multiplied each year as the supply of antique pieces declines. Here is a simple rendition in 2″ pine. Old Timey Furniture makes it in lengths of up to 84″.

Literature available, $1.50.

Old Timey Furniture Co.
Smithfield, N.C. 27577
(919) 965-6555

Hall Settees/Settles/Benches

Informal furniture of this sort can be used in many areas of an old house—in a living room, front hall, front porch, or a bedroom. It is furniture made for the use of more than one person, perhaps as many as three people. It is not meant to be as comfortable as an easy chair, but there is no reason why a bench or settle should not be inviting indoors or out. The settle or bench (the terms are almost synonymous) was used in old inns and hotels; the settee of the sort listed here was a precursor of the sofa, but without upholstery. All three kinds of furniture were used in all kinds of North American homes during the eighteenth and early nineteenth centuries. They weren't excluded from the mansions of the gentry as being too common. And, today, the same situation applies, making the supply of antique pieces somewhat limited.

Foyer Settees

Bishop White lived right across the green from Independence Hall during the important years of the eighteenth century. Two settees from his foyer have been copied in detail by Frederick Duckloe's craftsmen, a firm in business since 1859. Nineteen turned hickory spindles rise from a poplar plank seat and are connected by an 80″ ash steam-bent back. The arms are

solid cherry. The original pair was made by Philadelphia craftsman John Letchworth during the Revolutionary period.

Literature available.

Frederick Duckloe & Bros., Inc.
Portland, Penn. 18351
(717) 897-6172

Shaker Bench

In a Shaker community a pine bench like this would have been used principally in the dining room. There is no reason why it can not be placed in other rooms—depending on the overall style of furnishings. Placed against the wall, it will serve the needs of even those with lower back trouble—a common American affliction of the twentieth century. The seat is 9½″ x 48″.

Catalog available, $2.50.

Guild of Shaker Crafts
401 W. Savidge
Spring Lake, Mich. 49456
(616) 846-2870

Estate Bench

Attractive benches for use out in the open are extremely difficult to find today—antique or reproduction. Too many home owners have opted for something salvaged

from a city park, often a bench that has been encased in cement. Santa Cruz Foundry makes a 5-foot "Estate" bench which will complement any well-tended grounds. The seat and back are Douglas fir prefinished with Danish oil stain. The wrought-iron ends come in black or forest green. You might want to anchor the legs in some manner as lawn furniture of this sort can disappear in even broad daylight. The bench is priced at $147.

Literature available.

Santa Cruz Foundry
P.O. Box 831, 738 Chestnut St.
Santa Cruz, Calif. 95060

Custom Furniture

Nearly all of the craftsmen listed in these pages will undertake commissions. They particularly enjoy the opportunity to create a one-of-a-kind object. If you are trying to complete a set of chairs or want to exactly duplicate a particular piece, these craftsmen will guide you along the way. Such work is terribly expensive and may take some time to complete.

Up Country Enterprise

Up Country Enterprise is a limited edition producer of furniture in the English and colonial Philadelphia traditions. Each piece is undertaken as a distinct entity; there is no mass production of any parts. Only when an order is received does the work begin. Up Country also engages in custom projects which may involve reproduction of an antique, adaptation of a design, or execution of an original design.

Literature available.

Up Country Enterprise
Old Jaffrey Rd.
Peterborough, N.H. 03458
(603) 924-6826

D. R. Millbranth

D. R. Millbranth has moved his shop from Maryland to New Hampshire and there will continue to make custom-ordered furniture. His specialty is Chippendale as well as primitive pieces.

D. R. Millbranth, Cabinetmaker
Center Rd., RR 2, Box 462
Hillsboro, N.H. 03244
(603) 464-5244

Kits/Plans

Fortunate is the woman or man skilled as a woodworker. Plans and kits are available to those who, unlike this writer, paid attention to the shop teacher at school and were smart enough to know early that working with the hands can be a rewarding experience. For the very skilled, plans may provide sufficient guidelines for constructing handsome pieces of furniture. For others, kits may be the answer.

Woodcraft Supply

If you have the notion to build your own Windsor chair or Boston rocker, Woodcraft Supply has a package of plans, assembly notes, material lists, and an 8″ x 10″ photo of the original—all for $8 each. Their 160-page book, *Windsor Chairmaking*, a step-by-step guide, is also recommended and sells for $10.25.

Catalog available, 50¢.

Woodcraft Supply Corp.
313 Montvale Ave.
Woburn, Mass. 01801
1-800-225-1153

Shaker Workshops

You can get good quality furniture kits from Shaker Workshops. The woods are northern hardwoods and pine. Each kit contains all you will need to complete the project except a hammer and screw driver. The classic straight chair sells for $45. The slats are secured with pegs, not nails. The seats come in your choice of colored fabric tape.

When its leaves are down, this table takes up very little space. With raised leaves, it is 38" wide. You can order lengths of from 4' to 7'. Prices range from $300 to $330.

Catalog available.

Shaker Workshops, Inc.
14 Bradford St.
Concord, Mass. 01742
(617)369-1790

Cohasset Colonials

Cohasset Colonials is another firm which offers well-made kits. Here is a slant-top desk with a rock maple lid which drops forward as a writing surface. It is 27" wide and 19" deep and has a drawer in the frame. It costs $140.

This half round table has a radius of 18". The maple top is supported by tapered maple legs. It stands 28½" high and sells for $34.

Here is a Shaker tray kit for $52. It makes a great serving tray, but can be used in other ways. It folds up nicely and takes up very little space. The top is 30" x 19" x 2½".

Catalog available, 50¢.

Cohasset Colonials
Cohasset, Mass. 02025
(617) 383-0110

Ford Museum & Greenfield Village

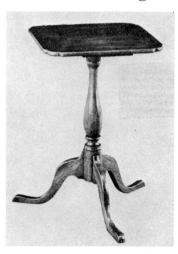

The original candle table from which this is copied is part of the Edison Collection at Greenfield Village. The Bartley Collection reproduces a number of pieces in kit form for the museum complex. The kits include all the things necessary to complete assembly and finishing.

Catalog available, $2.50.

Henry Ford Museum and Greenfield Village
20900 Oakwood Blvd.
Dearborn, Mich. 48121
(313) 271-1620

Crown of Fairhope

Assembled but unfinished pieces cost considerably less than finished. For instance, a finished $74.95 sculptured back chair can be bought unfinished for $59.95 from Crown of Fairhope. Similar bargains are available from manufacturers and retailers across the country. A basic course on finishing and refinishing furniture could be an excellent investment.

Catalog available, $1.

Crown of Fairhope
795 Nichols Ave.
P.O. Drawer G
Fairhope, Ala. 36532
(205) 928-2300

Odds and Ends

Reproduction craftsmen produce an almost endless number of objects in all sizes, shapes, and forms. Some are expert makers of looking glasses, spinets, swings, and such accessories as fern stands and hall trees.

Brumby Rocker

The Brumby Rocker people also produce a porch swing. Mortise and tenon joints make this oak swing sturdy, and an arched back makes it relaxing.

Literature available.

The Rocker Shop
1421 White Circle, N.W., P.O. Box 12
Marietta, Ga. 30061

(404) 427-2618

Wrought-Iron Corner Rack

Mexico House can supply many of the decorative requirements of a Spanish-style residence. Your plants will have room to grow in this wrought-iron corner rack. It's just over 5' tall and weighs only 20 pounds. The price is $39.95.

Catalog available, $1.

Mexico House
Box 970
Del Mar, Calif. 92014

Dressing Stand

Earlier and European forms of the dressing stand were often ornately carved and veneered. They were designed to display a lady's jewelry rather than to provide a place for its storage. Berea's craftsmen make a very modest stand. Only 9″ deep, it has a drawer on each side of a tiltable mirror and is meant to perch atop a dressing table. It is available for $260 in cherry or $267 in mahogany or walnut.

Catalog available.

Berea College
Student Craft Industries
Berea, Ky. 40404
(606) 986-9341

Spinet Harpsichord

If your bank account matches your taste for elegance and your eighteenth-century music room is without an instrument, you may be interested in a spinet harpsichord. Frank Rockette is a scholar-craftsman who meticulously builds an instrument which he believes has "considerable investment value due to the integrity of workmanship." The woods are exotic, the brass hardware is cast to his molds, and even the varnish is made in the shop.

Frank Rockette
Strawberry Banke Museum
Box 300
Portsmouth, N.H. 03801

Looking Glasses

Stephen Franklin carves 200-year-old looking glasses out of 150-year-old wood. He recreates four Chippendale styles in varying degrees of fanciness. These are available from a simple fretwork model to one with a gilt phoenix and carved side drapes and scrolls.

Literature available.

Stephen Franklin
Box 717
Buckingham, Penn. 18912

Supplies

Most of the basic supplies for refinishing and maintaining furniture are available at your local hardware store. Items of particular interest are listed herewith. You may want to recommend them to retailers in your area.

Lemon Oil and Tung Oil

Fine furniture is made to last, but it must be cared for. You can use lemon oil as often as you dust. It replaces the natural oils in the wood. Paint and hardware stores sell some varieties, or it can be ordered from a specialty firm such as The Hope Company. Hope sells a variety of refinishing products, too. They are the only source for 100% tung oil in the United States.

Literature available.

The Hope Co.
2052 Congressional Dr.
St. Louis, Mo. 63141
(314) 432-5697

Caning Kits

The old wooden rocker in the garage is not beyond hope. Perhaps all it needs is a new seat. The Newell Workshop stocks all kinds of cane, tools, and instructions so that even a beginner can do a perfect job. Caning kits are $4; refills are $2. It might be wise to send them a sample of the old cane to be sure the right size is in your kit.

It takes about two pounds of cord to restring an average chair. Newell stocks a twisted kraft cord which resembles natural rush. It also has a strong cord made out of Oriental sea grass. This is similar to natural rush except that the twisted strands are raised instead of flat.

Literature available.

Newell Workshop
19 Blaine Ave.
Hinsdale, Ill. 60521

Pressed Fibre Seats

An inexpensive alternative to caning is the pressed fibre seat. This is an appropriate form for many late-Victorian pieces. The seat is strong and relatively easy to install. The style shown here is 12¾" square and sells for $5.45.

Literature available.

Peco
P.O. Box 777
Smithville, Texas 78957
(512) 237-3600

Other Furniture Sources

Consult the List of Suppliers for addresses.

Beds

Bedlam Brass Beds
Berea College
Brass Bed Co. of America
Colonial Williamsburg
Davis Cabinet
Guild of Shaker Crafts
Magnolia Hall
Ephraim Marsh
Old Timey Furniture
Reid Classics
Townshend Furniture

Chairs

Cane Farm
Historic Charleston Reproductions (Baker)
Colonial Williamsburg (Kittinger)
Brian Considine
Country Bed Shop
Crown of Fairhope
Frederick Duckloe
Davis Cabinet
Guild of Shaker Crafts
Hitchcock Chair
Ernest Lo Nano
Magnolia Hall
Louis Maslow & Son
Nichols & Stone
Sturbridge Yankee Workshop
Superior Reed & Rattan

Chests/Boxes

Berea College
Colonial Williamsburg (Kittinger)
Brian Considine
Guild of Shaker Crafts
Magnolia Hall
Ephraim Marsh
D. R. Millbranth
Thomas Moser
Old Timey Furniture
Townshend Furniture

Cupboards/Cabinets

Berea College
Guyon
Magnolia Hall
Ephraim Marsh
Thomas Moser

Craig Nutt
Restorations Unlimited
Sturbridge Yankee Workshop

Looking Glasses/Mirrors

Berea College
Colonial Williamsburg (Friedman Brothers)
Brian Considine
Holmes Co.
Magnolia Hall
Ephraim Marsh
Rococo Designs

Rockers

Guild of Shaker Crafts
Sturbridge Yankee Workshop
Townshend Furniture
Robert Whitley

Settees/Settles/Benches

Bittersweet
Historic Charleston Reproductions (Baker)
Country Bed Shop
Guyon
Lennox Shop
Magnolia Hall
Ephraim Marsh
D. R. Millbranth
Thomas Moser
Old Timey Furniture
Townshend Furniture

Tables

American Woodcarving
Bittersweet
Historic Charleston Reproductions (Baker)
Colonial Williamsburg (Kittinger)
Country Bed Shop
Ephraim Marsh
Mexico House
Thomas Moser
Townshend Furniture
Robert Whitley

Customwork

Bittersweet
Brian Considine
Country Bed Shop
Noelwood
Craig Nutt
Robert Whitley

Kits/Plans

Albert Constantine & Sons
Furniture Designs
Minnesota Woodworkers
Peerless Rattan & Reed

SUPERIOR
COPPER WEATHER VANES,

Gilded with Pure Gold.

CHURCH CROSSES,
TOWER ORNAMENTS,
FINIALS, Etc., Etc.

Vanes made from any draw‌ing or design on short notice.

T. W. JONES,

Successor to Chas. W. Briggs,
"   " V. W. Baldwin.

170 and 172 Front St.,
New York.

Illustrated Catalogue of over
250 designs mailed free.

X Accessories

Maintaining the structural integrity of an old house is enough of a job without having to worry about suitable furnishings and accessories. It is understandable, then, that professionals in the building restoration business show little enthusiasm for the extras which make a house a home. These can be provided later if the owner is so inclined—and most are. This is why the first chapter of this book is devoted to structural needs and the very last to accessories. This organization of material serves to emphasize that the decorative values of old-house living are secondary to those of environment and structure. To merely embellish a crumbling building is about the same as painting a corpse before a viewing. Yet this is done in many renovation/decorating projects, and only the effect of "life," rather than its substance, is achieved. At worst, such a gussied up house becomes only a Hollywood set.

There are many reasons for this simplistic approach: the surface attractiveness of coverups such as paints, papers, and fabrics; a lack of interest in and knowledge of building technology; and, perhaps most important, economic limitations which preclude the kind of major structural work of returning a house to its original state and keeping it that way. If we don't have the time to do the work, we may not be able to afford to have someone else come in and perform it. Unless governmental aid is forthcoming in the form of tax breaks or outright grants for a truly historic home, there has to be some sort of compromise between past and future. While we may not be able to achieve period perfection (or even want to), we can at least get the props right and make sure that they are something more than a faint imitation of historic reality. There is no reason why the everyday objects we live with should not be as fitting and attractive as the house in which they are kept.

That is why space is properly devoted here to such a subject as accessories. Without pursuing antiquarian interests to an eccentric extreme, those who have learned to love living in a period setting should enjoy making use of other aspects of the material past—brooms made of straw that do not fall apart on first sweeping; fans that can cool a room almost as effectively as (and much more cheaply than) air conditioners; furniture and ornaments which make a porch or lawn as attractive a space for living as the inside of a house; pottery dishes that will not disintegrate when placed in the oven. There are other utilitarian benefits to be had from the craftsmanship of the past. But added to the tangible rewards must be the aesthetic. It is just plain nice to have attractive, well-made objects at hand whether we can explain their function or not. They are the immediate comforts of a good life.

Since we are bombarded daily with appeals to spend our hard-earned money on one piece of junk after another, there needs to be a constant sorting out of the good from the bad. It doesn't take very long to discover that most of the mail can be thrown into the fire. As George Funke, proprietor of Bassett & Vollum in Galena, Illinois, wrote this writer in a description of his historic house, "The stove is excellent for burning third class mail, too." He has the right attitude. You can't stop time, but neither do you need to fall victim to every fad and fancy for "the latest." We believe that the objects described in the following listings are not of the fleeting variety. Even the old-fashioned sugar cone used for table decoration has aesthetic appeal which has somehow survived the years.

Most of these secondary items for the old house are made by individual craftsmen and not large suppliers. (We have attempted to steer clear of ye olde gift shoppes and other such emporiums which often serve more nostalgic syrup than material substance). In the pages following are representative craftsmen who are producing objects that may become antiques of the future, regardless of the style in which they are working. A well-designed and crafted object will always retain intrinsic and extrinsic value.

Handmade Baskets

Baskets made of white oak splints are the specialty of Ken and Kathleen Dalton. They work and draw their materials from deep within the hills of southeastern Tennessee. Illustrated are round rib baskets from bushel size to those appropriate for eggs.

Brochure available.

Coker Creek Crafts
P.O. Box 95
Coker Creek, Tenn. 37314
(615) 261-2157

Similar kinds of baskets are produced by members of the Southern Highland Handicraft Guild. These are by Charlotte Tracy and illustrate stages of construction.

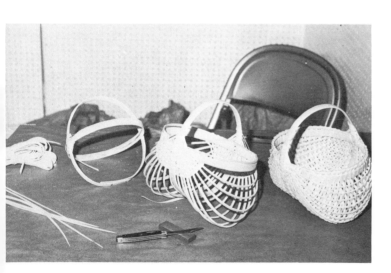

For further information, contact:

Southern Highland Handicraft Guild
P.O. Box 9545
Asheville, N.C. 28805
(704) 298-7928

Baskets of almost every sort can be found at the Cumberland General Store and through their mail order service. These are made of New England hardwood and are of the following kinds: bread, shopping, market, pie and cake, bicycle, produce, egg, feed, and fireplace grate.

Catalog available, $3.

Cumberland General Store
Rte. 3
Crossville, Tenn. 38555
(615) 484-8481

Boxes for Storage

Various kinds of wood boxes that fasten to the wall (such as those for knives or for candles) are handy containers to have around any house—old or not. The Candle Cellar & Emporium manufactures boxes of this sort in their workshop. They also have an adaptation of a workman's tool box (13¾ x 4 x 9½″) which can be used for holding garden tools, candles, mail, etc.

Brochure available, 25¢.

The Candle Cellar & Emporium
1914 North Main St.
Fall River, Mass. 02720
(617) 679-6057

The Shakers designed and produced some of the most beautiful and functional of wood containers. Several of these are now available from the Guild of Shaker Crafts. One especially handsome container is a dining room "deep tray" of pine with dovetailed corners. The original was used in the New Lebanon Ministry dining room for carrying water glasses. A berry box in pine is another appealing design. These were used for gathering and storing berries and nuts as well as herbs.

Catalog available, $2.50.

Guild of Shaker Crafts
401 W. Savidge St.
Spring Lake, Mich. 49456
(616) 846-2870

Brooms

Have you tried to buy a *real* broom recently? If so, you will appreciate knowing that old-fashioned brooms of straw *can* be found. In this illustration, Larry Kear, a member of the Southern Highland Handicraft Guild, is displaying his talents.

For further information, contact:

Southern Highland Handicraft Guild
P.O. Box 9545
Asheville, N.C. 28805
(704) 298-7928

Clocks

Unless you are a devotee of fine cabinetmaking and a precision jeweler, an antique clock may not be worth

the fuss. Most are notoriously unreliable instruments, and parts are sometimes hard to find. Millions of clocks were mass produced during the nineteenth century in much the same way that automobiles are manufactured today. Naturally, there are a goodly number of lemons. The handsome reproductions from The Royal Windyne Collection are made to last. Illustrated is the "Winthrop" model which strikes on the half hour and counts on the hour. It need be wound only once a month. The case is solid wood and the pendulum and hardware are of brass.

Catalog available.

Royal Windyne Ltd.
Dept. OHC
Box 6622
Richmond, Va. 23230
(804) 355-5690

Fans

The New York Times recently noted that city dwellers are amazed to learn that country and suburban people depend little on air conditioners; in the country most people simply turn on a fan—unless, of course, they live in the midst of the Sun Belt or in a tropical rain forest. Although it is not easy to live in a modern house or apartment without air conditioning, old-house dwellers can more easily rely on the cooling effectiveness of an electric fan, especially if their houses are well-insulated. The Cumberland General Store catalog features seven standard ceiling fans with non-adjustable wood or metal blades. They also feature the "Adaptair Option" which they recommend for cathedral ceilings. The blades are adjustable so that air can be pulled up or down.

Catalog available, $3.

Cumberland General Store
Rte. 3
Crossville, Tenn.
(615) 484-8481

The Royal Windyne brass-appointed turn-of-the-century ceiling fans were featured in the first *Old House Catalogue*. We are repeating them here because we feel that they represent reproductions which are made with the quality of antiques. They are available in 39″ and 53″ diameter sizes. According to the manufacturer, the Royal Windyne models use only as much electricity as a light bulb—about 90 watts; the average room air conditioner consumes 1,566.

Fences

Fences don't always make good neighbors, but they may help to keep the pets in place and certainly do dress up the yard. Americans were frequently exhorted in the 1800s to improve and extend fencing so that the countryside would present a neat, prosperous appearance. And just as frequently, this advice was ignored by the majority of country dwellers. Those living in small and large towns or cities, however, were more likely to enclose their properties. Many of these fences—urban or rural—have not survived the years in very good shape and need replacement or at the least considerable refurbishing.

The extraordinary firm of Kenneth Lynch & Sons is best known for its garden ornaments and weather vanes. Owner Kenneth Lynch, however, is very interested in fences and is preparing a new book on them, *To Keep In, To Keep Out.* He is ready to help you with at least two kinds of fencing—wrought-iron and stone—and can also supply gates.

Old Mansions Co., an architectural firm, is particularly interested in preserving period iron work. It stocks iron fencing and window guards. You can probably find brackets, crestings, and other decorative pieces here too.

Fountains, Urns, and Vases

Cast-iron urns in the Victorian and the Regency styles are expertly prepared by Steptoe & Wife. These can be placed on cast-iron plinths or used on other sorts of bases, as well as on the ground itself. Remember that these are hefty numbers weighing approximately 66 pounds.

A wide variety of fountains, urns, and vases in cast iron is available from Robinson Iron. This is a firm that values the past and makes a sincere effort to document all the period materials it produces. The "Venetian Fluted Urn" is an exact replica of one produced before

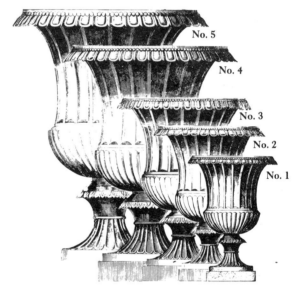

the Civil War. The Robinson catalog points out that "the top 'bowl' of the urn is made in a single piece. Only a master molder can make the urn bowl in one piece and even the masters have a failure rate of roughly 50%. Of course the technology for significantly reducing the failure rate is available, but this would require noticeable pattern modifications. We at Robinson have an intense desire to keep this particular tradition alive and well." Amen.

Garden ornaments of every possible sort in stone, lead, and wrought iron are indisputably Kenneth Lynch's eminent domain. There is no way to describe the riches which are available from his firm. You might want to inquire about the *Encyclopedia of Garden Ornaments*, a treasure trove of information that is available for $25. There are other books as well which are less costly and perhaps will suit your needs.

Kenneth Lynch & Sons, Inc.
78 Danbury Rd.
Wilton, Conn. 06897
(203) 762-8363

Garden Furniture

Some outdoor furniture has been discussed in the furniture section of this book, but the subject is one that is appropriate for "accessories" as well. The garden or lawn area of a home is probably the last concern when it comes to "furnishing," and it probably should be. As in the past, however, the outdoors can serve as a second living area—at least in the summer months—if properly planned and planted. Most old houses are generously endowed with trees and shrubs which may need only periodic maintenance to preserve their form. To place attractive garden furniture amidst them is an inviting prospect.

Tennessee Fabricating Co. mixes the new and the old. Its classic sets of tables, chairs, and settees are of ornamental metal but are cast in the patterns of the past.

Brochure available.

Tennessee Fabricating Co.
2366 Prospect
Memphis, Tenn. 38106
(901) 948-3354

About any style bench you can think of has been made by Kenneth Lynch. These are made of wrought iron, wood, cast iron, cast stone, marble, and granite. Many of the designs would suit the grounds of fine eighteenth and nineteenth-century homes.

A special catalog (book #9074) is available just on benches, $2.50 for paperback; $5 for hardcover.

Kenneth Lynch & Sons, Inc.
78 Danbury Rd.
Wilton, Conn. 06897
(203) 762-8363

Steptoe & Wife supply only cast-iron furniture of English Victorian design; tops of tables may be of aluminum or wood. Illustrated here is the Colebrookdale-style table and matching chairs. Naturally, you won't want to lug these from pace to place. The table weighs approximately 60 pounds and each of the chairs, 44.

Catalog available, $1.

Steptoe & Wife Antiques, Ltd.
3626 Victoria Park Ave.
Willowdale, Ontario
M2H 3B2 Canada

Metalware—
Common and Rare

Antique metalware is avidly sought by collectors. Early pewter, silver, copper, and brass bring extremely high prices, so high, in fact, that the supply of fine materials is extremely limited. Even good tinware is becoming scarce. There are, however, craftsmen making very fine reproductions which may be even more appropriate for everyday wear. Deanne F. Nelson is one of these. She is a goldsmith and silversmith working at the historic Swedish colony of Bishop Hill, Illinois. She makes sterling porringer shown here. The design on the handle is taken from an 1840 Bishop Hill hymnal cover. Its price is only $45.

Deanne F. Nelson
Box 43
Bishop Hill, Ill. 61419

Historic Charleston's pewter is made by Gorham. A porringer, bowls, and plates found in the historic 1739 William Elliott House form the collection of reproduction pieces. Modern pewter is lead-free and thus perfectly safe for serving of food.

Catalog available, $4.

Historic Charleston Reproductions
51 Meeting St.
Charleston, S.C. 29401
(803) 723-1623

Craftsmen at Greenfield Village and the Henry Ford Museum produce their own pewter pieces. The form and detail of antique models are faithfully reproduced. Such pieces as a wall candle sconce, candleholder, candle extinguisher, chamberstick, and a porringer are carefully hand-shaped and finished.

Catalog available, $2.50.

Henry Ford Museum and Greenfield Village
20900 Oakwood Blvd.
Dearborn, Mich. 48121
(313) 271-1620

William Stewart is a traditional tinsmith who has done work for the National Park Service and many historical groups and museums. He uses tinplate which is custom dipped exactly to the specifications used in the past. Stewart is a purist and will not make "adaptations." If it is cups or coffee pots or various sorts of table and kitchen ware that you are seeking, this is the man you should contact.

William Stewart & Sons
708 N. Edison St.
Arlington, Va. 22203
(703) 841-1776

Mirrors

Rococo Designs has slowly expanded its line of acid-etched, bevelled glass mirrors of late Victorian design. Earlier forms of mirrors or looking glasses are not hard to find as antiques or reproductions. The manufacture of late nineteenth-century accessories, however, is a relatively recent phenomenon and the buyer has every reason to be skeptical about the honesty and quality of such pieces. There is a lot of shlock being peddled which has nothing but a weak nostalgic appeal. That is not true of the designs from Rococo or of the execution of them.

Catalog available, $1.50.

Rococo Designs
417 Pennsylvania Ave.
Santa Cruz, Calif. 95062
(408) 423-2732

The Holmes Co. produces traditional eighteenth-century furnishings, including two mirrors or looking glasses. One is a hand looking glass with mother-of-pearl inlay in the handle; the second is a Chippendale wall mirror. Both are made of fine Honduras mahogany to which a soft gloss finish is applied. Neither have the hard, shiny look of a second-rate reproduction, a look which often is the result of an attempt to cover up an inferior wood.

Catalog available.

The Holmes Co.
P.O. Box 382
York, Penn. 17405
(717) 846-6807

190

Pottery

Good pottery containers of various sorts are not that easy to find. There is a great amount of work available that is interesting, but not really historically accurate. And there is also the vast quantity of hand-crafted ware that is thrown haphazardly from kilns everywhere in the country. The following firms are sources for attractive, useful reproductions that should stand considerable wear.

Beaumont Heritage Pottery produces only salt-glazed stoneware which varies in color from tan to grey with variations of brown tones. All the wares are handmade and can be treated as roughly as Pyrex. The designs in cobalt blue, as illustrated here, are carefully rendered. Potter Jerry Beaumont's group of craftsmen produces pitchers, jugs, covered jars, crocks, flowerpots, mixing and serving bowls, candle holders, mugs, steins, pie plates, spice jars, spoon holders, butter tubs, and water glasses.

Literature available.

Beaumont Heritage Pottery
Box 300, Atkinson St.
Portsmouth, N.H. 03801
(603) 431-5284

Spongeware in a color termed "Swedish blue" is most appropriately produced at the Colony Pottery in Bishop Hill, Illinois, by craftsmen Steve and Linda Holden. A pitcher set is illustrated here and includes a 1½ quart pitcher, four 8 oz. mugs, a creamer, and a sugar bowl. The interior and collar of each piece is glazed a glossy Albany slip brown. The exterior is a waxy white with decoration "sponged" in blue. The seven pieces are priced at $40. An extraordinary value.

Also available from the Holdens is a set of twelve

ceramic spice jars with corks included. Each has a capacity of approximately 4 oz. The set is offered for $50; individual containers are $5 each.

Colony Pottery
Box 18
Bishop Hill, Ill. 61419

Stoneware and earthenware have been traditionally produced in the Jugtown area of North Carolina for over two-hundred years. The wares are of exceptional quality, with the orange-glazed earthenware containers being the most original to the region. Local clays are used, and these are of a reddish-orange. Most of the pieces, however, have a brown, blue, or gray glaze. There is an almost endless number of forms available— jugs, pitchers, noggins, vases, bowls, plates, teacups, pots, jars, and candle holders. Illustrated is a salt-glazed stoneware pitcher. The photograph is by Charles Tompkins.

Catalog available.

Jugtown Pottery
Rte. 2
Seagrove, N.C. 27341
(919) 464-3266

Plates with sgraffito decoration have been produced by the Pennsylvania Germans for many years. This tradition has been continued by several craftsmen, including Dorothy E. Long. She signs and dates her pieces which are made for the Philadelphia Museum of Art's Museum Shop after originals in the institution's collection. These are of red clay with pale yellow, green, and brown decoration. The glaze used is non-lead, and the ware is ovenproof and dishwasher safe. Each is roughly 10" in diameter.

Illustrated at left is "Bird" ($66), patterned after a dish by Henry Roudebush, a potter active from 1804–16 in Montgomery County, Pennsylvania. The inscription translates as "I am afraid that my ugly daughter will get no husband." Above it is "Tulip" ($60), a plate copied from one by Johannese Neesz which was made in Tyler's Port, Montgomery County, in 1826. The translation on this reads: "I am made of potter's thoughts. When I break, I will be gone." At lower right is "Flowers" ($48), which is patterned after a plate thought to have been made by Johann Drey in Heidelberg Township, Lebanon County, c. 1800. When ordering, add $2.50 for cost of handling and shipping.

Catalog available.

The Museum Shop
Dept. OH
Philadelphia Museum of Art
P.O. Box 7858
Philadelphia, Penn. 19101
(215) 763-8100

Blue Hill is one of Maine's most handsome coastal villages. Rowantrees is very much a part of the pastoral scene. Founded in 1934 by Adelaide Pearson, it has been continued by Laura Paddock and, now, by one of her students, Sheila Varnum. You may find the brown-glazed, ovenproof beanpot of special use. There is also a wide selection of dinnerware.

Brochure available.

Rowantrees Pottery
Blue Hill, Me. 04614
(207) 374-5535

Venetian Blinds

Metal or plastic Venetian blinds are the norm these days, and wooden blinds are antique items. Norton Blumenthal decided that the situation needed to be changed and has arranged for the manufacture of blinds in clear-stained cedar or pine which are held by either nylon strings or tapes of cotton or rayon. Since they have to be custom-ordered, they are expensive. But after you root around the second-hand stores, you may find that there is no alternative but to start anew.

Norton Blumenthal, Inc.
979 Third Ave.
New York, N.Y. 10021
(212) 752-2535

Silhouettes

Silhouette cutting is one of the lost arts that has come alive again. The Laughons are masters of the techniques used to produce convincing heads and full-length portraits, as well as family groups with their house in the background. Itinerant silhouette artists once provided the home with appealing and relatively inexpensive portrait work. The Laughons do not amble around the countryside, but they will execute silhouettes from clear side-view photos or slides, as well as from life.

H. & N. Laughon
8106 Three Chopt Rd.
Richmond, Va. 23229
(804) 288-7795

Sugar Cones

These are not the variety available at the corner ice cream store, but rather giant inverted cones which are wrapped in blue paper. They are used for late eighteenth-century table centerpieces. You can see such copies at the Winterthur Museum.

Canada & Dom
Sugar Ltd.
P.O. Box 490
Montreal 3,
Quebec, Canada

Sundials

For any kind of sundial, turn to Kenneth Lynch. He has a whole catalog/book ($2.50 in paperback) devoted to

nothing but lead, stone, and wrought-iron devices. Ilustrated is #3525, a design of Fairfield stone with gilded lead numerals and a gnomon of bronze.

Kenneth Lynch & Sons, Inc.
78 Danbury Rd.
Wilton, Conn. 06897
(203) 762-8363

Tiles

Antique faience Delft tiles cannot be lavished as freely as other materials for floors and walls. But you may want to replace squares or introduce them in a fireplace facing or a small foyer area. Helen Williams is your expert, and, as she points out, only tiles made before 1800 are of the true hand-painted, tin-glazed variety. She has an extensive collection of these, and each measures roughly 5″ square. The most expensive are seventeenth-century blue and white designs with various scenes, animals, figures, etc. Those with tulips run $50 each. More affordable are eighteenth-century squares in solid white ($4) and tortoise shell ($9) or marble design ($8). Helen Williams also has some stock of antique English Liverpool transfer tiles and antique Spanish and Portuguese squares in blue and in polychrome. Illustrated are seventeenth-century blue designs.

Literature available.

Helen Williams/Rare Tiles
12643 Hortense St.
North Hollywood, Calif. 91604
(213) 761-2756

Weather Vanes

Although no longer used primarily for readings of wind direction, vanes serve an ornamental purpose for which no one need apologize. Not every old house or outbuilding should sport such an ornamental device, but some structures, particularly barns or the kind of attached or detached sheds once used for carriages and now automobiles, demand such attention. Vanes should be very securely affixed to a base, not only because they are buffeted by the elements, but also for security reasons. Whether antique or not, they are among the favorite objects of hit-and-run burglars.

Bruce Coutu of The Copper House handmakes copper vanes which are good reproductions of original models. He has a variety of styles and sizes available.

Catalog available, $1.

Bruce Coutu
The Copper House
Rte 4
Epsom, N.H. 03234
(603) 736-9792

E. G. Washburne vanes are handmade from their original cast-iron molds. Illustrated is one of the most typical of American designs, the galloping horse known as the "Kentucky." A complete vane includes a number of items other than the hammered figure. You must count on a steel spire, brass collar, large and small copper balls, and brass cardinals or letters.

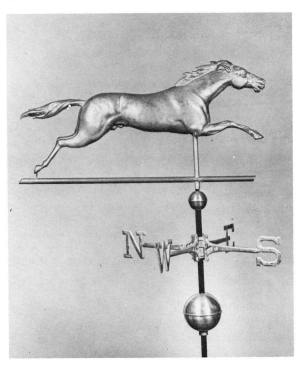

Literature available.

E. G. Washburne & Co.
85 Andover St., Rte. 114
Danvers, Mass. 01923
(617) 774-3645

Kenneth Lynch can provide you with a vane from almost any period and style—English, French, or American. Although often thought just a Colonial art form, vane making flourished in America and overseas throughout the nineteenth century. Some of the later ones are more properly called "bannerets." Illustrated is design #2504 in solid aluminum. Lynch also produces vanes in copper and other metals.

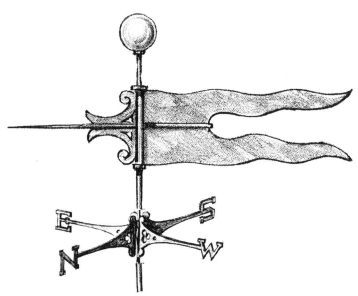

Catalog/book available, $2.50 paperback.

Kenneth Lynch & Sons, Inc.
78 Danbury Rd.
Wilton, Conn. 06897
(203) 762-8363

Woodenware

Wood bowls, plates, mugs, and utensils were the basics used in many Colonial kitchens; finer materials of china or pewter were used only in prosperous households. S. & C. Huber has faithfully reproduced basic containers and spoons—10½" and 7" plates, salt cellars, and hand-carved spoons. They are made of solid maple.

Catalog available, 50¢.

S. & C. Huber, Accoutrements
82 Plants Dam Rd.
East Lyme, Conn. 06333
(203) 739-0772

Other Sources for Accessories

Consult List of Suppliers for addresses.

Baskets

Cane & Basket Supply
Guild of Shaker Crafts
West Rindge Baskets

Clocks

Henry Ford Museum & Greenfield Village
Magnolia Hall
R. Jesse Morley, Jr.
Seth Thomas
Trotman Clock
Weird Wood (kits)

Fans

Gargoyles
United House Wrecking

Fences

The Cellar
Coker Creek Crafts
Gargoyles
Materials Unlimited
Renovation Source
Tennessee Fabricating
Wrecking Bar (Atlanta)

Fountains, Urns, Vases

Erkins Studios
Wrecking Bar (Dallas)

Garden Furniture

Gargoyles
Magnolia Hall

Kitchen Utensils

Bailey's Forge
Southern Highland Handicraft Guild

Metalware

Craft House, Williamsburg

Mirrors

The Cellar
Craft House, Williamsburg
Gargoyles
Magnolia Hall
Reale Mirror

Pottery

Henry Ford Museum & Greenfield Village
Craft House, Colonial Williamsburg

Shades

Perkowitz Window Fashions

Weather Vanes

Bailey's Forge
Cape Cod Cupola
J. W. Fiske Architectural Metals

Appendix A

The following is a list of retail outlets—arranged by state—carrying both Brunschwig & Fils and Scalamandre fabrics and papers. The majority of stores have branch outlets that may also supply these materials.

Levy's
El Con Center
Tucson, Ariz. 85702

Bullock's
7th and Hill Sts.
Los Angeles, Calif. 90014

Macy's San Francisco
Stockton and O'Farrell
San Francisco, Calif. 94108

W & J Sloane
216 Sutter
San Francisco, Calif. 94108

Denver Dry Goods
16th and California
Denver, Colo. 80201

May Co.-D & F
16th and Tremont Pl.
Denver, Colo. 80201

Woodward & Lothrop
10th and 11th, F and G Sts., N.W.
Washington, D.C. 20013

Blums of Boca
2980 N. Federal Highway
Boca Raton, Fla. 33432

Burdines
22 E. Flagler
Miami, Fla. 33131

Rich's, Inc.
Lenox Square
3393 Peachtree Rd., N.E.
Atlanta, Ga. 30326

Bonwit Teller
875 N. Michigan Blvd.
Chicago, Ill. 60611

Marshall Field & Co.
111 N. State St.
Chicago, Ill. 60690

Hochschild's
Howard and Lexington Sts.
Baltimore, Md. 21201

Hutzler's
212 N. Howard
Baltimore, Md. 21201

Filene's
426 Washington St.
Boston, Mass. 02101

Jordan Marsh
450 Washington St.
Boston, Mass. 02107

J. L. Hudson's
1206 Woodward
Detroit, Mich. 48211

Dayton's
700 On The Mall
Minneapolis, Minn. 55402

B. Altman & Co.
361 Fifth Ave.
New York, N.Y. 10016

Bloomingdales
1000 Third Ave.
New York, N.Y. 10022

W. &. J. Sloane
Fifth Ave., and 38th St.
New York, N.Y. 10018

The Higbee Co.
Public Square
Cleveland, Ohio 44113

Lazarus
S. High and W. Town
Columbus, Ohio 43216

Strawbridge & Clothier
8th and Market
Philadelphia, Penn. 19105

John Wanamaker
13th and Market Sts.
Philadelphia, Penn. 19101

Kaufmann's
Fifth and Smithfield
Pittsburgh, Penn. 15219

Dillard's
200 Houston
Fort Worth, Texas 76102

Joske's
4925 Westheimer
Houston, Texas 77027

Miller and Rhoads
517 E. Broad
Richmond, Va. 23219

The Bon Marche
4th and Pine
Seattle, Wash. 98101

197

Appendix B

Interior Designers

The design of any period interior is a serious matter of some expense. Although the work itself may be enjoyable and rewarding, it is not something which can be accomplished without expertise. *The Second Old House Catalogue* assists you to "do-it-yourself," but every home or apartment has special requirements which cannot be anticipated or documented in a book. If you feel that you need further assistance and can afford to enlist a professional, it would be best to contact a member of the American Society of Interior Designers. Many of the members have a thorough knowledge of period design. They are also in a position to obtain hard-to-get materials which are not generally available to the public—in particular, fabrics and special papers.

The following is a list of the ASID chapters throughout the United States. If you don't have a particular designer in mind, you might want to contact a chapter president or office regarding qualified professionals in period decoration in your area.

Alabama

Jim Mezrano, ASID
James Mezrano Associates
2841 Culver Rd.
Birmingham, Ala. 35223
(205) 879-4606

Arizona North

Mabel L. Helmick, ASID
1638 E. Cinnabar Ave.
Phoenix, Ariz. 85021
(602) 943-3837

Arizona South

Ronald C. Schuyler, ASID
Barrows
2800 E. Broadway
Tucson, Ariz. 85716
(602) 326-2479

California-Los Angeles

ASID California-Los Angeles Chapter
8687 Melrose Ave.
Los Angeles, Calif. 90069
(213) 652-2485

California-North

ASID California-North Chapter
300 Broadway
San Francisco, Calif. 94133
(415) 989-5363

California-Orange County

Daunine Vining, ASID
Daunine Vining & Associates
180 E. Main St., 140-A
Tustin, Calif. 92680
(714) 832-9855

California-Palm Springs

Marion Gardiner, FASID
370 Via Lola
Palm Springs, Calif. 92262
(714) 325-4496

California-Pasadena

Willis K. Hedrick
Willis Hedrick Interiors
441 S. Madison Ave.
Pasadena, Calif. 91101
(213) 796-5448

California-Peninsula

ASID California Peninsula Chapter
1612 El Camino Real
Menlo Park, Calif. 94025
(415) 323-3358

California-San Diego

Charles R. Wayland, ASID
Southwest Office Interiors
7480 Convoy St.
San Diego, Calif. 92110
(714) 565-7622

Carolinas

Howard R. Munroe, Jr., ASID
Carl Barnes Antiques and Interiors
2536 Reynolds Rd.
Winston-Salem, N.C. 27106
(919) 723-3594

Colorado

Victoria Degette, ASID
3113 E. Third Ave.
Denver, Colo. 80206
(303) 399-0280

Connecticut

Joan M. Arnold, ASID
Arnold-Brown
859 Post Rd.
Darien, Conn. 06820
(203) 655-2220

Florida-North

G. Dale Everett, ASID
1101 N.W. 39th Ave, A3
Gainesville, Fla. 32601
(904) 373-2566

Florida-South

Tulane Kidd, Jr., ASID
Tulane Kidd Interiors, Inc.
335 N. Federal Highway
Boca Raton, Fla. 33432
(305) 395-2848

Georgia

ASID Georgia Chapter
The Merchandise Mart, Suite 14A10
Atlanta, Ga. 30303
(404) 525-3778 (answering service)

Hawaii

Mary F. Philpotts, ASID
649 Sheridan St.
Honolulu, Hawaii 96814
(808) 947-1815

Illinois

ASID Illinois Chapter
620 Merchandise Mart
Chicago, Ill. 60654
(312) 467-5080

Indiana

Sallie Rowland, ASID
5619 E. 38th St.
Indianapolis, Ind. 46218
(317) 546-2451

Louisiana

John Eskew Campbell, ASID
P.O. Drawer 7087
Alexandria, La. 71306
(318) 445-0398

Maryland

Vicki Wenger, ASID
Rte. 1, Box 390
Old Annapolis Rd.
Frederick, Md. 21701
(301) 336-7600

Michigan

Frederick A. Sargent, ASID
Smith, Hinchman & Grylls Assoc.
455 W. Fort St.
Detroit, Mich. 48226
(313) 964-3000

Minnesota

Michael Johns Hopkins, ASID
1912 Franklin Ave., S.E.
Minneapolis, Minn. 55414
(612) 373-2073

Missouri-East

J. Randall Choate, ASID
618 S. Hanley
St. Louis, Mo. 63105
(314) 862-4520

Missouri-West/Kansas

Diane Wake Vogel, ASID
In Touch
7323 W. 97th St.
Overland Park, Kans. 66212
(913) 341-3702

Nebraska-Iowa

Leslie Berry, ASID
1146 S. 32nd St.
Omaha, Neb. 68105
(402) 341-8666

New England

F. Raymond Strawbridge, ASID
North House
West Main Rd.
Little Compton, R.I. 02837
(401) 635-2708

New Jersey

Stephen Greenberger, ASID

P.O. Box 427M
Morristown, N.J. 07960
(201) 538-4000

New Mexico

Ronald W. Nelson, ASID
3431 Florida N.E.
Albuquerque, N.M. 87110
(505) 881-3203

New York-Metropolitan

ASID New York-Metropolitan Chapter
950 Third Ave.
New York, N.Y. 10022
(212) 421-8765

New York State

Robert C. Frisch, ASID
Zausmer-Frisch Assoc.
219 Burnet Ave.
Syracuse, N.Y. 13203
(315) 475-8404

Ohio-North

Sheila Conner, ASID
The Dray Company
1154 E. Market St.
Warren, Ohio 44482
(216) 399-1843

Ohio-South/Kentucky

Robin A. Schmidt, ASID
Scoa Industries, Inc.
35 N. 4th St.
Columbus, Ohio 43215
(614) 221-5421

Oklahoma

Sydney Jane Winn, ASID
J. Richard Blissit Interiors
5550 S. Lewis, Suite 27
Tulsa, Okla. 74105
(918) 749-7711

Oregon

ASID Oregon Chapter
519 S.W. 3rd, Dekum Building
Portland, Ore. 97204
(503) 223-8231

Pennsylvania-East

Bernard Halkin, ASID
2104 Chestnut St.
Philadelphia, Penn. 19103
(215) 567-6364

Pennsylvania-West

Anne H. Ruben, ASID
Parke Interiors
4919 Centre Ave.
Pittsburgh, Penn. 15213
(412) 681-1313

Potomac (Washington, D.C., Northern Virginia)

John Richard Miller, FASID
6001 Joyce Dr.
Camp Springs, Md. 20031
(301) 423-8364

Tennessee

Dottie Sanders, ASID
Dottie Sanders Interior Design
160 S. McLean at Union
Memphis, Tenn. 38104
(901) 274-9263

Texas

ASID Texas Chapter
4007 Dallas Trade Mart
2100 Stemmens Freeway
Dallas, Texas 75207
(214) 748-1541

Texas-Gulf Coast

ASID Texas Gulf Coast Chapter
2607 Waugh
Houston, Texas 77006
(713) 526-6407

Utah

Bert F. Vieta, ASID
Gayl Baddeley Assoc.
430 E. South Temple
Salt Lake City, Utah 84111
(801) 532-2435

Virginia

Janet E. Kane, ASID
Janet Kane Interiors
1773 Parham Rd., Suite 202
Richmond, Va. 23229
(804) 320-2212

Washington State

ASID Washington State Chapter
107 S. Main St.
Seattle, Wash. 98104
(206) 624-0432

Wisconsin

Marie E. Crowley, ASID
Porter's
301 6th St.
Racine, Wis. 53403
(414) 633-6363

List of Suppliers

A

AA Abbington Ceiling Co.
2149 Utica Ave.
Brooklyn, N.Y. 11234

Accent Walls
1565 The Alameda
San Jose, Calif. 95126

Adams & Swett
380 Dorchester Ave.
Boston, Mass. 02127

Alcon Lightcraft Co.
1424 W. Alabama
Houston, Texas 77006

All-Nighter Stoves Works, Inc.
80 Commerce St.
Glastonbury, Conn. 06033

Allwood Door
345 Bayshore Rd.
San Francisco, Calif. 94124

Amerian Woodcarving
282 San Jose Ave.
San Jose, Calif. 95125

American Building Restoration, Inc.
9720 S. 60th St.
Franklin, Wis. 53132

American Olean Tile Co.
1000 Cannon Ave.
Lansdale, Penn. 19446

Ameritone Paint Co.
18414 S. Santa Fe. Ave.
Long Beach, Calif. 90810

Amherst Woodworking
P.O. Box 464
North Amherst, Mass. 01059

Townsend H. Anderson
House Joiner
R.D. #1, Box 44D
Moretown, Vt. 05660

Antique Center
6519 Telegraph Ave.
Oakland, Calif. 94609

Appalachian Fireside Crafts
Box 276
Booneville, Ky. 41314

Arch Associates/Stephen Guerrant,
  AIA
874 Green Bay Rd.
Winnetka, Ill. 60093

ArchiCenter
111 S. Dearborn
Chicago, Ill. 60603

Architectural Antiques
410 St. Pierre
Montreal, Quebec H2Y 2M2
Canada

Architectural Ornaments
P.O. Box 115
Little Neck, N.Y. 11363

Architectural Paneling, Inc.
979 Third Ave.
New York, N.Y. 10022

Laura Ashley, Inc.
714 Madison Ave.
New York, N.Y. 10021

Atlanta Stove Works, Inc.
P.O. Box 5254
Atlanta, Ga. 30307

Authentic Designs, Inc.
330 E. 75th St.
New York, N.Y. 10021

B

B & P Lamp Supply, Inc.
Box #P-300
McMinnville, Tenn. 37110

Bailey and Griffin
1406 E. Mermaid Lane
Philadelphia, Penn. 19118

Bailey's Forge
221 E. Bay St.
Savannah, Ga. 31401

A. W. Baker Restorations, Inc.
670 Drift Rd.
Westport, Mass. 02790

Baldwin Hardware Mfg.
841 Wyomissing Blvd.
Reading, Penn. 19603

Ball and Ball
463 W. Lincoln Highway
Exton, Penn. 19341

Bangkok Industries, Inc.
1900 S. 20th St.
Philadelphia, Penn. 19145

Barclay Fabrics Co., Inc.
7120 Airport Highway, Box 650
Pennsauken, N.J. 08101

The Barn People
Star Rte. 44
West Windsor, Vt. 05037

Barney Brainum-Shanker Steel
    Co., Inc.
70–32 83rd St.
Glendale, N.Y. 11227

Bassett & Vollum, Inc.
217 N. Main St.
Galena, Ill. 61036

Bates Fabrics, Inc.
1431 Broadway
New York, N.Y. 10018

Beaumont Heritage Pottery
Box 300, Atkinson St.
Portsmouth, N.H. 03801

Bedlam Brass Beds
19–21 Fair Lawn Ave.
Fair Lawn, N.J. 07410

The Bedpost
R.D. 1, Box 155
Pen Argyl, Penn. 18072

H. Behlen & Bros.,
P.O. Box 698
Amsterdam, N.Y. 12010

Bel-Air Door Co.
P.O. Box 829
Alhambra, Calif. 91802

Bendix Mouldings, Inc.
235 Pegasus Ave.
Northvale, N.J. 07647

Berea College
Student Craft Industries
Berea, Ky. 40404

Bergamo Fabrics, Inc.
969 Third Ave.
New York, N.Y. 10022

Berkeley Architectural Salvage
2750 Adeline
Berkeley, Calif. 94703

Lester H. Berry
1108 Pine St.
Philadelphia, Penn. 19107

The Birge Co.
390 Niagara St.
Buffalo, N.Y. 14202

Thomas A. Bisesti
409 Oakland St.
Springfield, Mass. 01108

Bishop's Mill Historical Institute
P.O. Box 150
Edgmont, Penn. 19028

Bittersweet
Rte. 12, P.O. Box 5
Riverton, Vt. 05668

Black Millwork Co., Inc.
Lake Ave.
Midland Park, N.J. 07432

Blaine Window Hardware, Inc.
1919 Blaine Dr.
Hagerstown, Md. 21740

Blair Lumber Co., Inc.
Rte. 1
Powhatan, Va. 23139

Jerome W. Blum
Ross Hill Rd.
Lisbon, Conn. 06351

Norton Blumenthal, Inc.
979 Third Ave.
New York, N.Y. 10022

Morgan Bockius Studios, Inc.
1412 York Rd.
Warminster, Penn. 18974

Bona
2227 Beechmont Ave.
Cincinnati, Ohio 45230

Bow & Arrow Imports
14 Arrow St.
Cambridge, Mass. 02138

Louis W. Bowen, Inc.
979 Third Ave.
New York, N.Y. 10022

Braid-Aid
466 Washington St.
Pembroke, Mass. 02359

Brass Bed Co. of America
1933 S. Broadway
Los Angeles, Calif. 90007

Brasslight
2831 S. 12th St.
Milwaukee, Wis. 53215

The Broad-Axe Beam Co.
R.D. 2, Box 181-E
W. Brattleboro, Vt. 05301

Broadway Supply Co.
7421 Broadway
Kansas City, Mo. 64114

Brookstone Co.
127 Vose Farm Rd.
Petersboro, N.H. 03458

Carol Brown
Putney, Vt. 05346

Bruce Hardwood Floors
P.O. Box 16902
Memphis, Tenn. 38116

Brunschwig & Fils, Inc.
979 Third Ave.
New York, N.Y. 10022

The Burning Log (Eastern Office)
P.O. Box 438
Lebanon, N.H. 03766

The Burning Log (Western Office)
P.O. Box 8519
Aspen, Colo. 81611

C

Samuel Cabot, Inc.
1 Union St.
Boston, Mass. 02108

California Redwood Assoc.
617 Montgomery St.
San Francisco, Calif. 94111

California Wood Turning
25 Lyon St.
San Francisco, Calif. 94117

Canada & Dom Sugar, Ltd.
P.O. Box 490
Montreal 3, Quebec
Canada

The Candle Cellar & Emporium
1914 N. Main St.
Fall River, Mass. 02720

The Cane Farm
Rosemont, N.J. 08556

Cane & Basket Supply Co.
1283 S. Cochran Ave.
Los Angeles, Calif. 90019

Cape Cod Cupola Co.
North Dartmouth, Mass. 02747

Victor Carl Antiques
841 Broadway
New York, N.Y. 10003

Dale Carlisle
Rte. No. 123
Stoddard, N.H. 03464

Constance Carol
P.O. Box 899
Plymouth, Mass. 02360

Carved Glass & Signs
767 E. 132 St.
Bronx, N.Y. 10454

Castle Burlingame
R.D. 1, Box 352
Basking Ridge, N.J. 07920

Celestial Design
1239 Blake St.
Berkeley, Calif. 94702

The Cellar, Antique Building Parts
384 Elgin
Ottawa, Ontario
Canada

Century Glass, Inc.
1417 N. Washington Ave.
Dallas, Texas 75204

Cherry Creek Enterprises, Inc.
937 Santa Fe Dr.
Denver, Colo. 80204

China Seas, Inc.
149 E. 72nd St.
New York, N.Y. 10021

Clarence House
40 E. 57th St.
New York, N.Y. 10022

The Classic Illumination
P.O. Box 5851
San Francisco, Calif. 94101

Cleveland Wrecking Co.
2800 Third St.
San Francisco, Calif. 94107

Cleveland Wrecking Co.
3170 E. Washington Blvd.
Los Angeles, Calif. 90023

Cohasset Colonials
335 Ship St.
Cohasset, Mass. 02025

Coker Creek Crafts
P.O. Box 95
Coker Creek, Tenn. 37314

Diane Jackson Cole
9 Grove St.
Kennebunk, Me. 04043

Cole and Son (Wallpapers), Ltd.
P.O. Box 4BU
18 Mortimer St.
London, W1A 4BU
England

Colonial Lamp & Supply Co.
P.O. Box 867
McMinnville, Tenn. 37110

Colonial Williamsburg, Craft House
Box CH
Williamsburg, Va. 23185

Colony Pottery
Box 18
Bishop Hill, Ill. 61419

Connaissance Fabrics and Wallcoverings, Inc.
979 Third Ave.
New York, N.Y. 10022

Conran's
The Market at Citicorp Center
160 E. 54th St.
New York, N.Y. 10022

Brian Considine
Post Mills, Vt. 05058

Conso Products
261 Fifth Ave.
New York, N.Y. 10016

Albert Constantine and Son
2050 Eastchester Rd.
Bronx, N.Y. 10461

John Conti, Restoration Contractor
Box 189
Wagontown, Penn. 19376

Cooke Art Glass Studio
222 Diamond St.
San Francisco, Calif. 94114

Copper Antiquities
Cummaquid P.O.
Cummaquid, Mass. 02637

The Copper House
Rte. 4
Epsom, N.H. 03234

Coran Sholes Industries
509 E. 2nd St.
South Boston, Mass. 02127

Country Bed Shop
Box 222
Groton, Mass. 01450

Country Braid House
Clark Rd.
Tilton, N.H. 03276

Country Curtains
Stockbridge, Mass. 01262

Country Floors
300 E. 61st St.
New York, N.Y. 10021

Craftsman Lumber Co.
Maid St.
Groton, Mass. 01450

Craftswomen
Box 715
Doylestown, Penn. 18901

Inez Croom
55 E. 76th St.
New York, N.Y. 10021

Crown of Fairhope
759 Nichols Ave.
P.O. Drawer G
Fairhope, Ala. 36532

Cumberland General Store
Rte. 3
Crossville, Tenn. 38555

D

Dahlman-Clift Lamps
10930 W. Loomis Rd.
Franklin, Wis. 53132

Dana-Deck, Inc.
P.O. Box 78
Orcas, Wash. 98280

Davis Cabinet Co.
Box 5424
Nashville, Tenn. 38106

R. H. Davis, Inc.
Gregg Lake Rd.
Antrim, N.H. 03440

The Decorators Supply Corp.
3610 S. Morgan
Chicago, Ill. 60609

Delaware Quarries, Inc.
River Road
Lumberville, Penn. 18933

Delft Blue
P.O. Box 103
Ellicott City, Md. 21043

Jack Denst Designs, Inc.
6–117 Merchandise Mart
Chicago, Ill. 60654

The Designing Woman
705 Rivermont Dr.
St. Louis, Mo. 63137

Devoe Paint Division
Celanese Coatings
1 Riverfront Plaza
Louisville, Ky. 40402

A. L. Diament & Co.
P.O. Box 7437
Philadelphia, Penn. 19101

Diamond K. Co., Inc.
130 Buckland Rd.
South Windsor, Conn. 06074

J. di Christina & Sons
350 Treat Ave.
San Francisco, Calif. 94110

Down Home Comforts
P.O. Box 281
West Brattleboro, Vt. 05301

Driwood Moulding Co.
P.O. Box 1729
Florence, S.C. 29501

Frederick Duckloe & Bros.
Portland, Penn. 18351

Dutch Products & Supply Co.
14 S. Main St.
Yardley, Penn. 19067

E

The Eighteenth Century Co.
Haddam Quarter Rd.
Durham, Conn. 06422

Eighteenth Century Hardware Co.
131 E. 3rd St.
Derry, Penn. 15627

Elon, Inc.
964 Third Ave.
New York, N.Y. 10022

Era Victoriana
P.O. Box 9683
San Jose, Calif. 95157

William J. Erbe Co.
434½ E. 75th St.
New York, N.Y. 10021

Erkins Studios
14 E. 41st St.
New York, N.Y. 10017

The Essex Forge
1 Old Dennison Rd.
Essex, Conn. 06426

European Marble Works
661 Driggs Ave.
Brooklyn, N.Y. 11211

F

Faire Harbour Boats
44 Captain Pierce Rd.
Scituate, Mass. 02066

Felber Studios
110 Ardmore Ave., P.O. Box 551
Ardmore, Penn. 19003

Felicity, Inc.
600 Eagle Bend Rd.
Clinton, Tenn. 37716

Felicity, Inc.
Cookeville Antique Mall
I-40
Cookeville, Tenn. 38501

Felicity, Inc.
Thieves' Market

4900 Kingston Pike
Knoxville, Tenn. 37902

Fife's Woodworking & Mfg. Co.
Rte. 107
Northwood, N.H. 03261

Finnaren & Haley, Inc.
1300 N. 60th St.
Philadelphia, Penn. 19151

Fisher Stoves International
P.O. Box 10605
Eugene, Ore. 97440

J. W. Fiske Architectural Metals, Inc.
111–117 Pennsylvania Ave.
Paterson, N.J. 07053

Floorcloths, Inc.
109 Main St.
Annapolis, Md. 21401

Focal Point, Inc.
4870 S. Atlanta Rd.
Smyrna, Ga. 30080

Folger Adam Co.
Box 688
Joliet, Ill. 60434

Follansbee Steel Corp.
Follansbee, West Va. 26037

Henry Ford Museum and Greenfield
  Village Reproductions
20900 Oakwood Blvd.
Dearborn, Mich. 48121

Stephen Franklin
Box 717
Buckingham, Penn. 18912

Friedman Brothers Decorative Arts,
  Inc.
305 E. 47th St.
New York, N.Y. 10017

Pamela S. Friend
590 King St.
Hanover, Mass. 02339

Frog Tool Co., Ltd.
541 N. Franklin St.
Chicago, Ill. 60610

Fuller O'Brien Paints

The O'Brien Corp.
P.O. Box 864
Brunswick, Ga. 31520

Fuller O'Brien Paints
The O'Brien Corp
450 E. Grand Ave.
South San Francisco, Calif. 94080

Fuller O'Brien Paints
The O'Brien Corp.
2001 W. Washington Ave.
South Bend, Ind. 46634

Furniture Designs
1425 Sherman Ave.
Evanston, Ill. 60201

Fypon Inc.
Box 365, 108 Hill St.
Stewartstown, Penn. 17363

G

Gargoyles, Ltd.
512 S. 3rd St.
Philadelphia, Penn. 19147

Gaston Wood Finishes
P.O. Box 1246
Bloomington, Ind. 47401

Gates Moore
River Rd., Silvermine
Norwalk, Conn. 06850

Genesis Glass, Ltd.
700 N.E. 22nd Ave.
Portland, Ore. 97223

Giannetti Studios
3806 38th St.
Brentwood, Md. 20722

Glidden-Durkee
900 Union Commerce Bldg.
Cleveland, Ohio 44115

Grampa's Wood Stoves
Box 492
Ware, Mass. 01082

Great American Salvage Co., Inc.
901 E. 2nd St.
Little Rock, Ark. 72203

Greystone Upholstery Corp.
502 Clewell St.
Fountain Hill, Penn. 18015

Robert Griffith, Metalsmith
16 S. Main St.
Trucksville, Penn. 18708

Bernard E. Gruenke, Jr.
Conrad Schmidt Studios
2405 S. 162nd St.
New Berlin, Wis. 53157

Guardian National House Inspection
P.O. Box 31
Pleasantville, N.Y. 10570

Guardian National Home Inspection
Box 115
Orleans, Mass. 02653

Guilfoy Cornice Works
1234 Howard
San Francisco, Calif. 94005

Guild of Shaker Crafts
401 W. Savidge St.
Spring Lake, Mich. 49456

Gurian's
276 Fifth Ave.
New York, N.Y. 10001

Guyon, Inc.
65 Oak St.
Lititz, Penn. 17543

H

Haas Wood and Ivory Works
64 Clementine St.
San Francisco, Calif. 94105

Hallelujah Redwood Products
39500 Comptche Rd.
Mendocino, Calif. 95460

John Harra Wood & Supply Co.
39 W. 19th St.
New York, N.Y. 10011

Harris Manufacturing Co.
763 E. Walnut St.
Johnson City, Tenn. 37601

Hartmann Sanders Co.
1717 Arthur Ave.
Elk Grove Village, Ill. 60007

Wilbert R. Hasbrouck
Historic Resources
711 S. Dearborn
Chicago, Ill. 60605

Heads Up, Inc.
3201 W. McArthur Blvd.
Santa Ana, Calif. 92704

Hearthside Mail Order
Box 127
West Newbury, Vt. 05085

Heirloom Rugs
28 Harlem St.
Rumford, R.I. 02916

Heritage Lanterns
Dept. OH78
Sea Meadows Lane
Yarmouth, Me. 04096

Heritage Rugs
Lahaska, Penn. 18931

S. M. Hexter Co.
2800 Superior Ave.
Cleveland, Ohio 44114

Historic Boulevard Services
1520 W. Jackson Blvd.
Chicago, Ill. 60607

Historic Charleston Reproductions
105 Broad St.
Charleston, S.C. 29401

The Hitchcock Chair Co.
Riverton, Conn. 06065

The Holmes Co.
P.O. Box 382
York, Penn. 17405

Home and Harvest, Inc.
4407 Westbourne Rd.
Greensboro, N.C. 27406

Homespun Weavers
Ridge and Keystone Sts.
Emmaus, Penn. 18049

R. Hood & Co.

Heritage Village
Meredith, N.H. 03253

The Hope Co., Inc.
2052 Congressional Dr.
St. Louis, Mo. 63141

Horton Brasses
P.O. Box 95, Nooks Hill Rd.
Cromwell, Conn. 06416

The House Carpenters
Box 217
Shutesbury, Mass. 01072

House of Moulding
15202 Oxnard St.
Van Nuys, Calif. 91411

Housesmiths
P.O. Box 416
York, Maine 03909

David Howard, Inc.
P.O. Box 295
Alstead, N.H. 03602

Howell Construction
2700 12th Ave., S.
Nashville, Tenn. 37204

S. & C. Huber, Accoutrements
82 Plants Dam Rd.
East Lyme, Conn. 06333

Hurley Patentee Manor
R.D. 7, Box 98A
Kingston, N.Y. 12401

I

International Consultants
227 S. 9th St.
Philadelphia, Penn. 19107

J

William H. Jackson Co.
3 E. 47th St.
New York, N.Y. 10017

Charles W. Jacobsen
401 S. Salina St.
Syracuse, N.Y. 13201

Janovic/Plaza
1291 First Ave.
New York, N.Y. 10021

Jo El Shop
7120 Hawkins Creamery Rd.
Laytonsville, Md. 20760

Jones & Erwin, Inc.
232 E. 59th St.
New York, N.Y. 10022

The Judson Studios
200 South Avenue 66
Los Angeles, Calif. 90042

Jugtown Pottery
Rte. 2
Seagrove, N.C. 27341

K

Katzenbach & Warren, Inc.
950 Third Ave.
New York, N.Y. 10022

Steve Kayne, Blacksmith
17 Harmon Pl.
Smithtown, N.Y. 11787

KB Moulding, Inc.
508A Larkfield Rd.
East Northport, N.Y. 11731

Kelter-Mace
361 Bleecker St.
New York, N.Y. 10014

Kenmore Carpet Corp.
979 Third Ave.
New York, N.Y. 10022

Kent-Costikyan, Inc.
305 E. 63rd St.
New York, N.Y. 10022

Kentile Floors
58 Second Ave.
Brooklyn, N.Y. 11215

Kittinger Co.
1893 Elmwood Ave.
Buffalo, N.Y. 14207

KMH Associates, Inc.

The Dam Site
Ceresco, Mich. 49033

Kohler Co.
Kohler, Wis. 53044

Kristia Associates
343 Forest Ave., P.O. Box 1118
Portland, Me. 04104

Bruce M. Kriviskey, AIP
3048–A N. Shepard Ave.
Milwaukee, Wis. 53211

John Kruesel
R.R. 4
Rochester, Minn. 55901

Kwal Paints
3900 Joliet
Denver, Colo. 80239

L

J. R. Lamb Studios
151 Walnut St.
Northvale, N.J. 07647

Larimer Drygoods Co.
Attn. RLC/RS
P.O. Box 17491 T.A.
Denver, Colo. 80217

Last's Paint & Wallpaper
2813 Mission St.
San Francisco, Calif. 94110

H. & N. Laughon
8106 Three Chopt Rd.
Richmond, Va. 23229

William A. Lavicka
(see Historic Boulevard Services)

Lead Glass Co.
14924 Beloit Snodes Rd.
Beloit, Ohio 44609

Lee/Joffa, Inc.
979 Third Ave.
New York, N.Y. 10022

Lemees Fireplace Equipment
Rte. 28
Bridgewater, Mass. 02324

L. R. Lloyd Co.
Box 975
Uniontown, Penn. 15401

Ernest Lo Nano
S. Main St.
Sheffield, Mass. 01257

London Venturers Co.
2 Dock Sq.
Rockport, Mass. 01966

Luigi Crystal
7332 Frankford Ave.
Philadelphia, Penn. 19136

Kenneth Lynch & Sons
Box 488, 78 Danbury Rd.
Wilton, Conn. 06897

M

MacBeath Hardwood Co.
2150 Oakdale Ave.
San Francisco, Calif. 94124

Nancy McClelland, Inc.
232 E. 59th St.
New York, N.Y. 10022

Magnolia Hall
726 Andover
Atlanta, Ga. 30327

Florence Maine
113 W. Lane, Rte. 35
Ridgefield, Conn. 06877

Maine Line Paints
13 Hutchins St.
Auburn, Me. 14210

Marble Modes, Inc.
15–25 130th St.
College Point, N.Y. 11356

MarLe Company, Inc.
170 Summer St.
Stamford, Conn. 06901

Ephraim Marsh Co.
Box 266
Concord, N.C. 28025

The Martin-Senour Co.
1370 Ontario Ave., N.W.
Cleveland, Ohio 44113

Louis Maslow & Son, Inc.
979 Third Ave.
New York, N.Y. 10022

Materials Unlimited
4100 E. Morgan Rd.
Ypsilanti, Mich. 48197

Mather's
31 E. Main St.
Westminster, Md. 21157

Maurer & Shepherd, Joyners
122 Naubuc Ave.
Glastonbury, Conn. 06033

Mayfair China Corp.
142 22nd St.
Brooklyn, N.Y. 11232

Mercer Museum Shop
Bucks County Historical Society
Pine and Ashland
Doylestown, Penn. 18901

Mexico House
Box 970
Del Mar, Calif. 92014

Michael's Fine Colonial Products
22 Churchill Lane
Smithtown, N.Y. 11787

D. R. Millbranth, Cabinetmaker
Center Rd., R.R. 2, Box 462
Hillsboro, N.H. 03244

Newton Millham—Star Forge
672 Drift Rd.
Westport, Mass. 02790

Minnesota Woodworkers Supply Co.
Industrial Blvd.
Rogers, Minn. 55374

Miss Kitty's Keeping Room Kolors
Turkey Run
Box 117-A, Rte. 1
Clear Brook, Va. 22624

Mohawk Industries, Inc.
173 Howland Ave.
Adams, Mass. 01220

Benjamin Moore & Co.
Chestnut Ridge Rd.
Montvale, N.J. 07645

R. Jesse Morley, Jr.
88 Oak St.
Westwood, Mass. 02090

Thomas Moser, Cabinet Maker
Cobb's Bridge Rd.
New Gloucester, Me. 04260

Mottahedeh & Co.
225 Fifth Ave.
New York, N.Y. 10010

George W. Mount, Inc.
P.O. Box 306
576 Leyden Rd.
Greenfield, Mass. 01301

Munsell Color Products
2441 N. Calvert St.
Baltimore, Md. 21218

Lehlan Murray
Box 18
Bishop Hill, Ill. 61419

Museum of Fine Arts
Museum Shop
Boston, Mass. 02115

N

Nassau Flooring Corp.
P.O. 351, 242 Drexel St.
Westbury, N.Y. 11590

National Home Inspectors Service of
  New England, Inc.
2 Calvin Rd.
Watertown, Mass. 02172

The National House Inn
102 S. Parkview
Marshall, Mich. 49068

Deanne F. Nelson
Box 43
Bishop Hill, Ill. 61419

Newell Workshop
19 Blaine Ave.
Hinsdale, Ill. 60521

New Hampshire Blankets
Main St.
Harrisville, N.H. 03450

Newstamp Lighting Co.
227 Bay Rd.
North Easton, Mass. 02356

New York Flooring, Inc.
1733 First Ave.
New York, N.Y. 10028

Nichols & Stone
Gardner, Mass. 01440

Noelwood Handmade Furniture
123 Virginia St.
Elmhurst, Ill. 60126

Craig Nutt Fine Wood Works
2308 6th St.
Tuscaloosa, Ala. 35401

O

Old Carolina Brick Co.
Salisbury, N.C. 28144

Old-Fashioned Milk Paint Co.
Box 222
Groton, Mass. 01450

Old-House Inspection Co.
140 Berkeley Pl.
Brooklyn, N.Y. 11217

Old Mansions Co.
1305 Blue Hill Ave.
Mattapan, Mass. 02126

Old Stone Mill
Adams, Mass. 01220

Old Timey Furniture Co.
Smithfield, N.C. 27577

Old Town Restorations
158 Farrington
St. Paul, Minn. 55102

Old World Moulding & Finishing, Inc.
115 Allen Blvd.
Farmingdale, N.Y. 11735

Open Pacific Graphics
#43 Market Square
Victoria, British Columbia
Canada

Ox-Line Paints
Lehman Bros. Corp.
115 Jackson Ave.
Jersey City, N.J. 07304

P

P & G New and Used Plumbing
 Supply
818 Flushing Ave.
Brooklyn, N.Y. 11206

Packard Lamp Co., Inc.
67 E. 11th St.
New York, N.Y. 10003

Megan Parry
1727 Spruce
Boulder, Colo. 80302

Pat's Etc. Co. (PECO)
Highway 71 at Alum Creek
P.O. Box 777
Smithville, Texas 78957

Peerless Rattan & Reed Mfg. Co.
97 Washington
New York, N.Y. 10006

I. Peiser Floors
418 E. 91st St.
New York, N.Y. 10028

Penco Studios
1110 Baxter Ave.
Louisville, Ky. 40204

Period Furniture Hardware
123 Charles St.
Boston, Mass. 02114

Period Lighting Fixtures
Dept. OH78
1 Main St.
Chester, Conn. 06412

Period Pine
P.O. Box 77052
Atlanta, Ga. 30309

Perkowitz Window Fashions, Inc.
135 Green Bay Rd.
Wilmette, Ill. 60091

Norman Perry, Inc.
P.O. Box 90
Plymouth, N.H. 03264

Pfanstiel Hardware Co.
Hust Rd.
Jeffersonville, N.Y. 12748

Walter Phelps
Box 76
Williamsville, Vt. 05362

Philadelphia Museum of Art
The Museum Shop
P.O. Box 7646
Philadelphia, Penn. 19101

Pilgrim's Progress, Inc.
Penthouse
50 W. 67th St.
New York, N.Y. 10023

Pittsburgh Paints
PPG Industries, Inc.
1 Gateway Center
Pittsburgh, Penn. 15222

Portland Franklin Stove Foundry, Inc.
57 Kennebec St.
Portland, Me. 04104

Potlatch Corp.
Wood Products, Southern Division
P.O. Box 916
Stuttgart, Ark. 72160

Pratt & Lambert
625 Washington
Carlstadt, N.J. 07072

Preservation Associates, Inc.
P.O. Box 202
Sharpsburg, Md. 21782

Preservation Resource Center
Lake Shore
Essex, N.Y. 12936

Preservation Resource Group
5619 Southampton Dr.
Springfield, Va. 22151

Francis J. Purcell II
R.D. 2, Box 7
New Hope, Penn. 18938

Q

Quaker Lace Co.
4th St. and Lehigh Ave.
Philadelphia, Penn. 19133

Quicksand Crafts
Vest, Ky. 41772

R

Rainbow Art Glass Corp.
49 Shark River Rd.
Neptune, N.J. 07753

Rambusch Decorating Co.
40 W. 13th St.
New York, N.Y. 10011

The Readybuilt Products Co.
Box 4306, 1701 McHenry St.
Baltimore, Md. 21223

Reale Mirror Mfg. Co.
16–18 E. 12th St.
New York, N.Y. 10003

Reed Wallcoverings
550 Pharr Rd.
Atlanta, Ga. 30318

Reid Classics
P.O. Box 8383
3600 Old Shell Rd.
Mobile, Ala. 36608

The Renovation Source, Inc.
3513–14 N. Southport
Chicago, Ill. 60657

Restoration & Reincarnation
250 Austin Alley
San Francisco, Calif. 94109

Restorations, Ltd.
Jamestown, R.I. 02835

Restorations Unlimited
24 W. Main St.
Elizabethville, Penn. 17023

Ritter & Son
46901 Fish Rock Rd.
Anchor Bay (Gualala)
Calif. 95445

Robinson Iron
Robinson Rd.
Alexander City, Ala. 35010

The Rocker Shop
P.O. Box 12, 1421 White Circle, N.W.
Marietta, Ga. 30061

Frank Rockette
Strawberry Banke Museum
P.O. Box 300
Portsmouth, N.H. 03801

Jane Kent Rockwell, Interior
 Decorations
48–52 Lincoln St.
Exeter, N.H. 03833

Rococo Designs
417 Pennsylvania Ave.
Santa Cruz, Calif. 95062

Rosecore Carpet Co., Inc.
979 Third Ave.
New York, N.Y. 10022

Rotar Services
5007 W. Lovers Lane
Dallas, Texas 75209

Rowantrees Pottery
Union St.
Blue Hill, Me. 04614

Royal Windyne Ltd.
Box 6622, Dept. OHC
Richmond, Va. 23230

S

The Saltbox
2229 Marietta Pike
Lancaster, Penn. 17603

Arthur Sanderson & Sons, Ltd.
Berners St.
London W1A 2JE
England

San Francisco Victoriana
606 Natoma St.
San Francisco, Calif. 94103

Santa Cruz Foundry Co.
P.O. Box 831, 738 Chestnut St.
Santa Cruz, Calif. 94115

Richard E. Sargeant
Hartland Forge, Box 83
Hartland 4 Corners, Vt. 05049

Raoul Savoie
657 Prospect Blvd.
Pasadena, Calif. 91103

Scalamandré
950 Third Ave.
New York, N.Y. 10022

Schrader Wood Stoves & Fireplaces
724 Water St.
Santa Cruz, Calif. 95060

F. Schumacher & Co.
939 Third Ave.
New York, N.Y. 10022

A. F. Schwerd Mfg. Co.
3215 McClure Ave.
Pittsburgh, Penn. 15212

Mrs. Eldred Scott
The Riven Oak
Birmingham, Mich. 48012

John L. Seekamp
472 Pennsylvania
San Francisco, Calif. 94107

Self Sufficiency Products
Environmental Manufacturing Corp.
P.O. Box 126
Essex Junction, Vt. 05452

Sermac
P.O. Box 1684
Des Plaines, Ill. 60018

Shaker Workshops, Inc.
14 Bradford St.
Concord, Mass. 01742

Shenandoah Mfg. Co., Inc.
P.O. Box 839
Harrisonburg, Va. 22801

Shepherd Oak Products
Box 27
Northwood, N.H. 03261

Sherwin-Williams Co.
101 Prospect Ave., N.W.
Cleveland, Ohio 44101

Silk Surplus
223 E. 58th St.
New York, N.Y. 10022

Silk Surplus
843 Lexington Ave.
New York, N.Y. 10021

Silk Surplus
449 Old Country Rd.
Westbury, N.Y. 11590

Simpson Timber Co.
900 Fourth Ave.
Seattle, Wash. 98164

Smith & Son Roofing
1360 Virginia Ave.
Baldwin Park, Calif. 91706

Southern Highland Handicraft Guild
P.O. Box 9545
Asheville, N.C. 28805

Spanish Pueblo Doors, Inc.
P.O. Box 2517, Wagon Rd.
Santa Fe, N.M. 87501

Spanish Villa
2145 Zercher Rd.
San Antonio, Texas 78209

William Spencer
Creek Rd./Rancocas Woods
Mount Holly, N.J. 08060

Greg Spiess
216 E. Washington St.
Joliet, Ill. 60433

Standard Trimming Corp.
1114 First Ave.
New York, N.Y. 10021

Stark Carpet Corp.
979 Third Ave.
New York, N.Y. 10022

Stencil Specialty Co.
377 Ocean Ave.
Jersey City, N.J. 07305

Stencilled Interiors
Hinman Lane
Southbury, Conn. 06488

Steptoe and Wife Antiques, Ltd.
3626 Victoria Park Ave.
Willowdale, Ontario M2H 3B2
Canada

William Stewart & Sons
708 N. Edison St.
Arlington, Va. 22203

Thomas Strahan Co.
121 Webster Ave.
Chelsea, Mass. 02150

Stroheim & Romann
155 E. 56th St.
New York, N.Y. 10022

The Structural Slate Co.
Pen Argyl, Penn. 18072

Sturbridge Yankee Workshop
Dept. OHC
Sturbridge, Mass. 01566

Sunflower Studio
2851 Road B½
Grand Junction, Colo. 81501

Sunrise Salvage
2210 San Pablo Ave.
Berkeley, Calif. 94710

Sunrise Specialty
The Galleria
101 Kansas St., Rm. 224
San Francisco, Calif. 94103

Sunrise Specialty
8705 Santa Monica Blvd.
Los Angeles, Calif. 94710

Superior Reed & Rattan Furniture Co.
500 W. 52nd St.
New York, N.Y. 10019

T

Pete Taggett
The Blacksmith Shop
P.O. Box 115
Mt. Holly, Vt. 05758

Tennessee Fabricating Co.
2366 Prospect St.
Memphis Tenn. 38106

Thermograte Enterprises, Inc.
51 Iona Lane
St. Paul, Minn. 55113

Richard E. Thibaut
204 E. 58th St.
New York, N.Y. 10022

Seth Thomas
135 S. Main
Thomaston, Conn. 06787

Thompson & Anderson, Inc.
53 Seavey St.
Westbrook, Me. 04092

Thonet
A Simmons Co.
Decorative Arts Center
305 E. 63rd St.
New York, N.Y. 10021

Thonet
A Simmons Co.
600 World Trade Center
2050 Stemmons Freeway
Dallas, Texas 75258

Thonet
A Simmons Co.
11–100 Merchandise Mart
Chicago, Ill. 60654

Thonet
A Simmons Co.
Los Angeles Home Furnishings Mart
Space 756, 1933 S. Broadway
Los Angeles, Calif. 90007

Tolland Fabrics
1114 First Ave.
New York, N.Y. 10021

Townscape
30 Public Sq.
Medina, Ohio 44526

Townshend Furniture Co., Inc.
Rte. 30
Townshend, Vt. 05353

Tremont Nail Co.
P.O. Box 111
Wareham, Mass. 02571

Trotman Clock Co.
Box 71
Amherst, Mass. 01002

R.T. Trump & Co.
Bethlehem Pike
Flourtown, Penn. 19031

Turco Coatings, Inc.
Wheatland and Mellon Sts.
Phoenixville, Penn. 19460

Jay Turnbull, A.I.A.
2007 Franklin St.
San Francisco, Calif. 94109

U

United House Wrecking
328 Selleck St.
Stamford, Conn. 06902

Universal Clamp Co.
6905 Cedros Ave.
Van Nuys, Calif. 91405

Up Country Enterprise
Old Jaffrey Rd.
Peterborough, N.H. 03458

Urban Archaeology
137 Spring St.
New York, N.Y. 10012

V

The Valentas
2105 S. Austin Blvd.
Cicero, Ill. 60650

Vanderlaan Tile Co., Inc.
103 Park Ave.
New York, N.Y. 10017

VanHouten & Brick
Millwork and Building Hardware
920 Ocean St.
Santa Cruz, Calif. 95060

Albert Van Luit & Co.
4000 Chevy Chase Dr.
Los Angeles, Calif. 90039

Vermont Castings, Inc.
Box 126, Prince St.
Randolph, Vt. 05060

The Vermont Marble Co.
61 Main St.
Proctor, Vt. 05765

Vermont Structural Slate
Fair Haven, Vt. 05743

Victorian Reproductions
1601 Park Avenue S.
Minneapolis, Minn. 55404

Village Lantern
598 Union St.
N. Marshfield, Mass. 02059

Villeroy & Boch
912 Riverview Dr.
Totowa, N.J. 07512

Virginia Metalcrafters
1010 E. Main St.
Waynesboro, Va. 22980

Virtu
P.O. Box 192
Southfield, Mich. 48075

W

Wagon House Cabinetmaking
Box 149
Mendenhall, Penn. 19357

Charles Walker Mfg. Co.
189 13th St.
San Francisco, Calif. 94103

Wallin Forge
R.R. 1, Box 65
Sparta, Ky. 41086

Wall Stencils by Barbara
R.R. 2, Box 462, Center Rd.
Hillsboro, N.H. 03244

Walton Stained Glass
30 S. Central
Campbell, Calif. 95008

E. G. Washburne & Co.
85 Andover St.
Danvers, Mass. 01923

The Washington Copper Works
South St.
Washington, Conn. 06793

Washington Stove Works
P.O. Box 687
Everett, Wash. 98201

Wasley Lighting Division
Plainville Industrial Park
Plainville, Conn. 06062

Waterhouse Wallhangings
420 Boylston St.
Boston, Mass. 02116

Watts & Co., Ltd.
7 Tufton St., Westminster
London SW1P 3QB
England

Waverly Fabrics
58 W. 40th St.
New York, N.Y. 10018

Weird Wood
Green Mountain Cabins
Box 190
Chester, Vt. 05143

Welsbach Lighting, Inc.
240 Sargent Dr.
New Haven, Conn. 06511

Western Art Stone Co.
541 Tunnel Ave.
P.O. Box 315
Brisbane, Calif. 94005

Western States Stone
1849 East Slauson
Los Angeles, Calif. 90058

Westlake Architectural Antiques
3315 Westlake Dr.
Austin, Texas 78746

West Rindge Baskets
Box 24
Rindge, N.H. 03461

The Robert Whitley Studio
Laurel Rd.
Solebury, Penn. 18963

Whittemore-Durgin Glass Co.
P.O. Box 2065OH
Hanover, Mass. 02339

I. M. Wiese Antiquarian
Main St.
Southbury, Conn. 06488

D. B. Wiggins
Hale Rd.
Tilton, N.H. 03276

Helen Williams/Rare Tiles
12643 Hortense St.
North Hollywood, Calif. 91604

Williamsburg Blacksmith, Inc.
Buttonshop Rd.
Williamsburg, Mass. 01096

Roy Wingate
560 Green St.
San Francisco, Calif. 94123

Noel Wise Antiques
6503 St. Claude Ave.
Arabi, La. 70032

Woodcraft Supply Corp.
313 Montvale Ave.
Woburn, Mass. 01801

Wood Mosaic
P.O. Box 21159
Louisville, Ky. 40221

The Wrecking Bar
292 Moreland Ave., N.E.
Atlanta, Ga. 30307

The Wrecking Bar, Inc.
2601 McKinney
Dallas, Texas 75204

Wrightsville Hardware Co.
N. Front St.
Wrightsville, Penn. 17368

Y

Yankee Craftsman
357 Commonwealth Rd.
Wayland, Mass. 01778

Yours and Mine Antiques
10400 Sonoma Highway
Kenwood, Calif. 95452

Selected Bibliography

Benjamin, Asher. *American Builder's Companion.* 1827 edition. New York: Dover Publications, 1969.

Bicknell, A. J., and W. T. Comstock. *Victorian Architecture* (reprints of Bicknell's *Detail, Cottage, and Constructive Architecture* [1873] and Comstock's *Modern Architectural Designs and Details* [1881]). Watkins Glen, N.Y.: The American Life Foundation & Study Institute, 1978.

Bicknell, A. J. *Village Builder.* 1872 edition. Watkins Glen, N.Y.: The American Life Foundation & Study Institute, 1976.

Blumenson, John J.-G. *Identifying American Architecture.* Nashville, Tenn.: American Association for State and Local History, 1977.

Chippendale, Thomas. *The Gentleman & Cabinet-Maker's Director.* 3rd edition. New York: Dover Publications, 1966.

Condit, Carl W. *American Building: Materials and Techniques from the First Colonial Settlement to the Present.* Chicago: University of Chicago Press, 1968.

Cooke, Lawrence S. *Lighting in America, From Colonial Rushlights to Victorian Chandeliers.* Antiques Magazine Library. New York: Universe Books, 1976.

Curtis, Will, and Jane Curtis. *Antique Woodstoves, Artistry in Iron.* Ashville, Me.: Cobblesmith, 1975.

Devoe Paint Company. *Exterior Decoration.* Philadelphia: The Athaeneum of Philadelphia, 1976.

Downing, Andrew Jackson. *The Architecture of Country Houses.* 1850 edition. New York: Dover Publications, 1969.

Early American Life Society. *The Architectural Treasures of Early America,* 8 vols. New York: Arno Press, 1977. (The 150 monographs of the early 1900s have been compressed into this edited modern set. Get the originals if you can as the reproduction is poor in these copies.)

Eastlake, Charles. *Hints on Household Taste.* 4th edition. New York: Dover Publications, 1969.

Eiland, Murray L. *Oriental Rugs, A Comprehensive Guide.* Greenwich, Conn.: New York Graphic Society, 1973.

Fowler, John, and John Cornforth. *English Decoration in the Eighteenth Century.* London: Barrie & Jenkins, 1974.

Grow, Lawrence. *The Old House Catalogue.* New York: Universe Books, 1976.

Grow, Lawrence, comp. *Old House Plans.* New York: Universe Books, 1978.

Harris, Cyril M., ed. *Historic Architecture Sourcebook.* New York: McGraw-Hill, 1977.

Hayward, Arthur H. *Colonial and Early American Lighting.* New York: Dover Publications, 1962.

Hussey, E. C. *Home Building.* 1876 edition. Watkins Glen, N.Y.: The American Life Foundation & Study Institute, 1976.

Isham, Norman M. *Early American Houses and a Glossary of Colonial Architectural Terms.* New York: Da Capo Press, 1967.

Lipman, Jean, and Eve Meulendyke. *American Folk Decoration.* New York: Dover Publications, 1972.

Little, Nina Fletcher. *American Decorative Wall Painting: 1700–1850.* New York: E. P. Dutton & Co., 1972.

Loth, Calder, and Julius Toursdale Sadler, Jr. *The Only Proper Style, Gothic Architecture in America.* Boston: New York Graphic Society, 1975.

Maass, John. *The Victorian Home in America.* New York: Hawthorn Books, 1972.

McKee, Harley J. *Introduction to Early American Masonry, Stone, Brick, Mortar and Plaster.* Washington, D.C.: National Trust for Historic Preservation, 1973.

McRaven, Charles. *Building the Hewn Log House.* Hollister, Mo.: Mountain Publishing Services, 1978.

Montgomery, Florence M. *Printed Textiles, English and American Cottons and Linens 1700–1850.* A Winterthur Book. New York: The Viking Press, 1970.

Mumford, Lewis. *The Brown Decades: A Study of the Arts in America, 1865–1895.* New York: Dover Publications, 1955.

Mumford, Lewis. *Sticks and Stones: A Study of American Architecture and Civilization.* 2nd revised edition. New York: Dover Publications, 1955.

Palliser, Palliser & Co. *Palliser's New Cottage Homes and Details.* 1887 edition. Watkins Glen, N.Y.: The American Life Foundation & Study Institute, n.d.

Petit, Florence H. *America's Indigo Blues, Resist-Printed and Dyed Textiles of the Eighteenth Century.* New York: Hastings House, n.d.

Pettit, Florence H. *America's Printed and Painted Fabrics, 1600–1900.* Hastings House, 1970.

Pierson, William H., Jr. *American Buildings and Their Architects: The Colonial and Neoclassical Style.* Garden City, N.Y.: Doubleday and Co., 1970

Saylor, Henry H. *Dictionary of Architecture.* New York: John Wiley & Sons, 1952.

Scully, Vincent. *American Architecture and Urbanism.* New York: Frederick A. Praeger, 1969.

Seale, William. *The Tasteful Interlude, American Interiors Through the Camera's Eye, 1860–1917.* New York: Praeger Publishers, 1974.

Stanford, Deirdre, and Louis Reens. *Restored America.* New York: Praeger Publishers, 1975.

Stephen, George. *Remodeling Old Houses Without Destroying Their Character.* New York: Alfred A. Knopf, 1972.

Vaux, Calvert. *Villas and Cottages.* 2nd edition. New York: Dover Publications, 1970.

Wall, William E. *Graining: Ancient and Modern.* Revised edition by F. N. Vaderwalker. New York: Drake Publishers, 1972.

Waring, Janet. *Early American Stencils on Walls and Furniture.* New York: Dover Publications, n.d.

Whiffen, Marcus. *American Architecture Since 1780.* Cambridge, Mass.: The M.I.T. Press, 1969.

Williams, Henry L. and Ottalie K. *Old American Houses and How to Restore Them (1700–1850).* New York: Doubleday, 1946. (The finest book yet written on the subject. Beg, borrow, or steal it.)

Index